Researching children's perspectives

 Researching children's
perspectives

**EDITED BY ANN LEWIS
AND GEOFF LINDSAY**

Open University Press
Buckingham · Philadelphia

Open University Press
Celtic Court
22 Ballmoor
Buckingham
MK18 1XW

e-mail: enquiries@openup.co.uk
world wide web: http://www.openup.co.uk

and
325 Chestnut Street
Philadelphia, PA 19106, USA

First Published 2000

A catalogue record of this book is available from the British Library

ISBN 0 335 20280 2 (hb)   0 335 20279 9 (pb)

Library of Congress Cataloging-in-Publication Data
Lewis, Ann, 1950–
    Researching children's perspectives / Ann Lewis and Geoff Lindsay.
    p.   cm.
    Includes bibliographical references and index.
    ISBN 0–335–20280–2 (hbk)   ISBN 0–335–20279–9 (pbk)
    1. Children – Research – Methodology. 2. Children – Attitudes.
I. Lindsay, Geoff. II. Title.
HQ767.85.L49   2000
305.23'07–dc21
                                                                    99–13289
                                                                    CIP

Typeset by Graphicraft Limited, Hong Kong
Printed in Great Britain by Biddles Limited, Guildford and Kings Lynn

 Contents

Contributors

Amanda Begley is a doctoral research student at the University of Warwick. She is supported by a research studentship from the Down's Syndrome Association and is researching the educational perceptions and aspirations of children and young people with Down Syndrome.

Gill Bendelow is Lecturer in Social Policy in the Department of Applied Social Studies at the University of Warwick. She has directed and worked on a variety of projects which have explored the views and opinions of children and young people in relation to health, illness and 'risk'.

Debra Costley's research includes an evaluation of an Integrated Learning System which aimed to raise reading levels of pupils with learning difficulties. Earlier work focused on the impact of the National Curriculum on pupils with moderate learning difficulties. Publications include 'Making pupils fit the framework' (*School Organisation* (1996) 16(3): 341–54) and (with A. Sinclair Taylor) 'Effective schooling for all: the special educational needs dimension', in J. Siraj-Blatchford and I. Siraj-Blatchford (eds) *Cross-Curricular Skills, Themes and Dimensions* (Open University Press 1995).

Jo Crozier is a part-time lecturer in Education at the University of Warwick. She is currently involved in a study of a local authority multidisciplinary intervention supporting disaffected young people in school. She has conducted research on gender issues in relation to school disaffection and disruption with a focus on girls' perspectives of their school experience. An

Appendices   199

account of this (written with J. Anstiss) is 'Out of the spotlight: girls' experience of disruption', in M. Lloyd-Smith and J. Davies (eds) *On the Margins: The Educational Experience of 'Problem' Pupils* (Trentham 1995).

Tina Detheridge has been involved, since the early 1980s, in the application of information technology (IT) to enhance the communication of children and adults with special educational needs. Her recent research, based at the University of Warwick, examined the role of IT in bridging the gap between communicative competence and communicative potential. Her current work focuses on the use of symbols and pictures for people with severe learning difficulties and limited communication skills. She is co-author (with Mike Detheridge) of *Literacy through Symbols* (David Fulton 1997) and lectures widely on this topic.

Julie Dockrell is Professor of Psychology at South Bank University, London. A qualified educational and clinical psychologist, she is currently directing two research projects on children's language development. She is co-author (with J. McShane) of *Children's Learning Difficulties* (Blackwell 1993).

Alan France is a research fellow at the University of Sheffield. He is presently working on the evaluation of the Joseph Rowntree Foundation's Communities that Care Programme. He has published widely in the field of youth studies around questions of citizenship. His most recent research is concerned with young people's beliefs about health, lifestyle and risk taking.

Caroline Jones has taught in primary schools since 1980. She is currently a part-time tutor at the Institute of Education, University of Warwick. She is studying for a PhD researching the identification and assessment of special educational needs in the early years.

Ann Lewis is Senior Lecturer in Education at the University of Warwick. Her current research includes a study of individualism and collectivism in young children, and evaluation of IT based approaches to overcoming reading difficulties. She is a chartered psychologist and was editor of *British Educational Research Journal*. Her publications include *Primary Special Needs and the National Curriculum* (Routledge 1995) and *Children's Understanding of Disability* (Routledge 1995).

Geoff Lindsay is Professor of Special Educational Needs and Educational Psychology at the University of Warwick. He is Director of the Special Needs Research Unit and a chartered psychologist. He is currently carrying out research into children with specific speech and language difficulties, baseline assessment of 5-year-olds, support services for secondary pupils presenting problem behaviour and ethical dilemmas of psychologists and psychotherapists. His publications include *Values into Practice in Special Education* (David Fulton 1997) and *Baseline Assessment* (with Martin Desforges, David Fulton 1998).

Mel Lloyd-Smith is Deputy Director of the Institute of Education, University of Warwick. He is currently involved in a study of a local authority multidisciplinary intervention supporting disaffected young people in school. He has published books and papers on the sociological perspective of special needs education and co-edited (with J. Davies) *On the Margins: The Educational Experience of 'Problem' Pupils* (Trentham 1995).

Judith Masson is Professor of Law at the University of Warwick and a specialist on child law and socio-legal research. She has recently completed (with C. Harrison and A. Pavlovic) a study of social services work with children in long-term care and their parents, *Working in Partnership with Children and 'Lost' Parents* (York Publishing Services 1997) and (with M. Oakley) a study of children involved in care proceedings.

Eleanor Nesbitt is Lecturer in Religions and Education at the University of Warwick. She has recently completed a longitudinal study of young Hindus' perceptions of their religious tradition. Her publications include '*My Dad's Hindu, My Mum's Side are Sikhs': Issues in Religious Identity* (National Foundation for Arts Education 1991), *Photographing Worship: Issues Raised by Ethnographical Study of Children's Participation in Acts of Worship* (Visual Anthropology 1992) and (with R. Jackson) *Hindu Children in Britain* (Trentham 1993) and *Hindus Today* (Goloka 1999).

Anne Sinclair Taylor is Lecturer in Education at the University of Warwick and is interested in educational policies and practice which enfranchise learners. She has undertaken research on pupils' perspectives of schooling and is keen to assert the importance of giving children a voice in all matters concerning them. Her publications include 'Less better than the rest: perceptions of integration in a multi-ethnic special needs unit' (*Educational Review* (1995) 47(3): 263–74), 'Child protection: relative values?' (*International Journal of Early Years Education* (1996) 4(2): 70–6) and 'From survival to reflexivity: locating child protection in initial teacher education', in J. Davies and P. Garner (eds) *At the Crossroads: Special Educational Needs and Teacher Education* (David Fulton 1999).

Jane Tannock has taught in primary education since 1970 and is the Head of Early Years in a large primary school. She is an Ofsted nursery inspector and president of the Solihull branch of Early Education (formerly BAECE). She has recently completed research into the effects of bereavement on the young child.

Jane Tarr is Senior Lecturer in Education at the University of the West of England. She has taught in special and mainstream schools and has a particular interest in special education and the arts. Her current research includes work on the perceptions of children, parents and professionals concerning concepts of special educational needs. Her publications include (with G. Thomas, J. Webb and M. Taysum) *The Monitoring and Evaluation of Schools' SEN policies* (DfEE/University of the West of England 1997).

Simon Warren has worked in education since 1988, both in community education and as a primary school teacher. He was a research officer at the University of Warwick on a number of funded projects including 'Community and collectivism: the role of parents' organizations' and 'Supporting refugee children in schools: a focus on home–school links'. He is a member and mentor in Second City Second Chance, a peer tutoring scheme for 'at risk' pupils in Birmingham and is involved in the National Anti-Racist Movement in Education. He is co-editor of *Education Today and Tomorrow*.

Simon Williams is a Warwick research fellow in the Department of Sociology at the University of Warwick. He has published widely in the fields of medical sociology and social theory, including recent work on lay evaluations of modern medicine, and emotions in social life. His current research interests centre on body, health and emotion with particular reference to children and young people.

Maureen Winn Oakley is NSPCC Research Fellow at the School of Law, University of Warwick. She has a PhD in social anthropology and is a family law solicitor. She has recently completed (with J. Masson) a study of children's perceptions of care proceedings and is currently researching children's views on advocacy services in the care system.

 Foreword

For many years research has been conducted on and with children in the field of education and related disciplines in the social sciences. Most of this work has demonstrated that studies of children and childhood cannot be achieved using a single discipline. The problems that confront children and young people call for multidisciplinary and interdisciplinary approaches. It is therefore pleasing to find that the editors of this volume have commissioned a range of researchers and practitioners to write about children and children's perspectives.

The focus of this volume calls for a different style of research. No longer can researchers assume that those social science methods that are used to study adults can be used in the same way to study children. Instead, researchers need to give some thought to ways in which innovatory methods of social investigation can be developed and used with children so as to gain access to children's perspectives of the worlds in which they live and work.

A range of issues and questions emerge about the problems to be tackled, the processes involved and 'solutions' that researchers develop within their projects. In this volume we gain some insights into all these aspects of research with children. The legal status of the child raises questions about the negotiation of research access, procedures of data collection and issues concerning copyright and confidentiality. In all these areas there are no easy answers but these chapters have the potential to point us towards strategies that can be used in the field when conducting research with children.

Status of the child and nature of the task

The status of the child will vary with respect to age, general cognitive ability, emotional status and specific knowledge at the time of the research. These interact with each other, and also with the task itself. This meeting may be considered to lie on a continuum of intrusiveness, which includes considerations of a potential discomfort and harm as a consequence of the procedure (e.g. nightmares) and as a consequence of reporting the research (e.g. media attention).

Factors affecting impact

Example 1
A third year undergraduate student completes an experiment. For 15 minutes, the student is presented with non-words on a computer screen which are read aloud, or matched by common characteristics. In this example the time taken is unlikely to be considered excessive by the student, who agreed to take part for a small monetary reward. The experiment does not intrude on the student's belief systems, nor cause pain or discomfort, other than, perhaps, a degree of boredom.

A similar experiment might be undertaken with a child of 7 years of age, perhaps reducing the time and the complexity of the task, but essentially maintaining the same method.

Example 2
An undergraduate is recruited to carry out a classic experiment in obedience (Milgram 1963). The student is told to deliver a very mild electric shock to another student in a second room, out of visual contact, if the second student makes an error on a task being administered. With each successive error the intensity of the shock is increased, on a scale clearly visible, and the discomfort of the second student is clearly heard.

As with the first experiment, it would be possible to replicate this with 7-year-old children. Indeed, this experiment might be practicable using children in infant school, or by replacing the second child by one of a number of animals.

Example 3
An 8-year-old child who is having great difficulty learning to read is placed in the experimental group of a new approach to literacy for a six week programme.

Example 4
A 5-year-old child is assessed by the teacher as part of the new, statutory baseline assessment process introduced in September 1998 for all children

1) Researching children's perspectives: ethical issues

GEOFF LINDSAY

Research with human participants is an intrusive process. This is the case, albeit to varying degrees, whether we are conducting an anonymous survey or an in-depth interview concerning personally sensitive material. It is intrusive in different ways, and hence the potential effect on the participant may vary. We cannot assume that research subjects simply cooperate with the researcher for a short period of their lives and then move on unchanged. This rather stark presentation of a view of research may appear unwarranted or overblown. Surely, some might argue, completing a questionnaire for a researcher, or a reading test as one of a class of pupils, is very different from discussing, as an adolescent, one's views on the school or doubts about sexual identity? Such a riposte has justification, but with respect to degree.

The position adopted in this chapter is derived from an interactionist perspective. Impact, for example, must be considered with respect to the participant in a context. In its simple form, the three components for consideration are the research participant, the research task and the interaction between the two.

I shall first present examples of research which differ on these dimensions. Next I shall consider the distinction between research as educational practice affecting children which is in process anyway. I shall then consider the main loci of influence engendering and ensuring ethical practice, and examine examples of ethical codes for their guidance. Finally I shall make suggestions for ethical guidelines for research with children on the basis of the previous analysis.

 **Part I** Theoretical
and conceptual issues

The methods of research that are used with children (and with adults) need very careful consideration. While the choice of method will always be determined by the research question, it is essential to take account of the age, social class, gender and ethnicity of children so that these key variables are considered in an explicit way when designing and conducting projects. In studies with children drawn from different social contexts it will be essential to consider how to modify the questionnaire, how to handle the interview and how to develop strategies of observation and participant observation. Many of these methods have been developed and used with adults but some consideration needs to be given to their adaptation for use with children. While the interview is the most commonly used method of social investigation it is not possible for it to be used in a 'standard' way. Instead, consideration needs to be given to the way it can be adapted in a range of projects for use with 5-year-olds as well as 15-year-olds. In these circumstances, researchers will be required to innovate.

As the researchers in this volume indicate, gaining access to children's perspectives can be obtained by innovative methods used by adults. They can also be obtained by children working with other children who themselves can gain insights into how a research team is developed and works. Altogether the contributions to this volume bring new insights to the study of children and childhood. The chapters also have the potential to influence other researchers and students interested in working with children to re-evaluate the ways in which studies can be designed, conducted, analysed, disseminated and published. This collection will help to advance our understanding of children's perspectives and the worlds in which they live.

Robert G. Burgess
University of Warwick
December 1998

in their first term in school. Decisions are made of the child's developmental status, on the basis of which the curriculum is modified to meet perceived needs.

These four examples have been chosen to highlight some basic issues in research practice. As will be shown below, ethical codes do not always provide explicit guidance on how to address the questions which arise from these initiatives.

Is it research?

Our present concern is research, but the practical element of the study may be similar to that which might occur as part of the child's education or general life experience. While the memory and obedience experiments in examples 1 and 2 are not (we hope) part of everyday school life, baseline assessment will be administered to all children at school entry. As I have argued elsewhere (Lindsay 1998; Lindsay and Desforges 1998) many baseline assessment schemes have not been researched adequately, if at all. The Qualifications and Curriculum Authority (QCA: personal communication) has indicated that evidence will need to be available when the schemes are presented for reaccreditation in about 2001, so all children subject to such schemes will in effect be part of a research study, even while decisions affecting their educational provision are being taken and implemented. Whenever an educational procedure is untried, or has limited evaluative data, there is a potential or implicit research activity in addition to its implementation. Take, for example, the National Curriculum assessments at the end of Key Stages. These certainly are not presented as research; indeed the results arising from them are published as factual representations of the standards in each cohort, and ultimately of each child taking part. Yet the evidential base for the assessments is limited and hence the children concerned might be considered to be part of a large scale experiment.

Such concerns are not limited to education. Policy and practice in child care, for example may also be criticized on the same grounds. There is therefore an interesting issue concerning the ethical interface between 're-search' and 'practice'. The focus of this chapter is research, but I shall return to the implications for 'practice' as the distinction between these two processes may not be clear.

Research and ethical codes

Conducting research is subject to guidance and control at a number of levels. The main dimensions to be considered are the content of the codes, the process by which they are invoked and guide research, and finally the procedures whereby any transgressions may be addressed.

Processes

There are six main focuses of influence whereby research procedures may be influenced: employer, local ethics committee, peer review, professional bodies, 'community of scholars' and national debate. These might refer to ethical codes, ethical guidelines, codes of conduct, research guidelines or similar phrases. The differences between these may be semantic only, or may be of more substance.

Employer

For many teachers the primary influence on any research will be their 'employer'. This term has several reference points which have changed since the late 1980s. Not very long ago the local education authority (LEA) would have been very influential in this role. While few LEAs had research sections, an officer or adviser would frequently act as a reference point for research proposals. Decisions might be taken by that person, or passed to a senior officer or the local education committee, particularly if the proposed research were considered 'sensitive'. With the post-Education Reform Act 1988 shift in the balance of power, such decisions now will often be taken by the school's governing body. However, where a research proposal concerns more than the teacher's own school, the involvement of the LEA will be required to coordinate responses.

External researchers, primarily those in higher education, will also frequently need to gain the approval of the individual school(s), and again coordination, support and advice from the LEA may be helpful.

Local ethics committee

The situation described above is rather ad hoc and reflects the relatively low priority of research in the day-to-day activity of schools. In contrast, medicine is an example of a profession where research and its conduct are taken very seriously. Typically there will be a local ethics committee functioning with clear procedure and authority which must approve any research activity and consider research proposals addressing a wide variety of subjects, from different professions such as medical practitioners, psychologists, speech and language therapists. Research may include issues covering cells, embryos or people from infancy to old age and other investigations and interventions. Although psychologists and teachers may not be required to present proposals to educational ethics committees, those who carry out joint research with health professionals will need to go through medical ethics committees.

Peer review

Research proposals submitted to a funding body will be subject to peer review. A proposal may be sent to several referees, each of whom will be asked to rate its worth on a number of dimensions, including ethical considerations. When presenting the outcome of research to a conference or journal, a similar peer review process will often occur. These procedures are powerful as negative reviews may result in research not being funded, or papers not being published.

Professional bodies

It might be argued that one of the indicators of a mature profession is that it has an ethical code governing its members' activities, including research. Medical practitioners have longstanding guidance based on the Hippocratic Oath, but now supplemented by specific guidance on practice through bodies including the royal colleges and the British Medical Association (BMA). The Law Society publishes extensive guidelines to practice, rather than an ethical code. For purposes of illustration, I shall examine the guidance offered by bodies for two professional groups, which overlap in membership: educational researchers and psychologists. Within the UK there are two major bodies which have set out codes: the British Educational Research Association (BERA 1992) and the British Psychological Society (BPS 1996). Each provides guidelines for their members, but their content (see pp. 10–17) and their standing is different. The BERA document sets out guidelines whereas the BPS document comprises a Code of Conduct, together with a series of guidelines for specific activities, reflecting the broader role of psychologists as practitioners in various fields as well as researchers. There are comparable codes or guidelines documents in other countries.

It is of interest to note that, according to Simons (1995), from its inaugural meeting in 1974 until 1992, BERA members refused to adopt a code of ethics; she believes that this was related to possible self-serving rather than public interest. None the less, the 1992 guidelines have an interesting tenor, 'one of trying to establish that researchers have rights at all' (Simons 1995: 441) and she argues that the current focus of discussion concerns

what defensible ethical procedures we can derive to try to ensure that the research we conduct can raise questions independent of political agendas, without political interference in the process and without findings being censored or publication restricted.

(Simons 1995: 442)

A major issue concerning such documents is the force with which they may be applied. Employment based procedures have in-built control mechanisms: unless the researcher meets the requirements laid down, the research may be prevented. Professional guidelines, however, are influenced by a different mechanism. First, such documents may be highly influential at the point of training, when the researcher's understanding and approach are being formed. Second, once in an appropriate post these guidelines provide useful support material to aid a researcher when faced with planning a project. Third, a code of conduct or ethical code may, if written into membership of an organization, have a more formal impact. For example, all members of the BPS must abide by its Code of Conduct. If a chartered psychologist is judged to have carried out research which offends against the Code that person may be sanctioned according to the judgement of seriousness of the transgression and any mitigating circumstances. As an ultimate sanction, the psychologist may be struck off the Register of Chartered Psychologists. Here the Code has 'teeth' and serves a regulatory purpose, not just guidelines. However, it should be noted that these teeth are somewhat blunted as the register has no statutory basis. Hence, psychologists who are struck off may not refer to themselves as chartered psychologists but there is no automatic restriction on practising.

'Community of scholars'

This focus of influence is the least organized and formal. Researchers will debate with their peers through a wide variety of processes including research seminars, conference papers with discussions and house magazines, and informal discussions with colleagues. In such transactions, researchers learn from each other, and in the case of public lectures and correspondence, from the wider society. In some cases the focus may be a point of ethics or an ethical dilemma; in others the discussion may include an ethical issue. The fundamental characteristics of these interchanges are informal and grounded in the view of the researcher as having integrity, and being willing to learn.

National debate

The final focus of influence to be considered concerns national initiatives on research as an activity. This is currently a highly topical affair in education, with reports sponsored by two government departments on educational research: *Educational Research: A Critique* sponsored by the Office for Standards in Education (Ofsted) (Tooley and Darby 1998) and *Excellence in Research in Schools* (Hillage *et al.* 1998) for the Department for Education and Employment (DfEE).

The sponsoring of these reports was apparently stimulated by concerns about the quality of educational research, but the current discussion will focus on the ethical dimension and will use the 'Tooley Report' (as it has come to be known) as an example.

The question of ethical practice in research is not discussed in such terms. However, there is much consideration of the concept of *partisanship*. Tooley and Darby (1998) present an analysis of papers in four British educational journals. One of their criteria concerns whether the research avoids partisanship in the focus, conduct and presentation of the research. This comes within a section analysing whether the research makes a serious contribution to fundamental theory or knowledge. The authors claim that, on the basis of their analysis of 264 articles in the four journals, 41 of which were read and critically examined in detail, one of the four major themes they identified was the *partisan researcher*. Tooley and Darby provide evidence for partisanship of various kinds; they also report research that they deem not to be partisan.

This concept of partisanship is not found in ethical codes as such. However, it is related to basic principles, especially *integrity* and *competence*, but note it could apply to either. For example, a researcher may be insufficiently competent, and hence fail to report all available findings to provide a balanced perspective; or, in enthusiasm, may focus on one set of results which supports the position the researcher holds; or, as a result of limited competence, may misinterpret a statistical analysis so presenting confirmatory rather than negative findings with respect to a position. All of these (and others could be listed) are questions of competence, but there is no intent on the researcher's part to mislead deliberately.

For example, in the late 1970s I noticed that a research publication had reported the statistical analysis of a dataset as indicating that the experimental and control groups were not significantly different on a key measure, whereas the correct interpretation of the statistics was the opposite. This error led to a fundamental flaw in the interpretation of the research. While no intent to mislead may be present, it should be noted that such behaviour is an ethical matter. Misleading or incorrectly interpreted results will misrepresent research. In the category of integrity, the question would encompass intent also. In the example above, the issue might concern the actions of the researcher when the error was drawn to their attention.

Tooley and Darby (1998) raise important issues about partisanship, which I have related to questions of competence and integrity. Their critique is a cause for concern, with a number of articles presented as examples of research which is partisan in focus, conduct or report. Also, given their selection criteria for the articles examined in depth, they argue that the themes they identify are likely to represent typical strands in the research literature.

Of course, it is also instructive to evaluate their report on the same basis. While the methods are presented with clarity, and appear to be appropriate in general, there are questions which the authors note. For example, there is a sound basis for the four journals selected but, different journals might have produced other findings. Interestingly, presented as a footnote, the authors note that 'the project's survey of specialised journals, not reported here gave a picture which was very different' (Tooley and Darby 1998: 42). The point concerns methodology, with the high proportion of qualitative papers in the present analysis being mirrored by the exact opposite in the analyses of 'key reading research journals', where 85 per cent were quantitative in nature. Hence, the conclusions of the report are limited – as the authors recognize – but there must be a question why these other analyses are not presented with similar forcefulness, especially given examples of exactly opposite results.

Comment

These processes may be considered on a continuum of formality and impact. At one end there are informal procedures built upon ad hoc or informal arrangements, of advice and guidance while at the other end of the continuum are procedures which may prevent research taking place or being published, and in some instances sanctions being taken against researchers judged to be unethical. In considering such processes it is also important to reflect upon the content of the codes/guidelines and their rationale: the principles which guide the content and implementation.

Content of ethical codes and guidelines

It may be argued that there should be one ethical code for researchers with children. If it were possible to distil the essential ethical principles it should be possible to devise a code which would be appropriate whether the researcher were a teacher, psychologist, sociologist or medical specialist. In practice this has not occurred, the reasons being practical rather than as a result of detailed analyses, debate and dispute. Rather, ethical codes and guidelines have been developed by a variety of bodies over time.

An example concerns psychology. The European Federation of Professional Psychologists Associations (EFPPA) sought to produce one ethical code to which psychologists in all member associations would be subject. Despite the high degree of overlap between existing codes (Lindsay 1992) the exercise was to prove problematic. Some countries had no code. Those codes which existed had difference of emphasis reflecting local situations. Producing one common code not only would require drafting of an agreed formulation, but also would need its ratification by each member association through its particular procedures. As a result, EFPPA determined to develop instead one meta-code, which stated the elements that each association's code must address rather than set out the code to apply to individuals.

These examples are not specific to research, which is just one activity to be undertaken by the professionals concerned here, and this presents another problem. It may be possible to devise a set of guidelines for research as an activity, and this is characterized by the BERA document, but there is no one group of professionals who are 'researchers' only.

As a result, while BERA and its US counterpart the American Educational Research Association (AERA) may develop guidelines whose content is exclusively about research, professional bodies must address research as just one of a number of activities. The approach of the BPS is instructive here with a single Code of Conduct, providing the general, 'bottom line' descriptions of behaviour which not only guide but also will form the criteria against which any complaint may be judged, and a series of guidelines.

BERA Ethical Guidelines for Educational Research

The BERA Guidelines comprise an introduction, a general statement and seven sections. The introduction sets the context, and interestingly refers to the political context. The opening sentence states:

> The British Educational Research Association has been aware for some time of a concern amongst the educational research community about increasing restrictions being imposed by government agencies on the conduct and dissemination of the educational research and evaluation which they sponsor.
>
> (BERA 1992: 1)

The document continues by warning about accepting sub-optimal contractual obligations, restricting researchers' freedom to publish, and warning of increasing restrictions on the conduct of the research itself. However, the opening clause provides a statement with broader reference:

> The British Educational Research Association believes that all educational research should be conducted within an ethic of respect for persons, respect for knowledge, respect for democratic values, and respect for the quality of educational research.

Only one of the seven sections in the Guidelines makes direct reference to participants as its focus. That section is reproduced in full.

Responsibility to the participants

7 Participants in a research study have the right to be informed about the aims, purposes and likely publication of findings involved in the research and of potential consequences for participants, and to give their informed consent before participating in research.

8 Care should be taken when interviewing children and students up to school leaving age; permission should be obtained from the school, and if they so suggest, the parents.

9 Honesty and openness should characterise the relationship between researchers, participants and institutional representatives.

10 Participants have the right to withdraw from a study at any time.

11 Researchers have a responsibility to be mindful of cultural, religious, gendered, and other significant differences within the research population in the planning, conducting, and reporting of their research.

(BERA 1992: 2)

Note that there is one specific reference to children, the others being guidelines with general applications. However, Guideline 8 is unclear in its advice. What is the implication of taking care in this context? The sentence as a whole implies its subject is one of consent, with the school being recommended as the agency for giving consent, or suggesting parents do so. The other guidelines in this section also have implications for children as research participants. The statements here may be seen as worthy in themselves, but they raise the question of implementation. For example, if participants 'have the right to be informed of the aims, purposes and likely publication of findings involved in the research and of potential consequences for participants' (Clause 7) how is this to be ensured? At what level of detail should the researchers explain? Is it enough to say that you (a 7-year-old) will be given an assessment of your reading in order that relative progress in schools of boys and girls may be examined, that the results will be published in a journal, and that there are no direct consequences for you personally? Is this sufficient, or not enough?

This simple example highlights the hidden complexity. Can an individual 8-year-old be allowed 'to withdraw . . . at any time' (Clause 10), and if so how will this be arranged?

In addition to this section, there are other clauses which have direct implications for individual research participants. For example under Responsibility to the Public, Clause 13 commences 'Informants and participants have a right to remain anonymous'. What meaning has anonymity if a teacher marks test results in the example above, or wanders into the room during a research interview or discussion group as described by France, Bendelow and Williams in Chapter 12?

The BERA Guidelines also recommend in their guidance on freedom to publish that 'The understanding should be conveyed to participants as part of the responsibility to secure informed comment' (Clause 15). Again, one might ask how a young child can be given sufficient understanding of the politics of publication in order to give *informed* consent.

Informed consent

This brief analysis indicates the importance of the concept of *informed consent*. Note the two elements: consent must be given, and it must be informed. Researchers may be considered to have extra responsibilities when the participants are children. It is necessary to ensure that a child fully understands not only the short term implications of the research but also the long term (e.g. being a 'case study' in a paper or on television). Stanley *et al.* (1995) have reviewed the literature on consent and argue that, even in adults, the general trend is for studies to show comprehension of consent information to be poor. However, they argue that the competence of minors to consent to research is probably often underestimated.

Factors to be considered in ensuring that the child is informed include age, general cognitive ability, emotional status and knowledge. Also, note that these interact. For example, a normally capable 15-year-old may not be in a position to give informed consent for a particular research into an issue relating closely to a significant aspect of the young person's emotional life. Vulnerability must be considered in a broader way than age alone, with the responsibility on the researcher to err on the rule of caution.

It is also important to consider the nature of the task. It may be agreed that there is an increasing need for informed consent with reduced anonymity and increased intrusiveness of the procedure. Hence a 20-minute group reading test is different in degree from a 20-minute individual assessment, or the implementation of a programme of counselling, or behaviour management to enable competing approaches to be evaluated.

The degree of exposure of the child is relevant, ranging from low or minimal exposure (e.g. the aggregated reading test results of a school) to the high exposure of an individual case study.

As an example of intrusive research, we have probably come a long way since an experiment by Landis (1924, described in Crafts *et al.* 1938) on emotional reactions. Landis (1924) compared 25 subjects, mainly adults but including one 13-year-old boy, a hospital patient with high blood pressure. The subjects were exposed to various apparatus to produce emotional responses. The purpose was to assess facial expressions of emotion. There were 17 situations, including the playing of jazz and technical music, and reading from the Bible. These might be seen as relatively benign depending upon your view of music and religion. Further situations included a deception leading to the subject sniffing ammonia rather than 'syrup of lemons' as indicated, being asked to write out a description of the meanest and most contemptible and embarrassing thing you ever did – and having this read out.

Other tasks included a mental multiplication (e.g. 79 × 67) but with distraction, presenting a set of French pornographic photographs and being asked to cut a rat's head off. Consider also this description of situation 14.

> A pail was placed beside the subject, and he was told, 'without looking into the pail, shove the cover to one side and put your hand inside to the bottom of the pail and feel around'. While the subject was doing this, he received a strong electric shock. The pail contained several inches of water and three live frogs.
>
> (Crafts *et al.* 1938: 108)

We might be horrified by such research and take comfort in its having taken place in the 1920s. We may not go so far now, but issues of informed consent, intrusiveness and abuse remain key ethical issues in research with children.

Ethical codes and guidelines: overview of content

Examination of other ethical codes and guidelines provides a useful entry into consideration of necessary components of a code for researchers with children as participants. In this section I shall examine the codes developed by psychological associations and societies, in particular the American Psychological Association (APA 1992), British Psychological Society (BPS 1996), Canadian Psychological Association (CPA 1992) and the European Federation of Professional Psychologists Association (EFPPA 1995).

In each case, research is only one area considered. Also, the origins and format of each varies. The 1992 APA Code, the latest revision of a code first set out in 1953, is set out as Ethical Principles of Psychologists and Code of Conduct. It comprises the presentation of six ethical principles followed by 102 ethical standards, specifying behaviour to be expected. The BPS Code of Conduct comprises a general statement followed by four sections, each comprising between five and ten specific injunctions. Compared with that of the APA, the BPS Code is more general in its statements. The Canadian Code follows the APA format with four principles together with specific statements which are associated with each principle. However, uniquely among these publications, the CPA Code is supplemented by discussion and guidance, including what to do if principles conflict, and the ethical decision making process.

The original APA Code approved in 1953 was devised from ethical dilemmas arising in psychologists' practice. In fact, inspection of the *American Psychologist* journal in years leading up to the codes being ratified reveals a debate about whether having a code was beneficial. For example, it was argued that a code should be unnecessary and scientists should be expected to behave in an ethical manner. For example, Hall (1952) in an article entitled 'Crooks, codes and cant' argued:

> I am opposed to a code because I think it plays into the hands of crooks on the one hand and because it makes those who are covered by the code feel smug and sanctimonious on the other hand.
>
> (Hall 1952: 430)

This view did not prevail; furthermore, the later versions came to be developed by expert committees building upon earlier codes, not directly from real ethical dilemmas. It is this first process which was also followed by the EFPPA Task Force charged with designing the meta-code. This comprises four ethical principles together with statements of behaviour, but unlike the APA and CPA Codes, these statements state what national associations' codes should contain, not how an individual should act.

Examination of the context of these codes with respect to research, and to children, reveals the following findings.

APA Code
The American Code has 26 statements directly addressing research issues. Children are not mentioned specifically in any. The nearest direct reference is in Statement 6.11 Informed Consent to Research where Clause (e) states:

For persons who are legally incapable of giving informed consent, psychologists nevertheless (1) provide an appropriate explanation, (2) obtain the participant's assent, and (3) obtain appropriate permission from a legally authorized person, if such substitute consent is required by law.

(APA 1992: 1608)

Other clauses which are relevant, but as part of a reference to 'special populations', include Clause 1.08 Human Differences, where psychologists, in any professional activity, are required to obtain appropriate training, experience and necessary supervision where differences of age but also gender, race, ethnicity and other factors significantly affect psychologists' work.

BPS Code

The British Code makes direct reference to children only in its section on obtaining consent. Psychologists are required to carry out 'investigations and interventions only with the valid consent of participants'. In Clause 3.5 it is required that they

recognise and uphold the right of those whose capacity to give valid consent to interventions may be diminished, including the young, those with learning disabilities, the elderly, those in the care of an institution or detained under the provisions of the law.

(BPS 1996: 2)

Clause 3.6 requires that, where the person is in no position to give valid consent, the psychologist must seek it from a person who has legal authority.

The BPS (1996) booklet also contains supplementary guidelines including Ethical Principles for Conducting Research with Human Participants (BPS 1996: 7–11). Children are specifically addressed only in the section on consent. The guidelines largely mirror the statement in the Code, but add that in cases where 'the nature of the research precludes consent being given by parents or permission from teachers, before proceeding with the research, the investigator must obtain the approval from an Ethics Committee' (Clause 3.3).

CPA Code

The Canadian Code has more references to children, although these are often tied in with other vulnerable groups. Also, the major point of reference is to consent, which is located within the section Respect for the Dignity of Persons. For example, Clause I.23 states:

Respect the right of the individual to discontinue participation or service at any time, and to be responsive to non-verbal indications of desire to discontinue if the individual has difficulty with verbally communicating such a desire (e.g. young children, verbally disabled persons).

(CPA 1992: 33)

Further statements are provided in the subsection Vulnerabilities. The Code requires that informed consent be sought from an appropriate person with legal responsibility in the case of children (and others) (Clause I.29). Also, even if consent is sought from an adult, the assent of the person should still be sought. Clause I.28 requires:

Not (to) use persons of diminished capacity to give informed consent in research studies, if the research involved might equally well be carried out with persons who have a fuller capacity to give informed consent.

(CPA 1992: 35)

EFPPA Meta-Code
Unlike the previous codes which address the behaviour of individuals, the EFPPA Meta-Code provides guidance to national associations on the contents of their codes. However, even less guidance is provided on children; indeed they are not mentioned at all. Relevant clauses concern the need for national codes to provide guidance on informal consent, and Clause 3.1.3 (iii) which requires recognition that there may be more than one client, with differing professional relationships with the psychologist. This may refer to parents and children, but is more an issue for practice other than research.

Comment
Examination of the BERA Ethical Guidelines and the codes of conduct of three major psychological societies (APA, BPS and CPA) and one European federation indicate that guidance on research with children is barely addressed as a specific topic. Rather, these documents address, in various ways, broader concerns. First, one dimension is the ethical principle, for example respecting the dignity of the person. Children, although not necessarily specified are subsumed. Second, the reference may be to an area of practice, e.g. research. Again, many points concerning the care to be taken, competence of the researcher and need to avoid deception or pain/discomfort have general applicability. Third, children and young people may be included in 'special populations'. These are of two kinds: the first reflects the diversity of society with respect to gender, ethnicity and the like, and age is one such dimension; the second concerns populations deemed vulnerable, including those developmentally young either through normal maturation or intellectual impairment.

These conclusions are unremarkable in one sense, but do raise the question: is it appropriate for there to be so little direct guidance on ethical concerns for research with children?

To answer this question requires a different approach. One method would be to examine the dilemmas, uncertainties and concerns of researchers undertaking research with children. This approach has been developed particularly in the work of Pope and colleagues in the USA (e.g. Pope and Vetter 1992) and Lindsay and colleagues in the UK (Lindsay and Colley 1995; Lindsay and Clarkson 1999). In these studies, the targeted population are asked to provide one or more examples of incidents which had been professionally challenging. Analyses of the responses are then categorized according to salient dimensions. In these studies, research was found to be a relatively frequent domain for dilemmas, albeit much less prevalent than, for example, confidentiality.

Ethical guidelines for research with children

In this chapter I have reviewed ethical considerations for research with children and young people. While some professional researchers (e.g. in medicine or psychology) may be subject to enforceable codes of conduct, other researchers (e.g. teachers) are subject only to guidelines to good practice. However, these guidelines and codes provide only limited specific guidance on the subject. In this section, therefore, I shall offer additional suggestions for consideration when researching children and young people.

Ethical principles

Ethical codes and guidelines either explicitly or implicitly derive from ethical principles. Expression of these principles may vary, with different elements included in each, but those which structure the EFPPA meta-code are helpful:

- respect for a person's rights and dignity
- competence
- responsibility
- integrity.

The first step, therefore, is to consider these principles and their general implications. For example, what follows from the principle 'competence'?

Standards

In deciding upon the specificity of the research exercise, the researcher will identify exact areas of practice. A researcher in this case would analyse the skills and knowledge required to undertake the research and ensure that these were available. If these were not, either they must be acquired through appropriate training, or another competent person should carry out the work. Hence, the researcher works from general principles to specific standards.

Coverage

This process should be repeated for each ethical principle: the published codes and guidelines relevant to the researcher are necessary but not sufficient. Each is too general to offer specific advice.

Interactions

Research on ethical dilemmas has indicated that practice cannot be made to fit written codes, however well they are devised. There may be two or more factors, which have different, even conflicting implications. In our research, the most dramatic has been the conflict between the need to maintain confidentiality and the social responsibility to inform when a threat to another's well-being is made whether in the future or past (e.g. revelations of abuse).

In research with children, it is necessary also to be aware of interacting and competing principles. For example, the difficulties in ensuring valid informed consent by a child may be offset by seeking it from the parent. A study where information is not released on any individual child may justify consent from the school rather than parent. The benefits to society as a whole may need to be weighed against a very low probability of a negative consequence for an individual.

The CPA Code advocates that, although it is not possible to provide a single absolute ordering of principles, the four it specifies should normally be the appropriate order of weight in any conflict:

- respect for the dignity of persons
- responsible caring
- integrity in relationships
- responsibility to society.

Supervision

Resolving a dilemma is not mechanistic. In many cases there is no 'obvious' answer, but rather a balance of judgement is required. In such cases, the support of another is good practice, and is often specified in professional guidance. In the case of, say, a teacher undertaking a research degree, there will be supervision from the tutor. Responsibility for different aspects of the research may be differentially allocated, the supervisor may take ultimate responsibility for advice, but the actions of supervisees remain their responsibility. This supervision does not absolve researchers of responsibility.

Furthermore, the researcher must, to behave ethically, avoid pseudo-supervision. This may be found in an informal supervision relationship when the researcher seeks a colleague who will collude with the researcher's preferred way of resolving the dilemma, rather than challenge and help the researcher to think through the issues. Hence, it is an ethical responsibility of all researchers to enter into at least a discussion of the ethical issues concerned with their work, and for this to be undertaken in an ethical manner itself.

Political context

In our study of psychologists, Ann Colley and I argued that there were two kinds of ethical dilemmas reported. The first were the traditional concerns of competence, gaining informed consent and the like. However, the second group comprised dilemmas arising from the psychologist's position *vis-à-vis* an institution (Lindsay and Colley 1995).

In the context of educational research, for example, dilemmas may arise in the publication of results which are unwelcome 'politically', whether the potentially embarrassed party is a school, LEA, Ofsted or another government agency. Indeed, approval for or facilitation of a research project may be influenced by political concerns. In such cases the researcher has a different problem. What is the price of social responsibility, and scientific truth, as against possible threats to one's career? Again, this is not specific to work with children, but given the political sensitivity of education, these issues will directly affect those who undertake research in this field. As I have argued elsewhere (Lindsay 1995) science is not value free. Examples of politically sensitive research with children include the implementation of baseline assessment given the lack of requirements for technical quality information on the scales; the validity of inspectors' judgements in Ofsted inspections of schools and university courses of initial teacher education; the validity of school improvement measures, including the choices of measures to judge school effectiveness, and the validity of trend analyses leading to schools being judged as 'improving' or 'failing'.

Conclusion

Research with children poses the same ethical questions that apply to other types of research. Practitioners should respect their participants, in their interactions, in the tasks they set, and in their treatment of information which they acquire. Researchers should be competent, know when to increase their competence by training, and when to seek the support of another skilled or knowledgeable researcher. They should have regard to scientific professional responsibility, and have a sense of social responsibility. Their concerns, therefore, address primarily the participants in their research, but also the wider scientific and professional community, and society as a whole.

There are also concerns specific to children and to young people. Primarily these are focused upon informed, valid consent, and ways of ensuring that this is attained, but the child is also included meaningfully in the decision making process. Furthermore, there is a duty to ensure that research is not carried out on children unnecessarily, and that the degree of intrusion is minimal (e.g. US Department of Health and Human Services 1995).

Researching children requires practitioners to be aware of the relevant ethical codes and guidelines, but, further, to be able to judge the relative importance of conflicting ethical principles. To do this successfully requires not only further clarification of the ethical dilemmas which arise in research with children, a research issue itself, but also that researchers, as an ethical position, should ensure that they seek support and supervision from knowledgeable mentors or colleagues which will challenge their thinking and practice. Perhaps it is now time to have ethics committees to guide research in education, analogous to those in the health service. These might be formed from representatives of LEA officers, teachers, researchers in higher education and parents. There is also a case for members who are at least close to being the subjects of the research, young people of 16–19 for example. Continuing professional development for researchers with children should include increasing sensitivity to identification and resolving ethical issues, and in ensuring that practitioners' research is not only valid and useful, but also ethical.

2 The UN Convention on the Rights of the Child: giving children a voice

ANNE SINCLAIR TAYLOR

In general it is adults who write about and debate the issue of rights for children. This might be interpreted as symptomatic of the power relationships, which confine children to subordinate roles in their societies, or might simply be seen as an inevitable phase in the process of change. As with any complex concept, defining what is meant by rights is problematic; adult conceptions and interpretations differ widely. Children's views may cover a different set of perspectives. Rights can be seen in civil, economic, political, cultural and social terms. This chapter explores how far legislation has moved rights for children in the UK forward in relation to education.

It can be argued that to be human confers personhood and absolute rights which should not be circumscribed by age, ability, nationality, gender or any other characteristic. However, in the UK legislation, such as the Disability Discrimination Act 1996 and the Sex Discrimination Act 1975, has been necessary to assert the rights of vulnerable groups – those who suffer from discrimination of varying kinds. Such legislation has tended to see marginalized groups as having discrete rather than complex and interacting problems. That is, it fails to address issues which compound disadvantage such as the way ethnicity can interact with disability to result in further disadvantage (Sinclair Taylor 1995b).

One document which attempts to delineate new rights for all European Union citizens is the Treaty of Amsterdam. 'The Treaty will outlaw all discrimination based on gender, race, religion, sexual orientation, age, or disability' and take action to 'combat social exclusion' (Palmer 1997: 10).

However, it fails to identify and include the unique needs of children and in so doing it signals the differential and marginal status which children continue to be afforded.

Children and the law

In Great Britain over the past century legislation relating specifically to children has been brought onto the statute books. For example the Prevention of Cruelty to and Protection of Children Act 1889 made explicit that cruelty to children should be viewed as a criminal act; the National Society for the Prevention of Cruelty to Children (NSPCC) was established in the UK a year later. In 1948 the first Children Act was implemented. This legislation emphasized children's best interests while at the same time asserted the importance of keeping families together. The thrust of the legislation was to protect children within a framework where adults, be they parents or professionals, dominated decision making.

Eleven years later, in 1959, the United Nations (UN) issued its first Declaration of the Rights of Children, which focused on care and protection of children in terms of nutrition, medical attention and education as well as their rights to be protected from exploitation. However, this legislation continued the trend of operationalizing a deficit model of childhood; children being viewed as the property of their parents, as passive recipients of decision making about their lives. It was not until the 1980s that a more active, participatory and individualistic role for children was placed on the agenda. Children began to be seen as potentially having views and ideas about their own lives and of having a right to genuine participation in decision making affecting them.

Constructions of childhood: the making of children

Children are designated by the UN Convention as being everyone under the age of 18. Children, however, are not a homogenous group, but comprise a wide variety of characteristics and dispositions; children live in highly variable family circumstances and widely differing communities; they attend schools that differ in terms of ethos and facilities. This results in some children's early lives being constructed in considerably more advantaged ways than others. Some children experience extreme cruelty, for example Rikki Neave, who suffered prolonged ill-treatment and eventual murder on 28 November 1994 in woodland near Peterborough. He was strangled with his anorak. His mother was cleared of murder but jailed for 7 years for cruelty, and responsibility for murder was not established. Equally there are cases of children themselves behaving in ways which horrify and disturb, for example, the child murderers of 2-year-old James Bulger in 1993. The media played an active role in the construction and demonization of these children. The *Daily Star*'s headline following their conviction was 'How Do You Feel Now You Little Bastards?' (25 November 1993). There was also the case of the children at the Ridings School in York who were perceived to be out of control and unteachable. The *Sunday Times* (3 November 1996) ran a piece entitled 'Anarchy Rules OK', asserting that the collapse of school discipline was illustrative of such deterioration throughout the UK.

Children, like adults, are viewed and depicted in differing ways depending on, for example, their gender, age, nationality, abilities or social class (discussed further by Lloyd-Smith and Tarr in Chapter 5). However there is a tendency, as refracted through the media, to focus on extremes. 'That English culture is deeply inimical to children and prefers to see them either as monsters, as in the popular *Toddler Taming* by Christopher Green, or as fantasy angels as in the Mothercare catalogue' (Neumark 1997: 6). The director of research at the National Children's Bureau (NCB) believes that 'teenagers are demonised in our society . . . we see them as feckless, troublesome and economically dependent – not as contributors' (J. Watts 1997: 22). Recent evidence shows that more children are living in poverty with families solely dependent on benefit. Such children are more likely to become marginalized, leave school without qualifications, experience unemployment and become known to the police (Howarth *et al.* 1998).

There are common factors which contribute to the vulnerability and uncertainty of children and young people's lives across the world, including war, poverty, divorce, crime, drugs and alcohol abuse, unemployment, homelessness, poor health and so on. However countries problematize and respond to the effects of these influences on children in differing ways, depending on the severity of problems and the resources and political will to address them. About 40 per cent of India's population live below the poverty line and only 25 per cent of the country's 350 million children go to school. In Latin America and the Caribbean 15 million children struggle for survival on the streets but Shelter estimates that approximately 156,000 children in the UK are homeless, with 2000–3000 sleeping rough (S. Moore 1993). For many children, childhood carries no special privileges; in fact disadvantages can outweigh advantages:

> For childhood to have a future, we must insist on their rights. While philosophers debate the feasibility of granting rights to those who are unable to exercise them, who among us would not insist that every child has the right to shelter, food, education, love? In other words the right to a childhood itself.
>
> (S. Moore 1993: 42)

The case for individual rights for children

The UN Convention on the Rights of the Child 1989 provided a landmark in the development of rights for children. As a result a number of organizations developed in order to lobby on behalf of, and provide advice for, children.

Peter Newell and co-workers at EPOCH developed their organization to exert pressure to have the UK statutory endorsement of physical punishment repealed (Section 1(7) of the Children and Young Persons Act 1969 gives parents, teachers and other persons having lawful control of the child the right to administer punishment to them). EPOCH's remit is to promote adoption of new legislation to remove the common law rights of parents (teachers have been prohibited since 1988) to hit their children. Precedents have been already been set, for example Sweden in 1979, Finland in 1983, Denmark in 1985, Norway in 1987 and Austria in 1989 have all adopted laws which prohibit parents hitting their children. In the UK evidence from a random sample of 700 parents showed that 62 per cent hit their 1-year-old children and that by the age of 7 years 75 per cent of children were either hit or threatened with implements. The majority of British parents interviewed seemed to believe that physical punishment was an inevitable and even necessary aspect of ordinary child upbringing (Newsom and Newsom 1990). Newell (1991) is calling for an end to the use of physical punishment by invoking relevant articles in the UN Convention 1989 which state that children should be seen as individuals with rights of their own. This has been strengthened by the European Commission's challenge to UK legislation on the use of 'reasonable chastisement'. EPOCH has a clear position on this issue: *Hitting People is Wrong – and Children are People Too* (EPOCH Worldwide 1996: 1).

Questioning the cultural acceptance of hitting children has articulated with the tragic and high profile child abuse tragedies which marked the 1970s and 1980s (such as the deaths of Maria Colwell in 1973, Jasmine Beckford in 1984 and Kimberley Carlile in 1986) and thus to cause the roles and status of children in society to be debated. These events have brought into sharp focus the issue of some families being dangerous places for children. They have shown that children's rights may be at odds with parents' rights; that children need the protection of being seen as individuals in their own right.

However, the case for rights for children is far from universally accepted. As G. Alexander (1995: 131) says, 'The concept of children . . . being seen as rights holders constitutes a fundamental challenge to a value system which at root believes that children should be seen and not heard'.

UN Convention on the Rights of the Child 1989

The UN Convention was landmark legislation in delineating rights for children, expressing vision and hope in terms of both their protection and *participation* in society. The Convention was adopted by the UN in 1989 and ratified by 177 nations by September 1995 (including the UK) and marked a significant development in thinking about children and their rights as individuals. The Convention asserts the political and civil rights of children, e.g. the right to freedom of speech or the right to due process in cases concerning juveniles. The majority of the Convention articles address, however, 'a series of civil, economic, social and cultural rights which go well beyond the usual jurisdiction of the courts' (Bennett 1996: 45). This makes the realization of rights for children across their societies a highly complex task involving not only state parties and families but also all services which involve and impact upon children, including education. This chapter examines children's rights to express their views in matters which concern them, by looking at their participation in educational decision making.

Content of the Convention

The UN Convention requires that services for children develop policies that are responsive to the wide range of needs and abilities that the term 'children' encompasses. The Convention is a wide ranging treaty that looks at the rights of children in all spheres of their lives. Its contents are summarized as follows:

- *Measures for implementation*: Articles 4, 42 and 44.6 oblige governments to take all possible measures to ensure implementation, to publicize its contents and to report on progress towards implementation.
- *General principles*: Articles 2, 3, 6 and 12 call for non-discrimination, best interests of the child, the right to life, survival and development and respect for the views of the child.
- *Civil rights and freedoms*: Articles 7, 8, 37a and 13–19 concern the preservation of cultural identity and of freedom of thought and association as well as protection from violence, abuse and neglect, torture or other degrading treatment.
- *Care within or outside the family*: Articles 5, 9, 10, 11, 18, 20, 21, 25 and 27 cover issues such as parental responsibility adoption and reviews of placements outside the family.
- *Welfare and health*: Articles 18, 23, 24, 26 and 27 cover welfare issues such as childcare services, standards of living and provision for disabled children.
- *Education and recreation*: Articles 28, 29 and 31 cover education, recreation and cultural activities.
- *Special measures of protection*: There are eleven articles which cover children with profound needs such as those caught up in armed conflicts or suffering from economic, sexual or drug related abuse.

For an accessible elaboration of the articles see Children's Rights Office (1995). Many of the above articles can be seen as being relevant to education. However, some articles are more obviously relevant than others:

- *Article 3*: the duty in all actions to consider the best interests of the child.
- *Article 12*: the child's right to express an opinion and to have that opinion taken into account in any matter or procedure affecting the child.
- *Article 2*: all rights in the Convention must apply without discrimination of any kind irrespective of race, colour, language, religion, national, ethnic or social origin, disability or other status.
- *Article 19*: the right to protection from all forms of violence, injury, abuse, neglect or exploitation.
- *Article 23*: the right of disabled children to special care, education and training to ensure the fullest possible social integration.
- *Article 28*: the right to education, including vocational education, on the basis of equality of opportunity.
- *Article 29*: the duty of the government to direct education at developing the child's fullest personality and talents and promoting respect for human rights.
- *Article 30*: the rights of children from minority communities to enjoy their own culture, language and practise their own religion and culture.

Broadly, in educational terms, the Convention asserts rights for children to participate in decision making, have equal opportunities in accessing an appropriate education (in an inclusive setting) and of being protected from harm. It offers a 'principled framework' within which to analyse UK education policies (Lansdown and Newell 1994).

Framework for analysis

There are many layers of influence on children's experiences of schooling from the macro, structural, political and ideological through to the community and individual school and class contexts. These layers fuse and interact to result in the individual conditions that comprise everyday classroom learning. I shall now look at the structural context in which education has developed and relate how tenets of the UN Convention articulate with these developments.

Structural context

The perception of the child as a small adult to be trained has survived robustly in contemporary Western thought and practice. Children are still expected to work extraordinarily long hours at school, in directive, authoritarian classrooms, so as to forge them into the disciplined workforce of the future. They are seen by many policy makers as units of human resources, the future guarantors of pensions, social values, even of nationhood and other ideologies.

(Bennett 1996: 48)

Educational standards were identified 'as the main cause of British economic decline' in the great debate of 1976–7 (Merson 1995: 303). It was claimed by the then Prime Minister James Callaghan that the education system did not prepare young people adequately as a workforce capable of competing in global markets. This belief is predicated on the view that children are commodities, to be trained to contribute to the wealth of the nation.

At a crude level these views objectify children and cause education itself to be conceptualized as a product. It also means that some children, namely those who are likely to contribute most, have greatest cultural capital; children who are least likely to contribute to the wealth of the nation will have least. There is a social Darwinism about this approach which works against Articles 2, 28 and 30, which emphasize non-discriminatory practice and social integration (D. Hamilton 1997).

Political and ideological context

The linkage of economic prosperity and education paved the way for the Education Reform Act (ERA) 1988, which introduced the National Curriculum, a centrally defined curriculum which focused on the basics which were defined as English, Maths and Science. The subsequent Education Acts tightened the focus further so that reading and number dominated and children tested against national criteria not only at ages 7, 11, 14 as well as 16 and 18 but also on entry to school through baseline assessment. Results are made public along with Ofsted inspections, and schools are judged as failing or succeeding in published league tables. Education has become a commodity that is weighed and measured for the benefit of the prime customers, parents. The rights of parents, not children, are articulated through various parent charters. Children have no formal rights to participate in educational decision making. As Lansdown and Newell (1994: 162) put it, 'Education as it currently stands has no principled framework within which to promote the rights of the child and lacks any commitment to promoting the best interests of the child'.

There are many examples where children could play a more active role at policy levels but recent initiatives in education not only fail to do this but also are reconceptualizing the very nature of children themselves. The discourse of many documents reveals, for example, that the term 'children' has been supplanted by 'pupils'. Indeed there is little mention of children or pupils in the guidelines for standards for Qualified Teacher Status (QTS)

(DfEE 1998). These documents emphasize subject mastery, i.e. the product of learning, for both student teachers (referred to as trainees) and children (pupils). The discourse underpins a product model of learning which fails to see children as active participants in decision making about their learning. It also sees students in a similar way. Those to be awarded Qualified Teacher Status must, when assessed, demonstrate that they, for example, 'monitor and intervene when teaching to ensure sound learning and discipline' or 'sustain the momentum of pupils' work through structuring information well, including outlining content and aims, signalling transitions and summarizing key points as the lesson progresses' (DfEE 1998: 13). This document is redolent of a didacticism which is in breach of Article 12 of the Convention.

While there is concern about the rights of all children, there is particular concern that the rights of children with special educational needs (SEN) may be being uniquely disadvantaged by provisions under the Education Act 1996. One of the key features of the preceding Bill was to ensure that the child with SEN had a voice in decision making, for example to make representations and exercise rights of appeal concerning educational provision. Indeed the Code of Practice on the Identification and Assessment of Special Educational Needs (DfE 1994a) makes explicit that children should contribute to decision making at all five stages of the Code; 'special educational provision is most effective when those responsible take into account the ascertainable wishes of the child concerned, considered in the light of his or her age and understanding' (DfE 1994a: 3). Information required from the child will be their 'personal perception of any difficulties' and 'how they might be addressed' (DfE 1994a: 24). However, under the Education Act 1996, which subsumed the 1993 Act, a child with SEN is disenfranchised and all former rights are vested in the parent. This is a retrograde step in terms of the Convention. Before this legislation children could make representations to the LEA on assessment of their SEN or to the Tribunal on appeal or on an appeal to the High Court. However, ground has now been lost, particularly Article 12, the right to a voice in decision making.

The Green Paper on Special Needs (DfEE 1997a) is heavy on inclusive rhetoric, which articulates greater rights for children with SEN to participate; however, it continues to operationalize a deficit model of SEN. Children are to continue to be allocated support and placed in educational provision which is based on their disability/need rather than their strengths. It works against Article 23, the rights of children to fullest possible social integration, by labelling children in deficit terms and using these to allocate special support. While thinking is underpinned by this discriminatory taxonomy and while a system of normal and non-normal schooling exists, full social integration will not be realized. Hamilton's (1997) critique of Ofsted's commissioned review of effective schooling sums up what I believe are the underpinning beliefs.

[They] are shaped not so much by inclusive educational values that link democracy, sustainable growth, equal opportunities and social justice but, rather, by a divisive political discipline redolent of performance based league tables and performance related funding.

(D. Hamilton 1997: 4)

Policies concerning inclusion cannot be decontextualized from a system that judges schools through value added accountability analyses. National targets for example, for 80 per cent of children to reach Level 4 in reading by age 11, plan in the prospect of failure for up to 20 per cent of children. This is not inclusive thinking. Inclusivity requires a system where individuals can progress according to their own talents and needs rather than some artificially imposed notion of achievement.

Community dimension

Provision for children is most tested at the sharp end when dealing with those in greatest need. What appears to be common to the more successful initiatives is an attempt to listen to children's views. For example, local authorities such as Devon and St Helens have set up youth councils 'to hear the views of unemployed young people at first hand . . . We know that young people will use services they feel they can trust, that will listen to them' (J. Watts 1997: 22).

Many charities which work on behalf of children have set up children's rights services or advocacy centres. For example, the Children's Society has set up a centre in Wales following the inquiry on abuse in north-east Wales. Its aim is to ensure children's access to 'independent services which not only listen but act upon their views or concerns' (J. Watts 1997: 22). So there is evidence of initiatives which enfranchise children into the decision making process. This is in line with Article 12 of the UN Convention on the Rights of the Child, which imposes on states duties to assure to children the right to express views on all matters which affect them.

While some local and charity based initiatives are moving towards an inclusive and enfranchising approach for particularly needy children, evidence points to education moving in the other direction. Community facilities including youth clubs and playgroups have suffered cuts. The use of school premises out of school hours has been affected by the change in funding arrangements brought about under the Education Act 1988. Schools are seeking to maximize their assets by charging for their use. This means that they 'are beyond many of the youth and children's groups which previously had access to them through the local authority. At the same time, some school playing field sites are being sold to raise funds' (Lansdown and Newell 1994: 183). While we see zero tolerance measures and curfews being brought in to tackle youth crime, we see a commensurate loss in the positive measures that might prevent children turning to crime. Article 31.2 points out the duty of providers to supply children with facilities and services for play and leisure, and ensure adequate funding for this. Current funding arrangements work against this endorsement.

School and classroom level

The Danish Ministry of Social Affairs states:

Children should be included in the planning and execution of activities in daytime childcare facilities, according to their age and maturity, . . . children in this way are able to gain experience of the connection between influence and responsibility on a personal and social level.

(Lansdown and Newell 1994: 183)

The Danish regulations explicitly state that schools have responsibilities in developing children's skills in learning to participate in decision making.

In the UK there has been an insistent move towards greater prescription in not only what to teach but also how to teach. Methods imported from the Pacific Rim which focus on whole class teaching are being held up as the secret ingredient to raising educational standards. Researchers who have examined comparative pedagogies point out that:

To identify a single model of teaching as the solution is premature and naïve . . . that to understand a teaching method, let alone exploit its full potential, you need to penetrate below the surface level of organisation, important though that is, to the deeper levels of discourse and values.

(R. Alexander 1996: 27–8)

Politicians, however, need simple solutions: prescription and didacticism have become essential elements for raising achievement, but there may be costs. What is being advocated is at odds with enfranchising methodology. Rather than placing the child at the centre of the curriculum, subject mastery has become dominant. In fact subject mastery is a theme which permeates policy throughout the education sector from teacher education to practice in special schools (Ofsted 1996). If schools are the arena where children can practise citizenship, authoritarian and didactic teaching methods will do little to encourage this. Article 12 states that schools and LEAs should ensure that children are provided with the opportunity to express their views on matters of concern to them and that their views are given due weight. Evidence from the literature (e.g. Rutter *et al.* 1979; Mortimore *et al.* 1988; DES 1989) supports the view that where children are given a voice and responsibility in their schooling, both behaviour and learning improve. This means that they need the opportunity to participate in democratic pedagogies (see Lipman 1980; Freire 1993).

Between 1990 and 1995 there was a 450 per cent increase in the rate of exclusions of children from school and a perception that behaviour of children was deteriorating. How exclusion rates articulate with pedagogy and wider educational issues is complex though, according to the Children's Society, pressure on schools to paint a good picture of themselves in the marketplace has led to non-conformist pupils being excluded more readily than hitherto (Chaudhary 1998: 7). Under the legislation it is parents, not children, who have the right to appeal against exclusions:

> it is still not the rule to help children in schools be creative, to make choices, to engage in real problem solving and to participate significantly in their environments – skills which may, in fact, serve better the societies of the future.
>
> (Bennett 1996: 51)

Child protection and schools

Teachers, after families, have most regular contact with children and therefore are in a unique position to identify and respond to abuse. Abuse can be defined specifically in terms of physical, emotional and sexual abuse and neglect. However, it can also be linked more closely to rights; that is be interpreted as any act of omission or commission by individuals, institutions or society as a whole which prevents the child from reaching their full potential or denies them equal rights. Using the narrower concept of abuse, at a conservative estimate 10 per cent of children in the UK suffer abuse and neglect; some argue that the figure is higher due to differences in interpretation of what constitutes abuse and problems of detection (Reder *et al.* 1993). Children who are maltreated are likely to develop behavioural and learning difficulties. 'School problems, both academic and behavioural, have emerged as the single most dramatic and consistent risk factor for school aged abused and neglected children' (Kurtz *et al.* 1993: 58). A more sophisticated level of assessment and intervention needs to be made than that implied in the Standards for Initial Teacher Education which have a dominant focus on subject mastery and behavioural control, particularly in relation to abused children. Equally by operationalizing policies and practices in classrooms which give children a voice, there will be a greater probability of picking up abuse in the first place (Tite 1993). In relation to abused children, there are powerful reasons for the promotion of listening classrooms and enfranchising practices.

Empowerment

Empowerment is a much debated concept. Empowerment is about locating the personal in the wider context and can be seen in terms of processes as well as outcomes (Stevenson and Parsloe 1993). Empowerment is about shifting the balance of power from service providers and scrutinizers across political, community and institutional levels to recipients (Thompson 1993). Some professionals view with alarm any shift in the balance of power between themselves and their clients. Teachers, for example, have voiced increasing concerns about children being less respectful and of their having less control over unruly pupils (Jones 1996). But how many of these perceived problems are linked to wider issues such as the pressure to achieve in league tables or prepare for and survive Ofsted inspections? How much relates to children's invisibility in the process of schooling other than as a recipient of other people's decision making? Giving children a say in their schooling, or any matters affecting them, gives them a stake in the processes at play. Anti-oppressive practice is about shifting responsibilities as much as exercising rights, ultimately liberating professionals from the constraints of total responsibility (Dalrymple and Burke 1996). It can buttress professionals from confrontation or even litigation as it can generate dialogues and critiques about interprofessional/personal communication. Democratizing systems allows responsibilities to be shared – a break in the 'us and them' mentality. Giving children a voice in decision making makes them visible and gives them a stake in that process, thereby reducing the chances of their wanting to sabotage it.

Conclusion

Educational developments have shown little concern for children's rights. In spite of the rhetoric on raising standards, the key stakeholders in the system, the children, have diminished opportunities to play their part in defining or contributing to what those standards are. It has been shown that the success of policies and practice is directly related to the sense of ownership of those who are most affected (Handy 1990). All policy reforms relating to children need to reflect this. It is timely for policy and practice to move on, to embody the spirit and intent of the UN Convention and ensure children are given a voice at all levels of decision making, including in the development and implementation of research.

The establishment of an Office of Children's Rights Commissioner, to promote the rights and best interests of children, in line with endorsements contained in the UN Convention, would be an important development in this regard. The role of the Commissioner would be to scrutinize law, policy and practice and comment on how it could be improved in respect of its influence on children. It would raise the status of children and ensure that politicians and policy makers took children's rights and interests seriously, for example, in transport, employment, health and housing policies as well as more obviously child focused education and social policies. A person with qualities such as the late Albert Kushlick would be ideal. 'His passion and concern for the disadvantaged and damaged flowed from a humanness and a decency within him large enough to make even the most seasoned cynic shiver' (Griffiths 1997: 12). Perhaps it is time to counter the instrumentalism of these times with integrity framed within a document which has some vision, such as the UN Convention on the Rights of the Child 1989.

3 Researching children's perspectives: legal issues

JUDITH MASSON

Including child participants in research, as respondents or interviewers, raises ethical and legal dilemmas about children's rights and the obligations of researchers. Until the 1990s the research community has mainly divided into two distinct groups: those, particularly in the fields of education and health, who researched children relying on the consent of their parents or teachers, but who rarely asked the children themselves, and those who excluded children arguing that the issues of competence, consent and risk made children inappropriate subjects or unreliable respondents for research. Both these approaches compromise research legally, ethically and in terms of research findings. Reliance on the consent of others denies the child respondent information which would be thought essential for an adult participating in research, opportunities to clarify the aims of the research, what their role in it might be, and to decide whether or not to participate. The exclusion of children's voices, particularly from research intended to influence policy development, is a flaw which severely (even fatally) undermines the validity of the perspectives and insights gained.

This chapter explores the legal dimensions of children's involvement in research, explaining the current position relating to the rights of children, parents and their carers. It focuses on the law in England and Wales; the position in Northern Ireland and in Scotland is similar. The relevant law is to be found in cases, and in the key statutes, the Children Act 1989 for England and Wales, the Children (Northern Ireland) Order 1995 which is in most respects identical to the law in England and Wales, the Children

(Scotland) Act 1995 and the Age of Legal Capacity (Scotland) Act 1991. Those researching in other Common Law countries, for example, the USA, Canada, Australia, New Zealand, will also find that similar concepts have taken root; elsewhere differences are likely to be greater. Wherever the research is to be conducted the researcher must be clear about both law and custom.

Although the relevant law is complex it is not uncertain (Alderson 1995: 74; Ward 1997: 20). Nor should it be seen as a barrier to the participation of children who are competent and willing to do so. To interpret the law in such a restrictive way undermines the rights that it enshrines for children. Although parents have rights because they are parents, there is no recognized tort of interference with parental rights (*F* v *Wirral MBC* 1991). Parents cannot claim damages from a person who has done something with their child of which they do not approve; penalties could of course follow if the activity was against the criminal law. But this would be the case even if the parent's consent had been obtained. Children's capacity to consent may not be clear cut, researchers who wrongly consider that a child has consented may be acting unethically, but their decisions could be challenged only by a child who had been harmed by the research.

Researchers may owe a duty of care to those they involve in their research and could thus be liable for foreseeable injuries which befall them in the course of the research. Interviewees injured tripping on steep unlit steps as they approached the interview venue or who fell when their chair broke could have a claim.[1] It is also possible to envisage claims by children arising out of their involvement in experiments. Particular care should always be taken that the practical arrangements are suitable; the law generally accepts that children may not be as careful, or as aware of risks, as adults. These are probably unlikely scenarios; usually researchers are not at risk of legal proceedings merely through involving children as respondents to social research. Indeed, unless research is a cover for malign activity, it is difficult to see what proceedings could be brought, or who could bring proceedings, against someone who spoke or corresponded with a consenting child. Including children as interviewers is more problematic in that it raises questions about children's employment and the special care that should be taken of young employees, but many of the precautions which should be taken are relevant to the safety of all interviewees.

There is a close relationship between law and ethics but not everything that is legal is ethical. Frequently law, when used as a tool of regulation, attempts only to set the minimum ethical standard. The aspirations of ethical practice are higher. Having clarified in their own minds that what they propose would be legal, researchers should also consider how it measures up against the ethical standards of their own professional body, of the funding organization and of any other body which is involved in facilitating the research. It can never be appropriate to defend proposed practice solely on the basis that it is legal. But nor can it be assumed that those who question the approach taken know or understand the relevant legal or ethical issues.

'Gatekeepers'

Children and young people are rarely free to decide entirely for themselves whether or not to participate in research. The enclosed nature of children's lives in families, in schools and in institutions means that they are surrounded by adults who can take on the role of 'gatekeepers', controlling researchers' access and children and young people's opportunities to express their views. Even where they have no power over a child's decision to take part in research, parents, carers and teachers generally control the places, homes and schools that provide the safest and most suitable venues for research interviews with children and young people. Arising from their position as parents, employees or carers, 'gatekeepers' have legal rights and responsibilities to safeguard children's welfare, to follow their employer's directions and comply with the ethical code of their professions. Their legal responsibilities mean that gatekeepers may face disciplinary action, including dismissal or removal of children from their care, if they fail to comply with the standards expected of them. Gatekeepers have a positive, protective function, sheltering children and young people from potential harm and testing the motives of those who want access. Researchers should expect gatekeepers to try to protect children and young people from ill conceived, valueless or potentially damaging research. They should be able to explain the purpose and value of their research and what steps they will take to minimize any possible risk of harm from participation in it. However, gatekeepers can also use their position to censor children and young people. Researchers need to understand both the source and limits of each gatekeeper's power so that they can negotiate opportunities for children to choose whether to participate in their research.

Children, childhood and parental responsibility

In England and Wales (and elsewhere in the UK) people under the age of 18 years are legally referred to as children. The use of the same word to cover all young people from infancy to the verge of adulthood may emphasize their incapacity but children are not powerless, nor without legal rights. Children are subject to the control of those who have 'parental responsibility' (see Figure 3.1) but parental responsibility itself declines as the child matures. Children are within the protection of the European Convention on Human Rights, now incorporated in the Human Rights Act 1998, and

Figure 3.1   Who has parental responsibility?

Mother, unless the child has been adopted or freed for adoption
and
Father, provided he is (or has been) married to the mother or he has made
a parental responsibility agreement with the mother he has a parental
responsibility order
and
A carer who has obtained a resident order Children Act 1989 (s.12)
and
Anyone who has obtained an emergency protection order Children Act 1989
(s.44) very limited duration
or
The local authority if the child is the subject of a care order Children Act
1989 (s.33)

as such have the same rights that are guaranteed to adults. Various statutes
recognize children's capacity to make specific decisions at particular ages
(Childright 1996). The term 'parental responsibility' is used in the Children
Act 1989 to encompass 'all the rights, duties, powers, responsibilities and
authority which by law a parent has in relation to the child' (s.3(1)). The
exact content of this power, the way it can be exercised and its extent are
not set out in the Act but have been determined through case law. For
researchers a key issue is whether and in what circumstances children can
agree to take part in research independently from their parents.

The ethical requirement for the relationship between researcher and
researched to be consensual raises the legal question who has the right
to consent to research participation by a child. Alderson (1995: 22) has
suggested that the 'safest course, though it can be repressive, is to ask for
parental consent and also to ask for children's consent when they are
able to understand'. The concern for safety here appears to be the safety
of researchers lest their actions are challenged in litigation (Alderson 1995:
74). This cautious view is at variance with the current law on parental
responsibility which limits the power that parents have over their mature
children. Emphasis on respecting children's rights suggests a bolder approach.

The right to make decisions about a child's life is one aspect of parental
responsibility. Common decisions for parents relate to the way the child is
brought up and include choosing the child's school. The decision whether
to participate in research is also included. In *Re Z* (1996) the court held
that a parent who gave confidential information about her child's medical
treatment or education was exercising parental responsibility. This case
concerned the making of a film about a therapeutic facility where the child
who had severe disabilities had received treatment, but the principle applies

to providing information orally or in writing. Parents who take part in research and provide information about their child, or who agree to their child participating in research, are exercising parental responsibility. Parental responsibility (the parental right to make decisions) is not absolute but is restricted by the parent's obligation to act in the child's interests and the rights of the mature child to make decisions independently.

Parental decisions are always potentially challengeable but this rarely happens except in the context of the acrimonious relationships of separated parents. A person who wishes to challenge the parent's decision applies to the court, which decides the dispute on the basis of what it considers to be in the best interests of the child (Children Act 1989 s.1).[2] Although the court could override a parental refusal, the only recorded example shows the court taking a paternalistic approach, viewing participation in a television documentary as contrary to the child's best interests. In *Re Z* (1996) the child's mother wanted her to take part in a television film about the care and treatment she had received in a rehabilitation clinic for children with severe disabilities but her father, who had long been in dispute with the mother, objected to this. The court, applying the principle that the child's welfare is the paramount consideration, barred the girl's participation. The court's view, that 'the welfare of the child would be harmed and not advanced by the publication of this film', was at odds with the view of the mother, who thought that her daughter's confidence and self-esteem would be enhanced by taking part. Research participation will involve far less exposure and thus avoid the adverse consequences of media attention which arose in *Re Z*. However, it may be very difficult to identify a clear benefit to an individual child from having taken part, except those associated with making a contribution or having a say, and thus to show that participation would be in the child's best interests.

Researchers who wish to include young children who are not old enough to decide for themselves about research participation must obtain the agreement of at least one person who has parental responsibility for the child. Although in the absence of court orders to the contrary (Children Act 1989 s.2(8)), the law recognizes separated parents as having equal power to consent, it is not ethical to privilege the view of a parent who is less involved in the child's day-to-day care. Researchers must engage with parents and provide them with the information that allows them to make good decisions about permitting their child's involvement in any proposed study.

Special considerations apply in respect of children who are looked after by a local authority, children in foster homes, residential schools, children's homes or elsewhere. The parents of these children retain their parental responsibility, although their opportunities to exercise it are obviously curtailed. Only where there is a care order does the local authority have parental responsibility for the child (see Figure 3.1) and then it holds it together with the parents. If children are only accommodated, the local authority can agree to research with the child only if this is reasonable for the purpose of safeguarding or promoting the child's welfare (Children Act 1989 s.3(5)). Local authorities are required to consult and consider the views of all parents (and children) before making decisions about them (Children Act 1989 s.22(4)(5)). Although this provision often appears to be honoured in the breach, researchers should expect to involve parents even though they do not have day-to-day care of their child.

Parental responsibility is not the determining factor for a child's participation in research where the child is mature. A child who has the capacity to understand fully a decision affecting his or her life automatically has the capacity to make that decision unless statute law states otherwise (*Gillick* 1986). Competence, the level of understanding required to make decisions, is directly related to the decision to be taken. Thus children are competent and can decide whether or not to participate in a research study, provided that they have a sufficient understanding of what participation entails and how participating may affect them. A considerably higher degree of understanding would be expected before a child could agree to take part in an experiment about the effects of sleep deprivation on exam performance than for a short interview about leisure activities. It is children's level of understanding, not their age, which is important. It cannot be assumed that all children of a particular age are, or are not, competent to decide. Competence can be encouraged by giving the necessary background information and providing opportunities to explore it before the issue of research participation is raised. However, this might require permission unless it was part of a normal activity which the child took part in at school, youth club or elsewhere.

Where children have the capacity to make a decision, parents' power over that area of their child's life is ended unless preserved by statute law. Consequently, a parent cannot consent to research on behalf of a competent child. Nevertheless mature children can explicitly allow parents or other adults to make decisions on their behalf.

Lack of competence to make decisions does not imply the inability to make a contribution through participating in research but it is clearly relevant both to issues of consent and the way the research is conducted. The law uses quite a different standard to determine whether a child can give evidence to a criminal court, a matter which is generally outside either the parent's or the child's control. A child can be a competent witness if he or she understands the importance of accuracy and honesty, and can give a coherent account of an event. Children as young as 4 years old have been accepted as witnesses in criminal trials, but would probably be called to give evidence only where an alternative source was not available. Views that children are unreliable and untruthful witnesses which dominated legal (and adult) thinking have been challenged by research (Spencer and Flin 1993). Considerable (but probably inadequate) care is now taken to ensure that child witnesses understand what they are being asked to do and that the process does not place too great physical or emotional burdens on them. These changes in criminal proceedings provide useful lessons both for researchers who wish to include children and those who think children's views need not be sought.

Consent and confidentiality

Having identified who must consent, consideration should be given to the nature of that consent. As far as medical practice is concerned, a concept of 'informed consent' has been developed in a number of countries. Where informed consent is required, only the consent of individuals who were fully informed of the relevant issues before they gave their consent is valid. English law has repeatedly refused to accept the need for informed consent for medical treatment, preferring to accept doctors' views about what patients need to be told. This approach leaves medical staff with considerable scope and frees them from the possibility of facing an action for assault on the basis that the patient's consent was obtained without disclosure of all the possible risks.

Using this approach researchers could argue against the need for informed consent to research. The contrary argument, for higher standards based on ethics rather than law, appears more persuasive. Researchers do not face the risks that informed consent would impose on doctors nor can they claim that their actions are designed and intended to benefit those from whom they seek cooperation. The fundamental importance of consent, freely given, to research participation reinforces the view that the researcher should always explain fully the purpose, process and intended outcomes of research and seek consent on that basis. Where general consents have already been given, for example as part of the arrangements for a child's care or education, these may not be adequate judged against high ethical standards. At the very least consideration should be given to the possible advantages to both researcher and participant of approaching each new study on the basis that fully informed consent should be obtained.

If consent is to be freely given, care also needs to be taken that children (or other potential respondents) do not feel obliged to participate. Where the person seeking children's participation is in a powerful position over them, as in the case of a teacher or carer, children may feel that they have to agree or, worse still, that they will be penalized if they do not. Researchers need to be alert to such possibilities, particularly where their access is arranged by those who provide services for children.

The notion of confidentiality has a very particular meaning among researchers which needs to be explained and agreed with those participating. Research confidentiality usually entails taking considerable care not to pass information to those connected in any way with the respondent and disclosing information only in ways which protect the identity of those who provided it. The location where the research took place is generally not identified, individuals are anonymized or given pseudonyms, and some facts, which might otherwise identify them, are changed or omitted. All research participants, including children and young people, need careful explanations of research confidentiality when (or before) their consent to participate is sought.

Where children are competent to make decisions, the law allows them the associated confidentiality which it would allow an adult. The confidentiality of younger children, who lack the capacity to consent, also needs to be considered. Although these children may keep secrets from their parents, they are not entitled to confidential relationships automatically. Where arrangements for children's participation have been made with parents or other gatekeepers, these people will of course know that an individual child has taken part, and what the focus of the research is. Natural curiosity and concern for their child may lead them to question the child or the researcher about what was said. This can put pressure on the child. Researchers need to consider this when negotiating access or consent for interviews with children and young people. Where parental consent is needed, it can be sought on the understanding that what the child says will not be passed to parents (C. Hamilton and Hopegood 1997). In such cases, parents may need to be reassured that certain types of information would be passed to them; where this is the case children should know that this will happen and what parents will be told. Some children may want to give the account of the interview for the researcher but others may prefer the researcher to explain on their behalf.

There are ethical considerations in research (and other work) with children which may mean that the same degree of confidentiality can not be guaranteed to a child as would be given to an adult. There are two areas of particular concern, where a child discloses that he or she is being seriously harmed or ill treated, and where the researcher identifies a condition, for example a medical condition or learning difficulty about which the parents could take action. Failure of the researcher to take appropriate action not only might lead to criticism on ethical grounds, but also in some limited circumstances could give rise to legal liability.

In the UK there is no legal requirement on anyone who knows that a child is being ill-treated to notify social services or the police as there is in some other countries, notably many states of the USA. However, guidance to doctors from the Department of Health (DoH 1994) and lawyers (Solicitors Family Law Association 1995) advises that the confidential nature of the relationship with the patient or client does not provide a justification for failing to pass on information where children are being abused. Researchers should be aware that the promise of confidentiality may have encouraged children to discuss their dreadful circumstances, and may feel betrayed if information is passed on without their knowledge. Where such issues could arise, the researchers need to consider the information and support they can provide for young people. Some young people may prefer the complete confidentiality of ChildLine to disclosure to an interviewer. This is a telephone advice and counselling service for children and young people, particularly those who are abused. Realistically most researchers will be unable to provide the kind of support required by a young person in the throes of a child protection investigation but with forethought they may be able to help them to access local services. In such cases interviewers may also need support. Employing researchers could even be liable for trauma suffered by interviewers who they knowingly required to conduct distressing interviews.

There will be some studies, particularly those involving the use of diagnostic instruments, where the researcher may obtain information about individual children which would be useful to children or their parents. In addition to any ethical duty to disclose this information, there could be a legal duty to do so, particularly for anyone conducting the research in the course of employment to provide services for children, for example a doctor or an educational psychologist. It is accepted that doctors owe a duty of care to their patients; a similar duty has been held to apply to educational psychologists carrying out assessments of, or providing advice about, individual children (*Christmas* v *Hampshire CC*; *Keating* v *Bromley LBC* 1995). Although it would be more difficult to establish that a researcher who was not otherwise providing a service owed a duty of care, an education authority which employed the researcher or permitted the research to take place might be held liable. Consequently, researchers need to consider whether and how to provide information about identifiable children. Where young people could take the necessary steps themselves, information should be provided to them directly but the researcher should consider whether they have the necessary maturity to handle it. In the case of younger children, parents should be given the information, as they too may need help to know what steps to take.

Protecting children participating in research

Current concerns about the victimization of children by those who have gained access to them through employment in schools or care homes, or through organizing children's leisure activities, have drawn attention to child sexual abuse occurring outside the home. Although children are generally at far greater risk of abuse within their families, no one who plans activities involving children and adults can disregard the dangers that some adults pose to children. Legislation requiring those convicted of certain offences against children to register with the police (Sexual Offenders Act 1997) together with new systems to check the criminal records of prospective employees (Police Act 1997) may appear to provide ways of determining that interviewers are appropriate people. However, both detection and conviction for these offences remains extremely low. Making use of the criminal record certificates (Police Act 1997 Pt V) can avoid exposing children only to convicted offenders; far greater care is necessary both in recruitment and the arrangements for research if children are to be safe.

Under the Police Act 1997 prospective employees will be able to obtain criminal record certificates which will disclose to prospective employers whether or not they have criminal convictions. For those whose employment (or voluntary work) involves regularly having sole responsibility for children (or vulnerable adults) it will be possible to have more detailed checks undertaken covering convictions occurring ten or more years previously and even details of offences which did not result in a conviction or a caution. These 'enhanced criminal records certificates' will replace the checking mechanisms available to local authorities and voluntary organizations and should be used for research staff working with children.[3]

Criminal records checks cannot ever replace good recruitment practices which seek to establish the prospective employee's suitability and work history from those who know them. Useful guidance was given to social services departments in the Warner Report (1992).

The arrangements for interviews also need to be considered. Both children and interviewers must feel and be safe during the research. Children may feel more comfortable if they can bring a friend or parent to an interview but this may also inhibit what they say and can make concentration difficult. There are cases where it will be appropriate for the researcher to arrange for chaperones, particularly where the research involves the child travelling to a laboratory or other facility where the research will be conducted. Particular care must be taken both in selection and training if the chaperone is not someone already known to the child. Using large public rooms or corridors allows the interview to be observed but not overheard but may not be practicable. Where children are interviewed at home, interviewers often have little choice about where they see a child. It may be difficult to find a sufficiently quiet place in living areas without disrupting family activities. Bedrooms are not usually suitable places for children to see strangers alone, although they may like to show them to visitors. The garden or the stairs can in some cases provide an appropriate place for an interview.

Children as researchers

More attention has been given since the mid-1990s to involving children in the research process either as part of advisory groups helping to design and direct studies about things which concern them or as interviewers of other children (Ward 1997). These initiatives raise further legal concerns about children's status and their safety. Children who are engaged as interviewers are working for the researcher and should be accorded no less consideration than adult interviewers. Even under minimum wage legislation it is likely to be legal to pay children less than adults, but where children possess special skills, such as the ability to obtain good rapport with other children, this should be recognized in the rate of pay as it would be for an adult. The strict regulation of children's work requires additional safeguards to be provided. Interviewers are often not regarded as employees but as sessional workers. However, where there is control over whom they interview and the contents of the interview, as would be the case where children are carrying out fieldwork, it is difficult to argue that they are not employees.

The Children and Young Persons Acts 1933 and 1963,[4] modified by the Children (Protection at Work) Regulations 1998, set out the limitations on work by those below the school leaving age of 16. Children below the age of 14 years may not be employed except in certain categories of light work specified in local authority bylaws. Although these categories may be broadly drawn they will not necessarily cover research work and may vary from place to place. Working hours are also restricted. Children under 15 years may not work for more than 2 hours on any school day or Sunday, or 5 hours on a Saturday. They cannot work for more than 25 hours a week in the school holidays. The Health and Safety (Young Persons) Regulations 1997 impose further safeguards for young people (i.e. those under the age of 18 years) and children (i.e. those below the school leaving age). Before employing anyone below the age of 18 years, employers must assess the risks posed by the work, taking account (among other things) of the immaturity and inexperience of young people. All employees have to be given 'comprehensible and relevant information' about risks and protective measures; where children are employed this information must also be given to a parent.

The concerns about the vulnerability of children being interviewed also apply where children are interviewers. Interviewees are at risk as they travel to interviews; where interviews will take place in private homes they may also be at risk from other household members, about whom little may be known. Those planning the research need to consider these risks with interviewers. Chaperones or drivers who wait outside provide a way of protecting interviewers both on the way to and during an interview but other arrangements such as pairs of interviewers will be more suitable for some studies. As well as physical risks, attention needs to be given to potential psychological harm from hearing disturbing accounts from other children. Young interviewers may well need more training and support than adults: under the regulations this is a legal requirement, not just a professional issue.

Conclusion

The law's relationship with children is generally protectionist. It seeks to shelter them from exploitation outside the family and control or punish those who would harm them. Protectionism has both advantages and disadvantages for children. It may help to keep them safe although it is often not effective. It has also justified controlling children and can lead to their marginalization. Researchers can help to counteract children's marginalization by involving them in research but in doing so need to take care not to jeopardize their safety nor exploit them. Research with children which does not take on board legal dimensions is likely to harm both children and research.

Notes

1 This claim would not necessarily be against the researcher. The person responsible for the building would have responsibility as the occupier.
2 In theory anyone may challenge the exercise of parental responsibility but the integrity of the family is protected by requiring those who are not parents, step-parents or long term carers of the child to obtain the prior permission of the court before making their application (Children Act 1989 s.10).
3 Employers and others seeking to use enhanced criminal records certificates will have to register with the Home Office and countersign each application for a certificate.
4 In Scotland the Children and Young Persons (Scotland) Act 1937 applies.

Case list

Christmas v *Hampshire CC; Keating* v *Bromley LBC* [1995] 2 FLR 276
F v *Wirral MBC* [1991] Fam 69
Gillick v *West Norfolk AHA* [1986] AC 112
Re Z (a minor)(freedom of publication) [1996] 1 FLR 191

4 Researching children's perspectives: a psychological dimension

JULIE DOCKRELL, ANN LEWIS
AND GEOFF LINDSAY

Adult: (pointing to oil slick on the road) Look, what's that?
Child: It's a dead rainbow

If this incident were taken from a research project one might examine the meaning of the exchange in various ways. We might ask what was the wider situation and how might it have affected the child's response? What was it about the child and the situation that made the adult ask this question at this time and in that way? Was this perhaps a well worn family joke? What was the adult seeking from the child: scientific understanding, any communication, reference to something other than the oil slick? Did the adult phrase the question in an appropriate way? Did the child hear the question correctly? Did the child have the linguistic skills to understand what was said (receptive language) and the skills to articulate a response (expressive language)? Was the child sufficiently motivated to give a considered response? These kinds of questions raise two central issues relating to researching children's views. The first relates to the reasons why the research is undertaken (the research question) and the second relates to fundamental methodological issue about the trustworthiness of the data (reliability and validity) of the information (data) collected. The theoretical concepts and debates underlying these points are the focus of this chapter. (See Robson 1993 for a lucid and accessible discussion of research terminology and wider research problems.)

The chapter begins with a review of approaches to children's development and the implications of these for researching children's perspectives. Then a series of methodological issues about which researchers must decide (such as whether to focus on naturalistic or artificial settings, how to minimize the gap between children's competence and 'performance', and the particular problems of trying to make valid comparisons about development across different ages) are discussed in the context of recent psychological research. The questions that these issues prompt are related to various methods of data collection and research designs. Our aim is to draw out the implications of developmental research for researchers planning studies involving children.

Traditionally, psychological studies of children and child development are concerned with issues relating to change: changes in children's skills, changes in children's understandings and changes in children's views. Studying change involves two related but distinct matters: identifying what it is that changes and identifying how change occurs. At one level we know what develops: children gain knowledge and become more competent in reasoning, language and a variety of other skills. To understand how these changes occur we need to devise empirical studies. In devising studies that are valid and reliable, psychologists are confronted with the cognitive and social factors that can hamper children's abilities or willingness to express their views. Similarly, researchers can be seduced by seemingly competent responses from young children which in reality do not reflect the knowledge or views that researchers assume.

The child in a social context

Before considering what psychology has to offer in the development of research methods and approaches with children, it is necessary to summarize our view of developmental psychology's contribution to understanding how children develop. In the past, developmental psychology has been influenced by a number of schools; it has been seen as deterministic in the sense that biological influences were considered to be pre-eminent (e.g. France, Bendelow and Williams, Chapter 12 in this book). Current explanations of development are characterized by three different but not mutually exclusive frameworks:

1 Development is viewed as determined by a series of in-built cognitive constraints and organizational principles that determine the hypotheses children entertain, the knowledge they acquire and the behaviour they produce.
2 Development is characterized by an internal set of cognitive restructurings which determine the ways in which children's thought processes and their understanding of the world develop.

3 Development is viewed as a social construction whereby the nature and content of knowledge and children's behaviour is influenced by the social and cultural context in which they find themselves.

A simple example might help to provide the flavour of these different views. From the first view the development of a child's language is determined by a series of innate rules. While accepting certain elements of the rules approach, the second perspective would see the language system becoming a problem space in its own right (see Karmiloff-Smith 1992). Finally, the social constructionists would place the major import on the opportunities and contexts that the child encounters.

All psychologists consider biological and environmental factors but the key issue is the different emphasis that is placed on their importance. This is commonly described as the nature–nurture debate. The former include genetic factors and biological influences during the period from conception through infancy and beyond, including the effects of disease, malnutrition, injury and evolution. The latter include the influences of the immediate family, the school and the immediate cultural environment as well as the influence of the wider society. A favoured model for understanding the impact of environmental factors is Bronfenbrenner's (1979) ecological systems theory. The essence of this theory is that environmental influences are nested one within the other, working out from the immediate behavioural environment (the microsystem), out through influences such as the family and school (the mesosystem), the wider social environments which do not include children but which affect them, including workplace, and social processes such as maternity leave (the exosystem), to the macrosystem comprising society's laws, values, customs and resources of the culture.

Furthermore, the emphasis now is on the bidirectionality of influences, whether at the level of behavioural genetics or interactions between different social influences. For example, children's behaviour in classrooms is interpreted not simply as reactions to the teacher, but rather as transactions, with the child's behaviour influencing and hence modifying the teacher's behaviour as well as the teacher's affecting the child's. Children's behaviour is also affected by their biological characteristics, but these too may be influenced by environmental factors. For example, the child with high levels of distractibility and activity – now often termed as having Attention Deficit with Hyperactivity Disorder (ADHD) – may be influenced by change of diet, medication, modified classroom arrangements and teaching approaches, or a combination of these. Hence the focus has changed to a more encompassing view of the influences on children. Each layer in the ecosystem has important influences and the relative power of each continues to be researched. An illustration of this is work by Judith Rich Harris (1995), who has argued that, contrary to what has traditionally been assumed, parental influence on children's developing personality (for example) is less strong than is the influence of the peer group. Equally, however, there are cases where within-child factors, such as autism, severely limit the ways in which environmental factors influence the developmental pathway.

There are direct implications for research. For example, when observing children's behaviour in classrooms, it is necessary to have not only a construct such as ADHD as a variable, but also the teacher's behaviour, the nature of the learning tasks and the setting. Further, it is important to view the child as interpreting what is happening, not simply responding to the researcher. In summary, there are many influences operating between and around the researcher and the child; thus all research results should be considered in the light of the context in which they were collected, whether this context refers to a particular task or a wider social system. One of the reasons that researchers spend a significant amount of time designing their studies and choosing the appropriate sampling frame is to collect a dataset which furthers understanding of development and can generalize to other situations.

Choice of methods of data collection

Psychological studies of children's perspectives can be addressed in a number of different ways. Measures can be direct or indirect. Direct measures involve asking the child, or a significant other, about the child's views and understandings of a situation or getting the child to solve a task that is known to address certain key developmental achievements, such as ego-centrism. Indirect measures, in contrast, include such measures as anxiety, test success, depression, crying, sleeping and so forth. Sometimes, the variables that we measure reflect directly the aspect of the child's behaviour in which we are interested. So, for example, if we were concerned about how a child was integrating with peers we might use a sociogram. In other situations the variables we measure are our own conceptualizations of a particular construct. If we take prosocial behaviour as an example again, in this case our variables are hypothetical constructs; we infer from the observed behaviour something about the underlying process in which we are interested. A problem for researchers is that children's behaviour or performance does not necessarily change (develop) in a straightforward and additive manner. This is hardly surprising given the range of influences that operate in development (as discussed on pp. 47–9) but these mean that we need to be creative about our approaches and understanding of what it is that is changing in development.

Developmental research has helped to illuminate the complexities involved in studying children. The following sections of this chapter are based on a series of questions that the researcher has to address, explicitly or implicitly, when planning the research.

Psychological aspects of methodological issues in data collection

These can be subdivided into three broad groups: first, questions about setting; second, questions about the child's capabilities; and third, questions about the most effective ways in which to put questions to children.

Is the setting for data collection to be naturalistic?

Attempting to tap children's perspectives and understandings require working through a series of questions to identify the most appropriate approach. As a first step it is important to consider the setting for the data collection. Children can be studied in either their natural environment or a formal setting. Natural contexts include homes, places of worship, classrooms, clubs, playgrounds, streets and day centres. Here the focus is on a naturalistic setting with the aim of avoiding anything that is controlled or contrived. In contrast, laboratories or special observational units are structured settings. Either choice has limitations as well as strengths. For example, working with children in schools means that although the children are in a familiar setting, the vagaries of the school timetable, unexpected special events, classroom dramas and staff absence may limit the researcher's work. Moreover, children may be concerned that information revealed will be fed back to teachers, parents or peers. In contrast, laboratories while supplying a degree of experimental control may also add artificiality and unfamiliarity thus limiting the generalizability of the findings. The advantage of such settings is that they provide a basis for making clear changes to test specific hypotheses. For example, the considerable advances in our understanding of children's working memory would not have been possible without the control allowed by experimental procedures (Gathercole and Baddeley 1992).

Diary studies

Methods of data collection in natural settings include observation and diary studies. Diary studies have been a principal source of information about early childhood for a long time. For example, Jean Piaget used the diary method to collect many of his data. For researchers in child language (e.g. Brown 1973; McTear 1985) diaries of children's early utterances form most of the data collected, especially in the early stages of acquisition. More recently diaries have been used to investigate such topics as children's homework and sexual behaviour (Dockrell and Joffe 1992). A diary considered as a research tool is in effect a kind of self-administered questionnaire. It is a convenient, cost-effective and relatively easy means of recording behaviours in naturalistic environments. Diaries can range from being totally unstructured to a set of responses to specific questions. They can also serve as a proxy for observing situations that are not amenable to the presence of observers, e.g. night-time waking. Parents have several advantages as observers above outside researchers: they may interpret the child's speech or actions better as they know the child and they can observe without disturbing the child or other members of the household. There is corroborative evidence that parents can be good judges of their child's early language skills (Klee *et al.* 1998). There are some disadvantages, however: parents may overinterpret their children's behaviour, training may be required to use the technique and diaries can be time consuming.

Observational studies

When we ask parents or teachers to complete diaries we are asking them to report back on their observations about particular behaviours or situations. Equally the investigator can carry out the observations. In research contexts we are interested in a sample of the child's behaviour (for example, temper tantrums during a specified series of time intervals, parental records of a child's sleep disorders over a four-week monitoring period, attainments on a slice of mathematical learning or a child's recall of best friends). Observations are time consuming both in terms of planning and execution.

The first step is to decide which behaviours to observe. If we were interested in whether a child was happy we would need to consider which of the various indicators of happiness (e.g. smiles, laugh, verbal expressions of pleasure, open eyes, hand clapping and so forth) we were going to measure. Second, we would need to decide whether we were going to record every occurrence of the behaviour (event sampling) such as the number of requests during free play. Alternatively we can measure whether the behaviour occurs at preset intervals (time sampling) such as every 10 minutes or every 30 seconds. Further, the intervals for sampling may be fixed or random. The sampling basis chosen may be highly significant as particular behaviours may typically occur in a pattern that the sampling overlooks or exaggerates. For example, classroom misbehaviour typically occurs more frequently around lesson changes than during the main body of lessons; consequently classroom observation at these different times would give very different impressions of the 'typical' frequency of misbehaviour. How we measure is intimately linked to the behaviours that are measured and the context of measurement (see Gardner 1994 as an example). Finally, we would have to demonstrate that someone else would record the same behaviours in the same way that we do. This is called inter-rater reliability and is an essential step in any observational study. Investigators are not immune to overinterpretation or misinterpretation of behaviour and often investigators will also require training with the particular measurement tools.

Interviews

Interviews are another form of data collection that can take place in a natural environment such as the child's school but within that the setting may be more or less structured. Some researchers have used children to interview other children (e.g. Pollard 1987) so aiming to increase the naturalness of the setting. Children can also be used to interview adults so that we can tap the child's views of the critical dimensions surrounding a particular topic such as a job or holiday. Other work (e.g. Gross 1993) entails an external researcher not known to the children interviewing them in the school, in a room set aside for the purpose. Here the context is clearly much more formal. The interview format is particularly important with vulnerable or disempowered groups, such as children. There is a particular need to be sensitive to the kinds of questions asked so as not to lead the children's responses.

In what size group will the child be observed or interviewed?

Related to choice of setting and method of data collection are questions about group size. Group size may influence the nature of the data collected in both observational and diary studies. If we were interested in the number of aggressive outbursts, numbers of children present during the observation could be critical. It would certainly be a parameter that should be controlled. Group size can be particularly significant where interviews are used as a method of data collection. Group interviews are widely used in market research for testing reactions to new products but they are also used with teenagers to gain their views on sensitive topics, e.g. sexuality, dating or parents. They have also been used with much younger children and in that context consideration needs to be given to matters such as group size, selection of group members, physical arrangements, recording and transcription, seating of group members and contamination of ideas between groups (discussed further in Lewis 1992). Group interviews allow the possibility that the discussions between individuals will spark off new ideas, criticism or developments. Other potential strengths of group interviews include the probing of consensus beliefs, the provision of social support in the context of 'risky' topics and a natural style of interaction. Group interviews may also be particularly valuable at the exploratory stage of research (see Lewis 1992, 1995).

A serious problem with group interviews is that some participants may dominate by either restricting the topics for discussion or dominating the discussion themselves. Some members of the group may be hesitant to offer a different or alternative perspective. Other potential disadvantages include difficulties for the interviewer in following through an individual's line of argument, inadvertent 'tidying up' of talk in the transcription process and group order effects.

Does the child's performance provide a 'true' indication of competence?

When we collect data from children we can only ever measure their performance. We use performance as an indicator of a child's competence. For example, if we are interested in children's road crossing behaviour we might observe what they do on certain occasions. This is a measure of their performance. Their competence or their 'true ability' at road crossing behaviour is only inferred from their performance. There are special problems with studying children that can lead us to either underestimate or overestimate their abilities. Children's performance as research participants will be determined by their developmental levels in relevant domains, and also by the nature of the task. It is often difficult to disentangle which of these factors is leading to successful performance or a child's failure to succeed. For example, there is now much research in the forensic field which suggests that children can be effective and accurate witnesses as adults, provided that the conditions for the investigation are appropriate (Bull 1995), and that they can similarly express preferences and so may be appropriately involved in giving consent (Melton *et al.* 1983; Stanley *et al.* 1995).

A major concern is to identify the reasons why a child might pass or fail a particular task, that is the accuracy of inferring from the behaviour the presence or absence of the capacity under investigation. However, children's performance is not always an accurate indication of their competence: this may lead to incorrect conclusions being drawn. The point applies equally to the research context in which we make judgements about, for example, children's beliefs, based on what they choose to reveal to the researcher. We can make two specific types of error. Errors that occur because we underestimate a child's competence (commonly called a type 1 error) and errors that occur because we overestimate a child's competence (commonly called a type 2 error).

There are several sets of causes underlying misjudgements. Several features may lead to an underestimation of children:

- *Linguistic*: children may fail a task because they do not understand the language that is being used or the meanings of specific vocabulary items. Many of Piaget's early studies were criticized for failing to consider this issue (Donaldson 1978; Neilson and Dockrell 1981).
- *Cognitive*: the task may rely on higher order factors so that the child is unable to work out the task demands. Misinterpretations of meaning can occur or may not be able to cope with all the task demands that are required. For example, the ability to complete a task at a later date (prospective memory) will be influenced by the situation in which the instruction is given. (Ceci and Bronfenbrenner 1985).
- *Memorial skills*: children may fail a task not because they do not understand the nature of the task but rather because additional demands are

placed on their memory system or information processing resources. A number of researchers have shown how children can succeed at complex inference tasks if no additional demands are placed on their memory (e.g. Bryant 1974).

- *Balance between text and context*: children are greatly influenced by the context in which tasks are presented or responses demand. Early investigations of these phenomena took place in Edinburgh in the late 1970s (see Donaldson 1978 for a review). The results of these studies clearly showed that children's performance was improved in situations that they could understand. More recently we have seen how children's abilities to understand the knowledge and intentions of others (commonly called a theory of mind) is also dependent on the context in which that knowledge is investigated. Dunn (1988) has shown how quite young children are able to demonstrate such skills in interactions with their siblings.

Other sets of features which may lead to overestimating or misrepresenting children's competence include the following:

- The child guesses or acts out some previously acquired response strategy. Children rarely sit there looking blankly at an investigator. They try and respond and one way to respond if you do not understand the situation is to guess from the nature of the materials how the problem might be solved. Guesses can sometimes be right and the tricky task is sorting out the guesses from the correct responses.
- The child can simply see a difference by direct perception rather than carry out the cognitive process we are studying. We need to ensure that the materials we use, e.g. pictures or questions, do not allow the child to solve the problem by processes other than the ones with which we are concerned.
- Irrelevant procedures can result in the experimenter unwittingly reinforcing a particular response or the child choosing only a specific location, agreeing with the last thing the experimenter said or changing a response if a question is repeated.
- Artifacts of the procedure including the nature of the response required can lead to spurious results. For example, hearing impaired children have been found to continue to give answers to multiple choice questions beyond their ceiling, so leading to a chance increase in score (Webster *et al.* 1981).

Should standardized tools be used to measure performance?

There is often an implicit assumption that if we use a standardized form of assessment, we shall get a 'true' measure of a child's competence. Such measures are usually carefully constructed and tested but they are also open to type 1 and type 2 errors. For example, the standardization process means that the child is being assessed against a particular population at a particular time and place. These may or may not be reasonable comparators for the child. There are also statistical constraints, for example, some reading tests provide different norms for boys and girls or for Scotland and England. It is beyond the scope of this chapter to explore these issues in detail but they are raised here in the wider context of the inevitably fuzzy 'best judgement' nature of conclusions about children's thinking in any research context.

What are the most effective ways and situations in which to put questions to children?

We have outlined a range of critical issues that need to be considered in investigating children's views. An obvious question to ask is whether there is a 'best' or most effective way to carry out research with children. Appropriate methods are directly linked to the topic of investigation and the hypotheses that are entertained. In some situations children will be reporting directly on their knowledge or beliefs. In these situations questions can be asked in several different ways. We can ask open-ended questions that allow children to structure the nature and extent of their responses. In general, questions that require only yes/no or very precise answers are to be avoided. A range of work has suggested that making a statement to a child tends to elicit a fuller response than does asking a question. This has been discussed by Edwards and Westgate (1994), who examine the repercussions of the conventional I-R-E structure (teacher initiation – pupil response – teacher evaluation) of much classroom talk. This has been contrasted with naturalistic talk in the home (see e.g. Tizard and Hughes 1984). Problematically a question that may seem neutral to an adult may seem very leading to a child. Asking 13-year-olds how often they see their friends may be seen as an attempt to discover if they spend sufficient time on their homework.

Difficulties particular to interviewing young children (3 to 6-years-old) include a tendency for the child to agree with the interviewer or to feel compelled to provide an answer even to 'nonsense' questions. M. Hughes and Grieve (1980) reported work in which 4-year-olds were asked to decide whether red was bigger than yellow, or milk was bigger than water, for example. The children gave a reply and did not say that the question was nonsensical. So, there is clear evidence that children will respond to questions even if they do not know what they mean. Young children will also tend to interpret questions very literally (see examples in Lewis 1995), be distracted by events outside the interview and want to find out about the interviewer. If the interviews take place in a school, then the conventions of teacher–child dialogue, such as that a repeated question is indicative of an incorrect answer, may also invalidate responses (Rose and Blank 1974). Similarly, work by Ceci (1991) has shown how recurrent probing for detail can lead children to supply details which they 'invent' in response to the questions. Further, the child's understanding of particular terms may not match the adult's. For example, young children questioned about the nature of severe learning difficulties appeared to confuse this with hearing difficulties. It is unclear whether this was a conceptual confusion or whether these children understood the concept but lacked the language with which to express their understanding (Lewis 1995).

What is the most appropriate form of response for children?

A critical issue to consider is the child's ability to respond to the, behavioural, oral or written language demands of the task. It is clearly developmentally inappropriate to require 5-year-olds to complete a conventional questionnaire. It might, however, be equally inappropriate for some 10-year-olds to complete questionnaires. Questionnaires can provide misleading information for a number of reasons. The child may not be able to recall the necessary information or the child may not have sufficient linguistic skills to understand the meaning of the question or may lack the written skills to produce a decipherable response.

Asking for verbal reports has different limitations. A key issue is to ask how faithful are verbal reports provided in interviews? Do the depth and subtlety that they provide allow for a reflection of the beliefs of respondents? Some cognitive psychologists have argued that verbal reports are not good indicators of actual thought processes (Nisbett and Wilson 1977). It is argued that the reports are a biased, generalized reconstruction. However, more detailed examination has shown that verbal reports can be accurate reflections of the process under investigation if the individual is recounting a specific event or set of events (Ericsson and Simon 1980). A parallel argument has been made by some social psychologists. Billig (1987) proposes that both the general and the specific levels of verbal data are useful since they investigate social interpretations and actual situations respectively. So a researcher might be interested in children's general view of homework and their specific view about last night's homework. Accordingly the data that are collected serve different kinds of purposes. For example, questions about the child's family may be interpreted very differently depending on whether the situation is settled, and neutral to positive, compared with the case of a child in fear (e.g. a child subject to abuse) or where the subcultural 'rule' is to give nothing away 'to authority'. These response tendencies will interact with the subject matter of the questions, but may also be more pervasive tendencies. Furthermore, the language used must be understood, an issue not only of vocabulary and sentence complexity but also of accent and rapport. For example a child tested by an American psychologist misinterpreted 'copper saucepan' as 'cup and saucer' reflecting both accent and a greater familiarity with the latter.

In some interviews pictures, scenes or objects can be introduced for discussion or sorting. This can be a particularly useful technique with children who are reticent or limited in their ability to communicate verbally (see Begley, Chapter 8 in this book). However, we must be very wary of using our own adult stereotypes to investigate children's views. For example, a good example of an accident for an adult might be a car crash but this might not be a child's prototypical response. Equally a picture of a child with Down Syndrome might be used to investigate views of special need but this might artificially limit the child's responses. So the use of non-verbal materials needs to be considered as carefully as verbal ones to mimimize the occurrence of error of commission and omission. We can also use a scaled response to investigate children's views, such as 'How much do you like working on your own?' with a rating of 1 (not at all) to 6 (very much), which could be used with a visual scale in which children manipulated materials to reveal the 1–6 position of their response. Ingenious devices based on rolling up or unrolling a 'toothpaste tube', drawing miniature curtains across the scale or rolling out a piece of fabric over the scale have all been used successfully with young children.

Researchers in child development have often turned to children's drawings as a means of understanding their views of situations and their cognitive level. The status of children's drawings for answering these two questions is rather different. Using drawings to make inferences about a child's personality or emotional state is highly suspect process. As Thomas and Jolley (1998) conclude that children's drawings on their own are too complexly determined and inherently ambiguous to be reliable as sole indicators of the emotional experiences of the children who drew them. Thus the use of drawings for such purposes is likely to be unreliable and lead to erroneous conclusions. A child may draw a person crying for many reasons.

Performance factors often play a crucial role in determining the information presented. While performance factors are also important in making claims about children's cognitive skills the use of drawings or notations to reflect the child's cognitive changes, although fraught with methodological problems, is quite promising. As we know by looking at children's drawings, their pictorial notations develop across the years (Thomas and Silk 1990). A number of authors have argued that investigations of children's early drawings and notations for numbers and words indicate that there are representational principles underlying early spontaneous notations. Such early notations are thought to provide clues to how the child's representation meshes with the environmental input, resulting in a creative and flexible system (Karmiloff-Smith 1992). So, although it might seem like a simple option to get children to draw so we can tap their views, such drawings need to be treated with great care and with as much precision as we would treat any other form of response.

Conclusion

In this chapter we have considered the critical factors that psychologists consider when investigating children's views and understandings. Two main issues were considered – the choice of investigative context and the child's response to that context. There are a range of methodologies that can be used to study children's perspectives. The choice of any particular approach should be governed by the research question, the age of the participants and potential generalizability of the results. Children are never passive participants in this activity; they constantly respond to the situations in which they find themselves and try to interpret (and make sense) of the demands that are placed upon them. They are very much active particip-ants in the research process. One of the key skills of an investigator is to disentangle how this active participation influences the results of the study.

5 Researching children's perspectives: a sociological dimension

MEL LLOYD-SMITH AND JANE TARR

One of the purposes of this book is to demonstrate the value of research which taps into the direct experience and perceptions of children and young people. There are indications in the field of education that evidence from this type of research is being increasingly used, a trend particularly noticeable in studies of special educational needs. One reason is that there is growing recognition in the UK that less able and non-conforming individuals are in danger of becoming more and more marginalized in a system built on the operation of market forces. Here, where parents rather than pupils are regarded as the consumers of education, public approbation and financial rewards are bestowed on schools whose able pupils score highest in statutory tests and public examinations. Although a range of outcome measures is used in quality assurance, the key indicator of effective schooling is widely regarded to be exam performance and the key impediments to a school's success are seen as the unsuccessful pupils and the disaffected.

In the education market, as Ball *et al.* (1994) have demonstrated, self-interest is the driving force: the self-interest of the parent-consumer and the self interest of the school-trader, pursuing policies to attract the ablest pupils with the most ambitious and supportive parents. There is evidence that resources for special needs are being reduced to meet other imperatives of market competitiveness. In this regime, it is possible to see a pupil as a commodity with a relative value and pupils with low value are clearly vulnerable. Commentators have used terms such as 'unsaleable goods' (Lloyd Bennett 1993), 'damaged goods' (John 1996) and even 'debris' (Parsons

1996) to describe perceptions of pupils who have been excluded from school. Understandably, therefore, concern has been voiced about the needs and rights of marginalized groups and renewed calls have been made to listen to their accounts of experience in a system designed for others (Tisdall and Dawson 1994; Lloyd-Smith and Davies 1995; Galloway *et al.* 1998). Researching pupil perspectives is a potent way of challenging assumptions made about marginalized groups within education, in the way that feminist and anti-racist research has revealed levels of discrimination and subtle social processes embedded in educational policies and practices (Troyna and Hatcher 1992; Woods and Hammersley 1993; Dawtry *et al.* 1995).

This chapter explores the issue of children's perspectives from a broadly sociological point of view and considers why there has been a relative neglect of children's views in educational research. The reluctance to give children a voice has historical and cultural roots and certain models of childhood can be identified which tend to justify this reluctance. There are alternative models, however; in addition to outlining these, an argument will be made for the reconceptualization of childhood. By doing this, it is proposed, the rights of children would be more effectively protected and greater encouragement given for developing the values and skills of citizenship.

Listening to children

Since the late 1980s new international and national legislation has come into being to assert and protect the civil rights of children. In the UK measures such as the Children Act 1989, the Education Act 1993 and the Code of Practice (DfE 1994a) have all introduced requirements that children be given the opportunity to contribute to decision making about their future interests. There is on the face of it an acceptance of an ethical imperative that children have a basic right to be heard.

For educational researchers and policy makers, justifications for giving a voice to children can be made on practical as well as ethical grounds. Ruddock *et al.* (1996) convincingly argue that in developing school improvement strategies, the views of pupils are of fundamental importance. Researchers' lists of factors in school success tend to be concerned with the actions of teachers, sometimes account is taken of the 'inferred experience' of pupils but seldom are pupils seen as analysts of schooling and monitors of its appropriateness. Ruddock and her colleagues became convinced, like other researchers whom they cite, that young people are capable of producing analytical and constructive observations and react responsibly to the task of identifying factors which impede their learning.

A telling conclusion from the Ruddock research is that when creating the conditions for learning, secondary schools 'do not adequately take account of the social maturity of young people, nor of the tensions and pressures they feel as they struggle to reconcile the demands of their social and personal lives with the development of their identity as learners' (Ruddock *et al.* 1996: 1). The implication is that improvement strategies focusing on teachers' perceptions of schooling and on the assumptions they make about their pupils' experience will be flawed. Without listening seriously to the recipients of schooling, the ostensible improvers may simply get it wrong. Evidence of effective change in school derived directly from research involving pupils is reported in Vulliamy and Webb (1991) who comment on a series of projects in which teacher-researchers used data from their own pupils. They note that the teachers came to value highly the pupils' views and found their attitudes towards them changing which, in turn, had a major positive impact on their practice in the classroom.

Davie and Galloway (1996) also point out the practical benefits of giving children a say in their education. They argue that the process provides a desirable model of cooperative working and helps to give a sense of ownership over what goes on in school, adding also that it is effective because children who have been involved in decision making will find it harder to complain later about what goes on.

From a sociological viewpoint, the principal justification for giving children a voice in educational policy making, in monitoring and quality assurance as well as in research is epistemological. The reality experienced by children and young people in educational settings cannot be fully comprehended by inference and assumption. The meanings that they attach to their experiences are not necessarily the meanings that their teachers or parents would ascribe; the subcultures that children inhabit in classrooms and schools are not always visible or accessible to adults. There is a growing body of evidence that children's experience of special provision may be markedly different from 'official' versions. The study by Sinclair Taylor (1995a), for example, of life in an on-site special needs unit, showed that the subculture within the school and the unit itself counteracted the fundamental policy objective, that is, the pupils experienced the unit as excluding and marginalizing, not inclusive as professionals in the school and local authority believed it to be.

An important role of sociological research is to challenge the meanings and models embedded in prevailing theory, to question taken-for-granted social assumptions and beliefs and to analyse critically formal discourses about social phenomena. In the context of schooling, researching the experience of children and young people provides an effective vehicle for these objectives. The practical difficulties in doing this are not inconsiderable, indeed, a lack of confidence in methodological tools may in the past have been a deterrent to research focusing on children's perceptions and interpretations of the world. Giving a 'voice' to school children does not, of course, only imply the collection of oral data. In his discussion of strategies for accessing pupil perceptions, Burgess (1995) draws attention to observation and 'documents of life', as well as photographs, film and video recordings.

Despite the pervasive rhetoric about the need to listen to children, however, there are powerful social and cultural tendencies to keep them in their place. Studies by Keys and Fernandes (1993) and Wade and Moore (1993) indicate a reluctance among teachers to consult their pupils. The questions remain therefore of why adults in many cultures have in varying degrees kept children isolated and why they have been reluctant or unable to regard children's knowledge and understanding as worthy of respectful consideration.

Constructions of childhood

Childhood is a social construction brought about through the influence of cultural mores and practised values experienced by the community groupings in which children may find themselves. This socialization process is the way by which children develop into unique individuals who also feel themselves to be a part of a cultural community. The level at which children feel a sense of belonging will vary according to the status which different cultural communities bestow upon them. The UN Convention on the Rights of the Child 1989 provides us with a framework through which to consider the position of children in our society (Newell 1991). The Convention, unlike the Declaration of 1959, is legally binding upon all states which choose to ratify it. State parties are required to report to the UN, two years after ratification and then every five years, on the steps they have taken to implement the articles stated in the Convention. The UN committee examining Britain's report in 1995 continued to be concerned about child poverty levels, child homelessness, inadequate sex education leading to high level of teenage pregnancies and the permitting of 'reasonable chastisement' as a means of disciplining children. The committee concluded that the best interests of the child were not reflected in education, health or social security legislation and that Article 12, the right of children to express their views on all matters of concern to them, was not being addressed adequately in legislation or practice (Lansdown et al. 1996). The magnitude of these areas for further development paints a grim picture of the place of some children in British society.

The adoption of the UN Convention (see Sinclair Taylor, Chapter 2 in this book) does mark an important move forward in that there now exists a set of minimum standards for children and they are recognized as a group to whom human rights law applies. Parents or adults working with children have a responsibility to ensure that the structures, systems and programmes put in place enable children to claim their rights, at least to the minimum standard stated within the UN Convention. The idea of children's rights, however, creates much controversy and a denial of children's rights is supported by some on the basis of age, vulnerability and dependency. This stance reveals the dominance of discourses derived from developmental psychology which in its adherence to the biological model tends to maintain the subordination of children.

In order to understand present practices in relation to the rights of children, it is important to ask why models of provision have developed that have excluded the voice of the child. This calls for reflection upon the theoretical and epistemological models created historically and socially which have served to bring about a multitude of assumptions about childhood and children, accepted as true by society and informing popular constructions of childhood. The debate is complex as the power relationships that exist between adults and children cloud the issues and shape the assumptions that are made. These power relations are built upon the view that childhood is a discrete category of human life: 'The child has its boundaries maintained through the crystallization of conventions into institutionalized forms like families, nurseries, clinics and schools, all agencies specifically designed to process the status as a uniform entity' (Jenks 1982: 11).

These institutionalized forms serve to maintain the power of adults over children and preserve the construction of childhood as a rehearsal for adult life which requires serious, controlled forms of socialization. The work of Foucault has explored the operation of power within social institutions and illuminated the ways in which the marginalized are controlled by processes set up, in this instance, to 'protect' them. Children are frequently moved from family life and placed in nurseries and schools for large amounts of time in their 'best' interests. Our culture has evolved in such a way that nurseries and schools are an essential element of childhood. Foucault (1980: 98) writes that 'each society has its regimes of truth' which control ways of thinking, creates subjects who think and feel in the same way and shape institutional goals and practices. It is an element of the socialization process that brings about these 'regimes of truth' and through the oppression of those marginalized by our society we effectively limit the level of critical analysis that can occur.

This chapter now describes and analyses four constructions of childhood which have been coined by Jenkins (1993), here expanded in order to develop an understanding of the different theoretical and epistemological models which have supported them. Each covers a specific perspective on childhood examining children as possessions, as subjects, as participants and finally as citizens.

Children as possessions

This concept of childhood holds the view that a child is the property of parents or other adults and has no rights independent of them. Exploration into wardship, that is the appointment of custody of children, in the Middle Ages in England reveals that the primary purpose of the process was the sharing out of the belongings of the dead man, the aim being to protect the property rights of adults, rather than the rights or needs of the child (Thane 1981). The stage at which the child is seen as a person in his or her own right is the age of majority, which has altered throughout the years. In the sixth century it was 10 years old and throughout the Middle Ages it varied according to the social class of the family. Since the thirteenth century it was generally accepted as being 21 years by most social classes and has now been reduced to 18 years. These changes reflect the changing perceptions of adults about the age at which children are able to behave in a rational manner.

The disciplining of children continues to cause concern in modern society. Foucault (1977) writes about discipline as a method of social control, the correct training of children serving to produce docile adult bodies. The primary site of childhood becomes the child's body:

> The classical age discovered the body as object and target of power. It is easy enough to find signs of the attention then paid to the body – to the body that is manipulated, shaped, trained, which obeys, responds, becomes skilful and increases its forces.
>
> (Foucault 1977: 136)

The legal position regarding the punishment of children was such in 1706 that it was deemed to be misadventure if the parent 'corrected the child or servant with a moderate weapon, and shall by chance give him an unlucky stroke so as to kill him' (cited in Jenkins 1993).

Parents and adults regarding children as their possessions or their property is one way in which they wield their power over them, legitimizing this by reference to notions of biological dependency and immaturity. Children exist essentially to fulfil the interests of the parent or adult. An analogy for the constant surveillance that exists over children was seen by Foucault (1977) in the Panopticon, a design of prison in which all cells are visible from central observation points. Foucault (1977: 201) described the social version of this as the 'automatic functioning of power'. The power relation is created by both the parent and the child in that permanent visibility creates such a curious state of consciousness. Foucault (1980: 98) develops his analysis, stating that power circulates: 'It is never localized here or there, never in anybody's hands . . . individuals are always in the position of simultaneously undergoing and exercising this power . . . [they] are the vehicles of power, not its points of application'.

The position of children as possessions or property can be viewed as a transitory state which alters as the beliefs and constructs of society change and evolve. The cultural and economic conditions of a specific time and place may justify the adults' view that their children are possessions but as these conditions alter, the power circulates and the balance shifts. In some areas of social experience this construction of childhood still exists, but society is changing its perceptions and the right of children to protection, provision and participation is growing and influencing current principles and practices, as will be shown on pp. 68–9.

Children as subjects

This construction of childhood perceives the child as a subject in need of protection by adults. In this respect the child does hold rights in terms of the provision of basic welfare and protection but these are decided by adults and enforced by adults. Parents can make many decisions they feel are in the best interest of children before ever consulting them. Children are perceived as dependent and incompetent, and therefore requiring protection from and within the adult world.

This model of the child as subject requiring protection has been fuelled by the work of Piaget, a former biologist who developed a powerful theory about stages of cognitive development. These were taken up by psychologists and educators as a structure by which they could understand the growth and development of children to adulthood. Piaget devised a four stage model of cognitive development, loosely linked to biological stages of development and incorporating generalized statements about characteristics and abilities. For example:

> Young children cannot make logical inferences, could not understand the principles of invariance of quantity, were unable to realize that other people have different points of view (socially and spatially) from themselves, were severely limited in the way they classified things in their environment, found measurement impossible.
>
> (Bryant 1984: 252)

Piaget did point out that 'children may grow intellectually by constructing their intellectual world for themselves' and yet his developmental stages remain to reinforce our perceptions that children will be dependent, irrational and vulnerable for a considerable length of time. The legitimacy of these principles has been questioned (Donaldson 1978; James and Prout 1997), but the strong hold of their positivist stance for a long time had an enduring influence on conceptions of childhood.

Education systems have many elements that reinforce developmental theories. Not only do the current standardized assessment tests pit peers against each other, but also a strong notion of the 'normal' child and age related development is encouraged. The concept of normalization has been taken further through Freudian theory, which views the process of childhood as the process of becoming a human being. Normal development is the management of id, an irrepressible, uncontrolled, mainly sexual drive, mastery of which leads to successful socialization. Childhood is examined and reflected upon in psychotherapy but never really gains any status in its own right. The Freudian perspective serves to reinforce the importance of the role of adults as protectors of children. The question arises: what are we protecting children from? It is quite reasonable that they will need a degree of protection as for many years they require a high level of physical care and attention but this can be exaggerated:

> Protection is mostly accompanied by exclusion in one way or the other; protection may be suggested even when it is not strictly necessary for the sake of children, but rather to protect adults or the adult social orders against disturbances from the presence of children. This is exactly the point at which protection threatens to slide into unwarranted dominance.
>
> (Qvortrup 1997: 87)

Placing adults as responsible for the protection and enforcement of children's rights conforms to the notion commonly held in western societies that children lack responsibility, competence and capability. The legislation regarding decisions about educational provision for a child with special educational needs (DfE 1994a) contains provision for consultation with children but responsibility lies clearly with the parents.

The health service provides little recognition of the rights of the child as again it is legally the parent who can determine whether or not their child below the age of 16 years will have medical treatment. The Gillick ruling in 1984, altered this legal position according to S. Lee (1986) 'by citing the DHSS memorandum that had advised doctors that they could offer under-16-year-old children contraceptive advice and treatment without parental consent in "most unusual . . . (or) . . . exceptional cases"' (Lee 1986: 48). The Gillick case involving four judges throughout the process, stated from the House of Lords that parents' rights over the child would cease and that the 'decision whether or not to prescribe contraception must be for the clinical judgment of a doctor' (Lee 1986: 48). The doctor decides whether or not the child has a level of maturity to understand what is proposed. This reflects a changing awareness of the level of responsibility that individual children can possess under the age of 16 years. However, without any clear guidelines on what constitutes a level of understanding the decision is left to busy medical practitioners who may not have time to establish an individual child's level of competence and understanding in specific situations and therefore act according to the main thrust of the legal statement that parental involvement would be required. (For further details on the Gillick ruling please refer to Kennedy 1988.)

The Children Act 1989 established the right of the child to be listened to and promoted the concept of social agencies working in partnership with parents. Family centred care has long been a common approach in social welfare work but the difficulty in managing any conflict between children and their carers still remains.

So despite visionary legislation in some areas, society continues to belittle the voice of the child and the power relationship between adults and children continues to cloud the issues of children's rights. John Stuart Mill, a political theorist, described this relationship as follows:

> The only purpose for which power can be rightfully exercised over any member of civilized community against his will, is to prevent harm to others . . . We are not speaking of children, or of young persons below the age which the law may fix as that of manhood or womanhood . . . the existing generation is master both of the training and the entire circumstances of the generation to come.
>
> (Mill 1964: 73)

While adults still continue to recognize the level of responsibility they hold regarding the next generation, children are now demanding to be heard, to be enabled to bring about change and to be valid agents in developing their world. This tendency leads to two alternative models of childhood which differ markedly from those which see children as possessions or subjects: children as participants or citizens.

Children as participants

This construction of childhood perceives children as participants in the decision making of adults and, in particular, having the right to be consulted about any decisions made about them. Participation refers to many types of involvement: economic, social, political and cultural, both within the community at large and in educational terms (Organization for Economic Cooperation and Development (OECD) 1997). In order to ensure such participation, the voice of the young person needs to be listened and responded to, but initially children must be encouraged to speak.

A vast conceptual leap is required to ensure that adults begin to consider the opinions and views of children seriously enough to encourage them to speak their minds and express their opinions. It is beginning to occur: the Children Act 1989 refers to parental responsibility rather than parental rights. It states that the interests of the child are paramount and that the wishes of the child should be heard. However, as noted earlier, the UN committee, when examining Britain's report of 1995 concerning the rights of the child, stated that Article 12, the right of children to express their views on all matters of concern to them, was not being addressed adequately in legislation or practice (Lansdown *et al.* 1996).

The role of education is vital as children need to learn how to participate in matters concerning them in order to develop a sense of personal autonomy. Knowing and understanding one's legal position is one way forward but feeling empowered to speak and take action requires a supportive environment. The Council of Europe's (1985) recommendation on

Human Rights in Schools identifies the importance of the climate of the school arguing that:

> democracy is best learned in a democratic setting where participation is encouraged, where views can be expressed openly and discussed, where there is freedom of expression for pupils and teachers and where there is fairness and justice.
>
> (Council of Europe 1985, cited in Starkey 1991: 259)

Clearly there needs to be a considerable change in the present adult–child power relationship if the climate described above is to become common-place in all schools and indeed within every family. Gradually systems and legal proceedings are changing to empower children to be a part of pro-cesses but there is a very real danger that they can be tokenistic. The whole approach to education, for example, needs to be based upon participation thus involving pupils in the creation of school policies and curricula at all levels. There has been little progress here, despite the rhetorical support of the Code of Practice 1994, which states that children who have special educational needs 'have the right to be heard and should be encouraged to participate in decision-making about provision to meet their needs' (DfE 1994a: 14).

Notwithstanding such legislation and its related official guidelines, the status of young people with disabilities continues, through the very language of 'need', to imply weakness and an incapability of developing independ-ence. Society continues to carry negative and deficit models of disability which result in the devaluation of young people and often degrees of social oppression. The recent focus on inclusive education has highlighted the plight of children with special educational needs as an oppressed minority group within the larger group of children. It is often the case that those on the boundaries of cultural groupings campaigning for change can eventu-ally bring about better conditions and a higher level of participation for the whole group. It seems rather unfair, however, that pupils with learning difficulties struggling for inclusion in mainstream education bear the brunt of the inequalities faced by children.

Children as citizens

This construction of childhood holds that the child is an active citizen and in this respect one who has the right to choose and to take action independ-ently of parents and adults. One needs to consider the generational position of children as it has major implications for their individual autonomy and agency. O'Neill (1995) states that the fundamental contradiction faced by children today concerns the contradiction between parents' and children's voices such that 'Only by overlooking the child/family bond can we imagine the child's political equality whereas the child's equality is a myth to which it is committed to "save" the inequality within and between families' (O'Neill 1995: 67).

There are, however, recent developments to increase the participation of children and young people in political life. *Hear! Hear!* (Willow 1997) is a document which provides examples of ways in which children and young people are being democratically included in political processes. Willow (1997: 12) states that 'to fail to consult or involve these children and young people because of an assumed innocence is patronizing and it does not take into account their experiences or competence in making difficult decisions'. One example of a way in which young people are actively involved in democratic processes and positive action is the Devon Youth Council established in 1993. This involves young people aged 14–25 years and since 1993 has become 'the recognized authority on the views of young people locally and is the first stop for those seeking the perspective and experiences of children' (Townsend 1996: 110). By working in partnership with other agencies, the Devon Youth Council has brought about participation of young people in projects addressing issues of crime, drug abuse and environmental awareness. It also talks of work with younger children (5–13 years) promoting the UN Convention and developing the knowledge and skills of younger children with regard to their rights and to enable them to take up a role in the Youth Council more effectively at the age of 14 years.

A report published by the Qualifications and Curriculum Authority (QCA 1998) proposes that education for citizenship should be a statutory entitlement within the curriculum and pupils should be empowered to 'participate in society effectively as active, informed, critical and responsible citizens' (QCA 1998: 9). Actual experience of participation as a child is essential in order to learn how to behave as an adult, but this document contains little mention of children's individual rights nor of children as citizens in their own right. It appears from this document and much educational legislation that the responsibility of adults to protect and provide for children in their care continues to be the dominant ideology and that the citizenship rights of children in reality are still distinct from the concept of human rights in which adults are assumed to be essential protectors and guardians. One result of this view of childhood is that young individuals remain ill equipped to adjust to the complex adult world and have to be slowly inducted through behavioural prescriptions.

Conclusion

The climate in British society may now be changing legally, politically, socially and culturally. Our systems of education would do well to recognize these changes and, as front line providers for children, model for other professionals a real process of including young people in decisions about their future, acknowledging and valuing their views and opinions. Children experience a wide range of social relationships and engage in life experiences which are often quite independent of adult concerns. Services responsible for provision for children in relation to education, social services, health, the environment and entertainment would benefit from encouraging the more proactive participation of children themselves.

The charity Save the Children (1996) conducted research into current planning for children entitled *Towards a Children's Agenda* and highlighted six major problems:

• failure to collect child specific information
• lack of recognition of children's productive contribution
• no participation of children in decision making
• using an inappropriate standard model of childhood
• pursuit of adult interests in ways that render children passive
• lack of attention to gender and generational relationships.

These lacunae in the planning process tend to reinforce the view formed by Franklin (1995: 5): 'Society constructs the children it needs. Instead of policies to protect children in the community, the government and media have preferred to promote policies to protect the community from children'.

This brings to the fore an urgent need for sociological research to unpack the complexities of society's present constructions of childhood and to explore the currently held 'regimes of truth' surrounding childhood innocence and immaturity. There is also a role for educational research to demonstrate the potency and value of listening to children in the evaluation of national policy, the promotion school improvement and the monitoring of provision for vulnerable and excluded groups. Giving children a voice will also empower them to greater levels of participation and involve them as young citizens. It is, therefore, part of the process of reconstructing childhood and a step towards ensuring that they are able to claim the minimum standard of rights outlined in the 1989 UN Convention.

Acknowledgement

Thanks are due to Carol Vincent for helpful comments on a draft of this chapter.

 **Part 2** Practical applications

⑥ Children and young people and care proceedings

MAUREEN WINN OAKLEY

What did children and young people think of those who represented them in care proceedings, namely the guardian *ad litem* and the solicitor for the child, and what was their understanding of this legal process? Did they feel that the adults were listening to what they had to say and did they feel that they had a choice about participating, or did they feel that they were left uninformed and excluded from the process?

Children and young people caught up in care proceedings are particularly vulnerable. Their future depends on both the social welfare and the legal systems as well as their parents and family. Communication between them and these systems is vital. There has already been research into the court processes in child protection and into the views of the adults involved, both professionals and lay, yet little is known of the views of the children and young people involved even though the proceedings are to do with their care. (See Masson, Chapter 3 in this book, for an examination of the legal dimension to researching children's perspectives.) Together with Judith Masson, I developed a study to redress this imbalance and give a voice to the children and young people concerned. Obtaining knowledge about representation that is derived from focusing on children and young people's views and experiences will add further dimensions to understandings which have depended upon the views of adults. Focusing upon the views of the children and young people is a theme that runs throughout the research.

The legal system and the research project

When social services departments have child protection concerns about the care of certain children and young people, they may decide to make an application to the court for a care or supervision order to enable them to monitor and support future care. Once children and young people are subject to such public law proceedings, they are automatically made parties to those proceedings and are provided with two professional representatives for the duration of the court's involvement.

One, a guardian *ad litem*, will usually have a background in social work and will be appointed by the court to look into the issues surrounding the welfare of the child and to make recommendations, in a report to the court, based upon what would be in the child's best interests. The other, a solicitor, will usually be a member of the Children Panel and as such will specialize in childcare cases, and will be appointed to ascertain the wishes and feelings of the child or young person with a remit to ensure that the court is made aware of this information. The solicitor will apply for a legal aid certificate to be issued in the name of the child to meet the child's legal expenses.

While both representatives have separate roles, they are expected to liaise to discuss the case and both, either jointly or separately, are expected to arrange to meet with the child or young person to introduce themselves, to listen to what the child or young person has to say, and to inform the child or young person of the proceedings and of any developments as the case progresses. Both professionals are expected to attend the court hearings in order to represent the child or young person; this is irrespective of whether the child or young person attends. Some young people may wish to attend the court hearing, and the representatives may facilitate this, but ultimately this matter is a decision for the court.

In the main, therefore, the child or young person's understanding of the court process, the role of these two representatives, and the part the young person can play in the proceedings, will hinge upon the meetings the child or young person has with their guardian *ad litem* and their solicitor. In planning the research, I therefore arranged to be present in order to observe interaction when the representatives met with their young clients and when the latter attended court. Individual interviews were carried out with the children and young people, the guardians *ad litem* and the solicitors once the court cases had concluded so as not to affect the case in any way.

The fieldwork took place over a 15-month period, in two areas of the English Midlands in 1996–7 and involved 20 children and young people and their respective representatives. The project concentrated upon children and young people over the age of 8 years so that they would be able to give their consent to participate in the research. We took the view that those who could understand what researchers do, and the nature of the research relationship, had the legal right to consent to participating in the research (see the legal case *Gillick v West Norfolk* 1986). Only one young person, a 17-year-old man, chose not to participate in the research and also failed to instruct his solicitor in the discharge proceedings. He said he was 'getting on with life'. His guardian managed one brief meeting with him because she tracked him down at a dog race.

Why do the research?

The 1990s began with a new legal statute concerning children and young people. The Children Act 1989 had been drafted and debated in Parliament against a background of concern about child abuse. The Act's implementation in 1991 brought with it a focus upon the interests of children, particularly for those involved in public law proceedings. In the same year the UK ratified the UN Convention on the Rights of the Child, thus supporting the right for children to express their views freely and for those views to be respected (Article 12). Indeed the Solicitors Family Law Association's *Guide to Good Practice for Solicitors Acting for Children* endorses this UN Convention and in particular Article 12.

Researchers were also becoming more aware of the absence of children's voices from narratives about their lives, the invisibility of children in official statistics and the lack of knowledge of children's and young people's perceptions among policy makers and service providers in areas such as health, education, social services and the legal system. A more collaborative approach to qualitative research was developing. The focus became research *with* rather than *about* children.

The importance of listening to children was a theme taken up by the National Society for the Prevention of Cruelty to Children, which funded this project. The NSPCC had, in the mid-1990s, run a national campaign aimed at parents and those providing services to children. Chris Brown, then director and chief executive of the NSPCC, stated: 'If we are to serve children effectively we must be prepared to listen and learn from what children have to say to us' (NSPCC Annual Report 1989).

Researching the court process in respect of child protection is not an easy option. Knowing the system beforehand is a necessity for researchers. Proceedings concern many different agencies and hence there are numerous consents to be sought. Researchers need to be aware of the professionals involved and the legal protocol, and to be sensitive to the issues. The court proceedings themselves are conducted in private: only parties to the proceedings are invited so there is no public attendance. Obtaining research access to such hearings not only involves the consent of the professionals taking part but also the consent of each of the parties to the proceedings.

A considerable amount of tact and patience is required by researchers when seeking access to the children and young people involved in such proceedings; however, if researchers regarded these barriers as insurmountable, children and young people's experiences would remain personal, private and hidden. Indeed, adult perspectives of care proceedings have already been well researched. See for example the perspectives of the various professionals involved (Murch and Hooper 1992; Hunt and Macleod 1997) and those of parents and other family carers caught up in care proceedings (Lindley 1994; Cleaver and Freeman 1995). There is no research about the perceptions of children and young people subject to such proceedings other than a study by a professional working within the system (Clark 1995).

The need to focus upon children's own perceptions was highlighted in a study that looked at children and social workers. The researchers concluded that the professionals were not always correct in their views of children's perceptions. Clearly, the message from this research was that adults must learn to listen to children in person (Butler and Williamson 1994). Indeed, the Utting (1997) report on children in care was highly critical of adults' failure to listen to what children had to say.

We wanted to analyse the perspectives of the representatives in representing the children and young people. Taking on board young people's opinions arguably calls for a greater child's rights perspective. Representatives, particularly the solicitors representing young people in care proceedings, would need to consider this perspective in putting forward young people's wishes to the court and in facilitating their attendance at such proceedings. However, deciding what is best for the child or young person is not only the remit for the guardian *ad litem*, but also the very cornerstone of the Children Act 1989 itself – 'the welfare of the child is paramount'.

It was possible that some legal professionals would lean towards a more protectionist or paternalistic view without being aware that such a perspective may deny the children and young people a voice. Indeed, some legal professionals, particularly those involved in the higher courts, have been unhappy about children's and young people's participation in legal proceedings, particularly proceedings concerning their care (see for example remarks *per* Waite in the case *Re C* [1993] and also remarks by the Official Solicitor in the case *Re W* [1994]). It has also been argued that numerous perspectives can be identified as existing within childcare policy covering the rights of the child, the rights of the family and the rights of the state, such as that supporting state paternalism and child protectionism (Fox Harding 1991).

A video has been produced to inform young people about their care proceedings (DoH 1995). The background research for the video sought the views of adults, professionals and carers, but did not seek to obtain any direct feedback from any children and young people who had experienced such proceedings. Apparently the views of such young people were not sought because the professionals felt that it would be abusive to do so. But how do we know what young people think unless we ask them? Research by Sawyer (1995) has suggested that excluding young people from issues that affect them can be abusive in itself.

With the above in mind, we set out to obtain the views of the children and young people involved in the cases identified during the period of the research. The numbers are not great and we do not claim that the study is representative of all those children and young people involved in such proceedings. Indeed the majority of care proceedings involve children much younger than 8 years of age. However, the study is a window upon the way that children and young people perceive those who represent them and their understanding of this legal process.

The research was investigative and we were keen to know whether young people identified with their guardian *ad litem*, their solicitor and whether they could give any definition of their respective roles. We also wanted to tap young people's knowledge about the court proceedings, and find out what information, if any, they had about the process. Running through the research was a concern as to whether the child or young person identified the proceedings as being *for* or *about* them.

Laying the groundwork

Preparation for the fieldwork required that we canvassed views about the project from a number of professional gatekeepers involved with the legal process and at the different levels of court, in particular because decisions in the higher courts dictated policy in the lower courts.

The advisory group

Preparation for the research project also involved the setting up of an advisory group. Members included practitioners with expertise in the guardian *ad litem* service, social services and childcare law, including a practising guardian *ad litem*, a Children Panel solicitor and a specialist in children with special needs. On the academic side there were a number of senior researchers who headed research projects in the law, children and child protection. Being able to discuss ideas and developments proved invaluable to the researchers. Feedback was freely given.

All advisory group members were adults: this is admitted as being a weakness. Discussions did take place about the appropriateness of young people on the advisory group, and a number of issues debated including some concern that young people may feel intimidated by other adult, professional, members or be seen as 'token' members. Knight (1998) had similar discussions in her research involving independent visitors for young people with disabilities; however, she opted for one advisory group of adults and another of young people.

Increasingly there is now a move for adults to consider input from children and young people when seeking advice about the services they provide. A number of children's charities have raised this issue. Locally, some independent visitors schemes now have young people on their management committees, as do children's rights and youth advocacy organizations such as the National Youth Advocacy Service (NYAS). Indeed in January 1998 some young members of NYAS agreed to give a presentation to those professionals attending the Annual Guardian ad Litem Panel Managers Workshop in London. Their play depicted the way that young people felt excluded from their care proceedings. One actor, now a young adult, was unable to perform on the day because the memories of such a negative experience upset her too much.

Piloting

Methodology includes piloting the research ideas. Individual interviews were undertaken with children and young people who had been involved in care proceedings, as well as interviews with solicitors and practising guardians *ad litem*. Piloting research ideas with young people similar in status to those to be included in the research fieldwork was felt to be very important, particularly so as the research was investigative, very little being known about how young people felt about their solicitor, their guardian *ad litem* or about the legal process.

Contact was made with some young people who had been involved in care proceedings but whose cases had now completed. Direct contact was attempted wherever possible, such as through young people's groups or through local newsletters and magazines for young people. Other contact was made through solicitors, guardians *ad litem*, children's rights officers or advocacy representatives. Some young people who did help pilot the research had heard about the research through the NSPCC 'grapevine' and volunteered themselves. Two people, whose legal cases had been completed over a year, were still very angry about the failure of some of the legal professionals to communicate with them and had felt excluded from the legal process. Far from being reticent to talk about their experiences, they stated that they were keen to pass on their feelings to me, as a researcher. Indeed, they suggested that this 'unburdening' could have a therapeutic input and so would be positive for them.

Doing the fieldwork

When an application for a care or supervision order is received by the court, the local guardian panel is contacted to request the appointment of a guardian to the case. The guardian then ensures that a solicitor is appointed to represent the child. We had negotiated research access with two guardian panels with the arrangement that once a request for a guardian arrived, and the child was over 8 years of age, the researcher would be contacted too.

Initially guardians assessed cases for their suitability and then asked children and young people if they were willing to participate. Cases that were not included in the active study were noted in brief together with the reason for non-inclusion. We are aware that guardians *ad litem* were given a substantial amount of power in assessing the suitability of the case for the research, and we acknowledge that there may be a bias here; however, without the guardians' input there would not have been access to and consent from the 20 children and young people who did participate.

Once a case had been identified, I commenced obtaining consent from the professional and lay adults involved in the specific case. Having negotiated research access with the director of social services (or equivalent) I informed other social services personnel such as team managers, social workers and foster carers, as well as parents and the solicitor for the child. A number of other adults became involved too, for example an educational psychologist, headteachers of residential special schools and those in charge of secure accommodation units. All were concerned with protecting children and young people from intrusive researchers. Indeed, several appropriate cases failed to be included in the research because some adult gatekeepers would not agree; these included guardians *ad litem*, solicitors, parents, social workers and teachers.

As the fieldwork researcher, I accompanied both the guardian and the solicitor, jointly and separately, to observe the visits they made to the children and young people. I did not attend on the first visit that the guardian made to the child so that the guardian could build professional rapport as well as refer to the research. I did not attend some visits because the guardian or solicitor requested this or because they coincided with other visits. If the representative took the young person out, I went too. If the representative travelled to see the young person at the child's home, with foster carers, in a children's home, at residential school or at a secure accommodation unit, then I would also travel, usually meeting the representative outside first. If the young person attended court, I obtained access and attended too. In all there were 63 visits.

Observation

Direct observation allows the researcher to 'see it like it is' and proved to be a very enlightening research method. Observing meetings allowed me to pick up whether issues were focused on the needs of the child or those of the adult and to observe whether issues raised were 'framed' according to legal importance. Being focused on the child or young person was an important theme for the research. As observer, I was keen to note whether issues raised by young people as being important issues were recognized by the representatives as such. One young man continually asked his representatives to obtain his skateboard from home. He raised this issue every visit but it was months before he got his wish.

The two main research methods employed in this research were observation and then interview. Deutscher (1973) has argued that observed actions can be ambiguous but that a combination of different approaches reduces overall error. Indeed, while I was able to observe where the meetings took place, who was present and what factors 'appeared' to have a positive or negative affect upon the interaction, I was also able to follow up such observations, at the interview stage, by checking out specific details with interviewees. For example, I observed that one girl attended a meeting in her Brownie uniform, and in interview it emerged that she was missing part of her Brownie meeting because the appointment with her guardian had been arranged for the same time.

In another case, a teenager asked her solicitor to leave after a few minutes because she had her homework to do. At interview I learned from the teenager that her foster carer refused to allow her to watch television until she had done her homework. The meeting with the solicitor took place on the evening that she wanted to watch her favourite television programme. The teenager said that she would have concentrated upon her meeting with her solicitor had it been at a different time.

The study found that meetings between young people and their representatives were not always arranged with the young people direct but often made with carers on their behalf. Some young people thought that their representatives should telephone after school hours and speak to them direct to ensure that proposed meetings were convenient. Maintaining some control over their lives and hence normality in their lives was important for them.

Observing the interaction between young people and their representatives also highlighted the case of those vulnerable young people with special needs. One teenager with learning difficulties stated that she wanted to go to court and meet the judge. The solicitor had decided that her client was not competent but was aware that she continually requested that she be allowed to attend the court hearing. The teenager astounded both the solicitor, and myself as observer, by arguing that a young man in a recent episode of the television programme *Kavanagh* had attended court and had been able to speak to the judge in person because he was not legally represented. This reasoning led the solicitor to arrange a court directions appointment to consider her client's request. In interview the solicitor confirmed that this experience made her question her own preconceptions about the capabilities of young people with learning difficulties.

In all the cases that I observed the representatives went out to visit the child or young person. The majority of the children and young people were pleased about this because it 'showed they cared': they had made a positive effort to be with them. This was true of young people in secure accommodation too because 'criminal lawyers' only ever met them at court. Needing to be able to talk to your representatives so that they could hear what you had to say was important to young people too. One young person later complained that her discussions with her guardian were constantly interrupted by her 3-year-old brother, who did appear to me to be somewhat loud and overactive. 'It would have been better because [younger sibling] is always leaping about'.

Another young person talked with his guardian *ad litem* while his mother sat on the settee nursing a younger sibling. On this occasion I observed that he did not engage with his representative and continued to play a computer game. He later ran away from home. In interview he told me that he had been unable to talk about his feelings because his mother was present and he had run away because he did not want to live with her.

All the notes of the observation meetings were made in the car immediately after the meetings had ended, which enabled me to keep a record of the number of visits made in each case and then to ask the representatives why some cases warranted fewer visits. One disturbing result was that a number of representatives acknowledged that proceedings discharging care orders were seen to be relatively straightforward and hence warranted fewer visits to the children and young people. This assumption was worrying. The young man who had run away from home had been having his care order considered for discharge. Indeed in 1973 the case of Maria Colwell had already alerted professionals nationwide to the need to be diligent when considering the discharging of care orders. Maria died after leaving care; a committee of inquiry reported as a result (Department of Health and Social Security (DHSS) 1974).

My making notes of the meetings was important. Whereas the guardian *ad litem* and the solicitor would make their own notes of each meeting on their work files, each professional was task driven and kept notes according to their personal remit. Non-legal issues may not have been noted down as such issues may not have been seen as significant. For example I made notes of observations during final visits when some representatives gave small gifts to the children and young people. These moments were personal and probably would not have been referred to on work files.

Representation in care proceedings is a process which can last many months. Observation enabled me to record the young people's changing reactions to and views about the process. Such experiences might not be readily recalled, particularly so as children are not task oriented and are unlikely to write down issues from the meetings. Observation also enabled me to witness how guardians dealt with explaining their report to young people. One guardian referred to it only verbally, another brought one printed page that referred to the child's wishes and feelings, another had a copy of the report but had obscured some parts of it.

Direct observation enabled me to witness whether any written information was given to the young people about the proceedings. Some solicitors handed over business cards to young clients, although these contained little information other than their representative's name and address. Some guardians used pamphlets that were written for children in general. Witnessing such acts and discussing this information with all interviewees led me to make a study of the literature available to those young people involved in care proceedings (M. W. Oakley 1998). Indeed considering what information was available for young people became an important issue.

As an observer, I considered whether my presence would affect anyone else; one solicitor did confirm in interview that she was disconcerted because she felt as though she were under a test of good practice. No children or young people referred to this point although most young people in the care system become acclimatized to having strangers invade their lives. On the contrary, two young people insisted that I join in games that they were playing with their guardian so as not to be left out.

Observing meetings between the child or young person and their representatives over a period provided the opportunity for the child or young person to get used to me as a researcher; this made it easier to establish rapport. I was responsible for following each case throughout and interviewed the young person and each representative. Children and young people therefore knew that I already had some insight into their case and had some knowledge of the meetings with the guardian *ad litem* and the solicitor.

Being an observer made access to interviewing easier, because carers of the young people were happy for me to arrange interviews with the young people after the court proceedings had ended. Teachers at one residential school, having met me on a number of visits, arranged a meal for me on the day of the interview. Another carer insisted upon taking my photograph to place in the child's life story book.

When young people attended court their representatives facilitated my access to the hearing so that I could observe, which enabled me to see the effect that the proceedings had upon the young person at first hand. One young person attended a directions hearing at court to consider her request to attend the final hearing. Her request was denied but she told me afterwards that she was satisfied that she had attended a court hearing and spoken to the magistrate herself. 'I had been listened to by the people at court.'

Interviews

All interviews were tape recorded after the interviewee consented to this. One young person refused; she had previously been tape recorded when a witness in a criminal case against her abusive parent and did not feel comfortable with being recorded again. One guardian also refused on the grounds that her voice sounded like 'Mickey Mouse'. Most interviews with the young people took place where the child or young person was living. One was arranged at McDonald's at the young person's request. Good practice now dictates that researchers do not shut themselves in bedrooms alone with young people. Interviews should be in a place where the young person feels comfortable. Young people naturally appreciate researchers and other adults arriving on time. Interviews with children and young people ranged from 10 minutes to 90 minutes. Interviews with representatives lasted 1–2 hours.

I had a checklist as a prompt because some questions were unstructured. Other questions were semi-structured and open ended so as not to place an adult perspective on the young person's data. It was left to the young person to define the issues and what was important to them. Open-ended questions allowed the young people to answer in their own words. Piloting had highlighted the fact that young people valued their own language and felt alienated by adult words or professional jargon. Research by the South Glamorgan Advocacy Scheme (1994) drew attention to this when young people referred to 'advocacy' as being an adult word. This had affected their involvement with the service and presumably with the research.

If children and young people asked me questions, I responded. It was made clear to all the young people that participation in the research would not affect the outcome of their legal proceedings in any way. Indeed, all interviews were done after the proceedings had concluded so as not to risk the research data being embroiled in an active court case, although one interview did take place on the day the final hearing was being heard at court because the young person was waiting at her foster carers, with her bags packed, ready to move to be with her aunt, who lived abroad.

Children and young people may be overwhelmed by the interview questions (Rubin and Rubin 1995). I constantly assured them that there was no right or wrong answer and that it was fine for them to say 'I don't know' or 'I don't want to answer that'. The young people also knew that they could end the interview with me whenever they wanted.

Other research techniques

As researchers, I had considered asking the children and young people to keep diaries noting meetings, events, development, feelings about the case or thoughts about their representative. This suggestion had to be rejected because the diaries may have become evidence in the active proceedings. It would have been useful to have young people refer to particular issues, events and times but again research confidentiality could have been at risk.

Other methodological points

Children and young people are special too

Ethical considerations of research concerning children and young people have meant that children should be well informed about the research and given time to consider participating, before consenting to do so (M. W. Oakley 1997). I was aware of the ethical considerations of doing research with children and young people (Alderson 1995). However, researchers generally do need to consider whether they can offer young people 100 per cent research confidentiality. As an NSPCC researcher I am aware that confidentiality may be compromised by a young person disclosing abuse. Researchers need to ensure that young people understand that they may have to pass on certain information if it appears that the young person is at risk, but that this would be done only with the young person's knowledge.

Neither adults nor young people were paid in this research. (There was no research budget for such an expense.) It may be that consideration should be given to whether children and young people are paid for participating in this type of research. If researchers are considering paying adults, they should also consider payment for young people. Payment need not necessarily be monetary. One researcher hired a room in a hotel and supplied food and a bouncy castle for all her participants while giving feedback on the research (Knight 1998).

Feedback from young people

Two teenagers referred to the interview after it was completed. They had felt positive about the research although one had been concerned about the questions to be asked. Both commented that they had enjoyed the experience and found it refreshing that I had accepted their replies without question. The young people mentioned that their representatives did not necessarily accept their responses first time and would often ask them to repeat or reconsider answers or would reinterpret them for them.

Feedback to young people

Part of the research methodology is to ensure that young people receive feedback about the research project if they want it. The research results may be aimed at adults, for example to assist in the training of professionals, but this should not negate the need to keep young people informed about the research. An A4 page summary was sent by post to the young people who requested feedback.

Some young people involved in the care system can be difficult to trace some months on. Several interviewees had already moved a number of times prior to the research commencing; many had had a change of social worker. This is not untypical (C. Shaw 1998). There should be an onus on researchers to ensure that feedback is given to young people wherever possible; for example an article in *Who Cares* magazine would reach children in care.

Conclusion

As a researcher I consciously tried to examine the process from the children and young people's perspectives: what did they understand about the process, how involved did they feel in it and to what extent did their representatives address their concerns?

The research found that children and young people have agendas separate from those of their professional representatives. Young people are often concerned about present day-to-day issues rather than past or future care. Being able to assume some normality in their lives is important to them, as is having some control. Professionals need to bear this in mind when interviewing children and young people. Like adults, they appreciate the courtesies of speaking to them directly to arrange interviews and of arriving on time.

Young people do not necessarily confine their agendas to legal issues although they were generally concerned about where they were going to live and what contact they would have with family and friends. They are not task driven and do not frame replies to fit in with the representatives' focus about whether an order should be made at court.

Young people involved in care proceedings are vulnerable young people and are often isolated from family and friends. They rely upon others, such as guardians *ad litem* and solicitors to assist them in understanding what is happening. Children and young people with special needs can be particularly vulnerable. Preconceptions about their lack of ability may mean that professionals, including researchers, may fail to take into account their capacity to understand. If representatives hold back from engaging with children and young people in care, they may be signalling a lack of commitment to the young people, who in turn may disengage from the representatives and the whole legal process. Adults must learn to engage with young people and learn about their experiences by ensuring that the voices of children and young people are heard.

Case law

C (a minor) (care: child's wishes), Re [1993] 1 FLR 832
Gillick v West Norfolk and Wisbech Area Health Authority and Another [1986] 1 FLR 224
W (secure accommodation order: attendance at court), Re [1994] 2 FLR 1092

7 A matter of life and death: a reflective account of two examples of practitioner research into children's understanding and experience of death and bereavement

CAROLINE JONES AND JANE TANNOCK

Any subject may be potentially sensitive (Renzetti and Lee 1993), but the decision to research children's perspectives on death and bereavement, a particularly sensitive topic, derived from an urge to consider whether 'death education' should be part of the curriculum in every school. If so, what in the light of firsthand research evidence should be the nature of that curriculum? Farberow (1963) equates sensitive topics with those areas of life normally surrounded by taboo or laden with emotion. However, R. Lee (1993: 4) suggests that this is a rather narrow interpretation and defines sensitive research as 'research which potentially poses a substantial threat to those who are or have been involved in it' including, on occasions, the researcher. Researchers bring their own opinions, values and beliefs to the research and the concomitant impact on the research setting is well known. However, less well explored is the effect of the research on the researcher, particularly where children or sensitive topics are involved. In the first project, which is discussed later in this chapter, such was the unexpectedly powerful effect of the children's views that the findings were never written up. Instead, the data lay buried in Caroline's filing cabinet. This 'unspoken practice of self censorship' is arguably 'more prevalent than most people admit' (Adler and Adler 1993: 261).

This chapter presents a reflexive account of two complementary approaches to exploring children's views about and experiences of death and bereavement, using a range of data collection methods. The chapter is divided into three sections. The first presents the contexts of each research project and considers the rationale in selecting the different methods of data collection. These pieces of research were conducted independently by us as classroom practitioners and combine to highlight a number of methodological issues relating to researching sensitive topics with young children. Teacher research is interpreted here as a study conducted by an individual teacher using his or her own school or class as the focus of the study (Anderson *et al.* 1994). The second section considers ethical issues and focuses on the relationship between the teacher-researcher and pupils-subjects. It points to a potential overlap between the child as a participant in research and a child in therapy. The advantages of collecting children's views on sensitive topics are juxtaposed with the limitations, for example the fluidity of children's views and the uniqueness of each child's situation, raising issues of generalizability, validity and reliability in gathering children's views. The third section reflects on the potential impact on the researcher of exploring sensitive subjects.

We make no apology for the subjective nature of this account. As Miles and Huberman (1994: 1) suggest: 'Words, especially organised into incidents or stories have a concrete, vivid, meaningful flavour that often proves far more convincing to a reader – another researcher, a policymaker, a practitioner – than pages of summarised numbers'.

Background and context

In England and Wales census figures show that approximately 200,000 children or 3.3 per cent of those under the age of 16 have experienced a significant bereavement and that each year 7000 children aged 1–14 years die (Wagner 1993). In addition, 20 per cent of children under 16 have to deal with separation from a parent, as they experience their parents' marriages break up.

In four local primary schools, totalling 800 children, including the school in which Caroline's project was conducted, a total of three teachers, three mothers and two pupils had died within the previous two years. In the school in which Jane's study was conducted, nineteen pupils had been bereaved of a parent or sibling within ten years, with many more bereaved of grandparents. Presumably, these schools are not untypical.

In both schools the teachers and headteachers had reacted to the shock of a death by taking advice from educational psychologists, making counselling available, sharing memories, and saying a prayer in assembly. However, it became apparent that responding after the event was no easy task for teachers, educational psychologists, parents or children. We suspected that somehow things would have been slightly less traumatic if talking about death had already been part of the teaching and learning experience. People working with bereaved families strongly believe that schools should teach about death, just as they teach about sex, birth and marriage. Leaman (1996) makes the point: 'It is remarkable that this common feature of humanity, the fact that we will all eventually die, is entirely ignored by schools'.

Other sensitive issues such as divorce, racial harassment, AIDS, cancer, suicide or bullying are often neglected in schools until after the event. As practising teachers, we were becoming increasingly aware of the frequency with which children encountered varying levels of loss, ranging from moving house or falling out with a friend, to separation of parents or the death of a grandparent. We supported the idea of developing preventive approaches to help children experiencing loss, rather than waiting for problems to occur. As Hornby (1995) suggests, it is important for teachers and other professionals who work with children who have been bereaved to develop preventive approaches rather than waiting for problems to occur. In order to do this, teachers need to understand the tasks involved in the process of mourning and to be familiar with the principles of grief counselling. Within this context, we also found the traditional boundaries between teaching, research and therapy became blurred.

By coincidence, both research projects were conducted in primary schools within the same LEA. Caroline's study was a small scale teacher research project, carried out with a class of 25 pupils, aged 7 and 8, in the 'normal' classroom situation. It was originally intended to explore within the classroom ways of creating a culture which would uphold children's rights to express feelings and opinions on sensitive topics. Jane's piece of research, five years later, involved a total of 96 children evenly grouped by age, ability and gender between the ages of 4 and 11. The aim was to find out how children across the primary age range perceived death and to make comparisons between the responses of the various age groups. Jane (Head of the Early Years Department at the school) recalls that her initial interest in the topic was prompted by overhearing some children discussing death. She was amazed at the horrific imaginings and misconceptions. She was also faced with distraught parents who sought her assistance in explaining to their young son, a child in her class, the death of his little sister. Furthermore Jane confronted the certainty that one day she would have to support her own daughter on the death of Jane's husband, who was terminally ill. She soon discovered that as a teacher and as a mother, she was not alone in feeling 'thrown in at the deep end', with no previous knowledge or experience upon which to draw.

Methods of data collection

At the embryonic stage of the research we knew that collecting and analysing children's views would be essential. As the main purpose was to explore, confront and portray the children's perceptions of death and bereavement, it was important that as far as possible, the ideas and views were based on the children's thoughts and not dictated by us. However, as Hudson (1998) suggests, in both documentation and literature, claims to listen to the voice of the child may be merely rhetorical. In this case, we gave careful consideration to various techniques as we endeavoured to select methods of data collection that would allow the children's views to be heard. Work reported by Lewis suggests that group interviews are a 'viable and useful technique' (Lewis 1992: 413) and that group situations, in which children have valued the contribution of others, may generate a greater range of responses than do individual interviews. However, some would argue that the group interview would be of 'little use in surfacing intensely personal issues' (Powney and Watts 1987: 106). Hence, Caroline decided against any type of discussion or question and answer scenario but chose to use children's writing as a means of gathering data:

> I planned to gather the data as part of the normal classroom situation without the extraneous paraphernalia of a tape recorder or the structure of a questionnaire. Also, it would have been difficult to find time to talk to the children individually in any depth. Writing 'en masse' avoided the problem of children influencing each other's responses, such as may be the case in group or individual interviews over a period of time . . . asking them to write seemed a logical and natural way forward as writing is one of the main features of children's primary school experience.
>
> (Research diary)

In contrast, Jane chose to employ a variation of the group interview, presented in the form of a tape recorded storytelling and discussion session. It involved tape recording children's responses and noting reactions during the telling of a story about the death of a dog (*I'll Always Love You* by Hans Wilhelm) and the follow up discussion. The group sessions ran for no longer than 30 minutes, on the same day each week and at the same time. The children sat on chairs in a semicircle where they could see the pictures in the book, shown as it was read; they could also make eye contact with each other and with the adult if they wished. The adult would pause if children made comments during the course of the story. If necessary, at the end of the story she would encourage discussion by asking the children how they thought the little boy might have felt when his dog died. This was the only key question planned. Otherwise her sole contribution was to ask 'Does anyone want to say anything?' Immediately following the session Jane made brief notes to assist, if needed, the transcription of the tapes.

The decision to conduct the study in this way was partly due to the large number of children involved. However, it was mainly based on the notion that group situations offer a more supportive, less threatening environment than a one-to-one interview and were therefore appropriate when researching such a sensitive topic. Group interviews may also increase the reliability of the data in revealing consensus views (Lewis 1992). Jane commented that the selected method caused minimal disruption within the school environment: 'A familiar aspect of the classroom curriculum . . . The setting and situation were kept as normal as possible with the sessions taking place in a regularly used "quiet room" with which the children were familiar' (Tannock 1997: 27).

In addition to the recording and analysis of the children's responses in the storytelling sessions, Jane initiated a separate piece of action research in order to observe and study the effects of intervention on the bereaved children in the school. This research was based on six planned group activity sessions, attended by six children and their parents. Sessions included writing, drawing, puppet making and role play and were attended by the school nurse. The educational psychologist attended as a non-participant observer, making notes throughout the sessions. Unlike the storytelling project this research took place outside the normal classroom situation. In these circumstances Jane played a dual role: on the one hand, she was setting up a specific research group situation, on the other she was providing an outlet for children and parents to explore and express their feelings and reactions to bereavement in a non-threatening environment. It appeared that where respondents were revealing sensitive, essentially private emotions or information, the dividing lines between research and therapy became indistinct. Ostensibly, the information was being revealed freely by the children. However, in researching sensitive topics, the personal nature of the children's comments may give rise to certain ethical decisions which will need to be made before, during and after the research process.

Ethical issues: access, consent and confidentiality

Any research project is likely to raise ethical issues including access and confidentiality. As the projects were largely within the normal classroom framework, in a familiar school, access to the children was unproblematic. Nevertheless, in spite of the apparent 'normality' of the situation we knew it was essential to gain informed consent from children and parents. Informed consent is defined by Diener and Crandall (1978) as the procedure that allows individuals to make an informed choice as to whether they wish to participate in an investigation. The underlying assumptions are that participants take part, are given full information about the research and freely volunteer to participate. Cohen and Manion (1994) suggest that researchers should gain permission from first the adults responsible for the children and second the children themselves. The researcher could have to apply to a number of people to gain access to children in schools, including the LEA, headteacher, governors and the class teacher. Having gained this access the need to ask the children could be overlooked. However, informed consent is an important principle to abide by when working with children and particularly when researching sensitive or normally private topics. Some commentators suggest that children, even as young as pre-school, should be given an explanation appropriate to their level of understanding: 'Our feeling is that children should be told as much as possible, even if some of them cannot understand the full explanation. Their age should not diminish their rights' (Fine and Sandstrom 1988, cited in Cohen and Manion 1994: 353).

In both studies the children had the choice to opt out, Caroline noting that, 'as far as the children were concerned, the choice of opting out at any stage was open to them. An alternative activity was on offer for them to choose'. With the consent of the headteacher, Caroline had discussed the study with parents on parents' evening. Parents were supportive because this was not the first study of this nature the researcher had conducted in the school. Apart from one member of staff who stated that she did not think it was 'right to talk about these things', colleagues were keen to discuss the implications relating to their own teaching. Jane explained her proposed study and received approval from the parents, children, the headteacher and her staff, the governors and the director of education.

Once consent has been obtained, confidentiality may still be a poignant issue. R. Lee (1993) in discussing research into sensitive topics comments that although participants in all research studies should expect their confidentiality and privacy to be maintained, this is particularly important where the information given is of a sensitive or intimate nature.

The fluidity of children's views and the influence of time and place need to be considered at the planning stage. Children's responses on a Friday afternoon after playtime are likely to be different from their responses on a Monday morning after assembly. As Ball (1993: 38) concludes, time is a neglected dimension of ethnographic research. We planned the timing carefully. As stated previously, Jane ensured that each group session took place on the same day at the same time each week and lasted 30 minutes. This increased the security of the children and reduced the likelihood of responses being influenced by varying time and place.

Caroline planned to build the research into the children's routine by having a series of six writing lessons, to set the convention and routine of the planned session on death, which was to occur in the fifth week. Each session was timetabled to be on Friday between assembly and morning breaktime, as this was usually uninterrupted. The breaktime provided a natural cutoff point as well as a release for the children after a concentrated session of writing.

Relationships between the teacher-researcher and pupils

Another important consideration in planning a research project is the influence of the relationship between the teacher-researcher and the pupils. When sensitive topics are involved, this relationship becomes a key feature in the decision making process, not only regarding issues of access, confidentiality, timing and consent, but also in achieving reliability and validity. Some believe the quality and validity of interview responses of children are likely to be higher when the data are gathered as part of a longer term involvement (Walford 1991: 96). Conversely, an established adult–child relationship may invite accusations of bias in constructing, analysing and interpreting the data which could, in turn, influence the findings or conclusions. Although bias can enter the conduct of experiments and the designing of questionnaires for surveys (Yin 1994), it could be suggested that in teacher research, bias is even more likely unless extreme care is taken. Lewis (1992: 417) warns that 'the teacher-researcher needs to consider carefully whether or not the children's inter-relationships as well as his or her relationship with the children will distort the responses and so render data invalid'.

Ultimately, the issues of reliability and validity may depend largely on the skills of the researcher. Miles and Huberman (1994: 38) ask: 'How valid and reliable is the person likely to be as an information gathering instrument?' It is important to consider how the children see the adult, how researchers see themselves and how much or how little the adult will be saying. Piaget (1929: 8) commented: 'It is so hard not to talk too much when questioning a child, especially for a pedagogue'. Caroline experienced a similar predicament: 'The temptation to walk round and drop hints was incredible but I sat on the teacher's chair and didn't move' (research diary).

Elliot (1991) claims that teacher-researchers tend to use quantitative methods in order to avoid 'personalized' situations 'in which colleagues and pupils find it difficult to divorce an individual's position and role as researcher from his or her other positions and roles within the school' (Elliot 1991: 62). One solution could be to involve another adult in the data collection. However, it has been argued that to a young child, any adult in school could be assigned the same status as a teacher or seen as 'a teacher in disguise' (Bell *et al.* 1981, cited in Powney and Watts 1987: 48). A note from Caroline's diary illustrates the quandary of the dual role:

On the one hand, I considered myself a teacher, on the other, a researcher. Words on one child's Christmas card indicated similar confusion regarding my status, 'To Mrs Jones, sometimes teacher, sometimes helper'.

Jane did involve another adult in the research, asking a parent to conduct the story sessions. The reason for this was not concerned with the pupil–teacher relationship, but represented an attempt to reduce possible bias. She noted: 'I did not want the children's reactions to be affected by any prior knowledge of my interest in the topic' (Tannock 1997: 27). Undoubtedly, children behave and respond differently to different people and the relationship of a researcher with a group of children may not be easily replicated by another researcher. However, circumstances in education are rarely replicable and as Griffiths (1985) states:

> Just as two different artists will approach the same scene with the same materials yet produce different pictures, so the same may be said about two researchers approaching the same scene with the same methodological tools. Neither can be judged in terms of right or wrong even though the images which they identify may well be different.
>
> (Griffiths 1985: 211–12)

We were conscious of the main pitfalls of the research. The unique nature of bereavement made a pilot study difficult and also each child's experience could be regarded as atypical. Indeed, it has been claimed that 'It is not possible to generalise about children's responses to bereavement because every child and every death is different' (Wynnejones 1985: 88). Some may view critically the perceived lack of precision, lack of objectivity and rigour in the studies or raise doubts about the extent to which qualitative research deriving from children's views can be generalized. However, a parallel can be drawn with case study researchers, who acknowledge that their findings may relate to one set of experiences and may not be generalizable to other situations. Walker (1989) suggests that the problem for case study workers is not whether it is worth studying one particular event but whether they can do so in a way that captures their audience. The value of case studies rests on their 'usefulness as models for others in exploring their own unique situations' (Elliot 1990: 59). Readers discover what is there that can be applied to their own situation and what cannot. These studies were close to the situation, whereas experimental design or survey research is not. Culture, meanings and processes were emphasized rather than variables, outcomes and products. However, the closeness to the situation can itself have an impact on the research.

Research as therapy

Both studies highlighted contrasts and similarities between research and therapy. Initially, in therapy the location and the adult may be unfamiliar.

The 'expert' has to spend time and use a variety of strategies to build up trust and the agenda is to meet the needs of the child. In these teacher-researcher projects, children were working with trusted adults in a safe, familiar environment and were given the freedom to opt in or out of the activity, to speak, write or draw about their feelings without feeling threatened or judged. While the agenda was set primarily to meet the needs of the research, the pupils had taken control and grasped the opportunity to fulfil their own needs. The sessions provided a safe outlet for the children's feelings and thoughts. As in therapy sessions, research sessions with children may reveal unexpectedly powerful, hidden or complex anxieties, theories and thoughts. In Caroline's study, for example, one 7-year-old girl wrote: 'Sometimes I get worried when I go to bed. I think I am going to die. I think someone is going to put a knife in me'. Another child, also aged 7, revealed her feelings when her teacher had died two years earlier: 'I felt like all the happiness had drained out of my body'.

During the six bereavement involvement sessions, Jane, working with the school nurse and educational psychologist, noted apparent psychological and personal benefits. These included one 7-year-old, Leanne, who had changed from not being able to talk about her mother to being able to talk in detail; Michael, aged 6, who played hospital role play and revealed that he would not talk about his mother because it made him cry; Claire, aged 4, who became able to explore her feelings and talk openly in a play situation about her brother's death; Jason, aged 8, who exhibited anger in his imaginative play. In the taped group discussion, it was noted that one child's voice apparently 'broke with emotion'. These findings indicate a clear need for further research into the potential advantages and disadvantages of methods which combine research and therapy in seeking children's views.

Impact on the researcher of researching bereavement

Researchers may avoid educational research that involves topics of a sensitive nature for fear of upsetting children. Sheldon (1994: 43) contends that it is a basic instinct to protect children from distress: 'Protecting vulnerable children is a natural, biologically-based impulse felt by most adults'. Even during a fairly brief interview, especially in the case of an unresolved situation or a sensitive issue, it can be difficult for interviewers not to feel responsible for and often upset by interviewees' problems. Interviews concerning sensitive topics can produce distress in the respondent and stress in the interviewer (R. Lee 1993). Researchers need to be meticulously prepared to deal with their own emotions by giving careful thought to the personal impact of sensitive data.

As noted earlier, children may benefit from the opportunity offered through research to express themselves, perhaps for the first time. Interviewing on sensitive topics, particularly with children, can pose problems for the researcher who is torn between trying to remain 'objective' without appearing aloof or insensitive. The interviewer may be one of the few informed people who has sat down and listened and apparently understood the difficulties. The interviewer then has to leave the situation, presumably, without offering advice or hope (Powney and Watts 1987).

> That we learn through human relationships forces us into a kind of emotional/rational schizophrenia . . . It becomes necessary to live in both worlds, motivated and affected by genuinely subjective feelings, that grow up in all human contact, yet able to draw back sufficiently to treat one's subject in sociological terms.
>
> (Harper 1992: 151)

At the stage of confronting the children's views, Caroline found she was unable to remain detached, unable to suffer 'the agony of betrayal' (John Lofland, cited in Adler and Adler 1993: 255). Her research diary illustrates the dilemma:

> As I began to read what they had written I realised the project was doomed. Until that point I had felt 'objective', only now did I acknowledge that I could not treat their words as 'data'. There was no way I would make the results of their efforts open to public scrutiny. I had not considered the potential emotional impact of using children as 'subjects' . . . Suddenly, I cared too much.

The second study also had a significant impact on Jane. She coped with her husband's death while continuing to support bereaved families in school. The findings increased her determination to be proactive in the field, by talking to teacher colleagues and becoming a trained counsellor.

Conclusion

These reflective accounts allow a number of conclusions to be drawn relating to researching sensitive topics with children. First, researching sensitive issues with children is a complex task which requires particular knowledge and skills on the part of a researcher. This account demonstrates that researching sensitive topics can make substantial demands on the researcher and requires 'skill, tenacity and imagination' (R. Lee 1993: 210). A commitment is needed to raise the profile of researching sensitive issues with children in order to develop spontaneous, relevant and appropriate opportunities to include sensitive issues in the curriculum. High priority should be given to developing comprehensive training and guidelines for teachers and researchers, building on children's natural experiences. If these feelings and experiences were harboured in these two schools alone, how many more children are waiting for the opportunity to express their worries and articulate their perspectives on sensitive topics? More discussion and research is needed on the similarities and differences between therapy and research with children.

Second, in spite of accusations of lack of methodological rigour attracted by this type of research, and the restricted nature of the sample and environment, this chapter illustrates some suitable methods for practitioner-researchers to explore a situation from a child's perspective. It demonstrates and respects that, in spite of or perhaps even because of their range of individual differences, children are capable of making valid contributions to research. Although in the late 1970s pupils' perspectives were among the most under-researched in education (Barton and Meighan 1979), there is a gradual shift towards giving children opportunities to be consulted and involved in research projects. Using 'naturalistic' methods with children is an area which needs further research. Perhaps the time has come to jettison questionnaires and structured interviews and explore alternative ways of researching children's perspectives through writing, discussion, story, music, model making, art, drama or puppets. As King (1987) asserts, we would be foolish if, with appropriate care, we did not use the children's discussion, reading and writing skills for research purposes.

Third, the impact of the research on the researcher should be further explored. According to May (1993), values and the researcher's experiences should not be 'bracketed away' but form part of the 'foundation of good social research' (May 1993: 48). As Jane reflected on the research for this chapter, she acknowledged a 'chicken and egg' situation. She discovered she was not alone in confronting death in the classroom and asked herself, 'Did the personal impact come as a result of carrying out my research or rather, was the research borne out of some strongly felt personal experience?' Personal motivation for research may be omitted in the final account. In addition, we rarely see reflective reference relating to the short or long term consequences of the research on the researcher's personal or professional life.

Fourth, we met by chance through a mutual colleague, yet other researchers could plan to use complementary or even contrasting methods in order to research the same topics, gradually building on each other's work. Researching sensitive topics with children has the potential to become a uniquely collaborative enterprise between 'academic' researchers, educational psychologists, teachers, parents and children. Even small scale, in-depth studies of classrooms can help to modify, challenge and alter the assumptions from which we work when we interact with children and help us build an understanding of the concerns of children (Stephen Rowland, cited in Webb 1990: 260). This chapter ends with a challenge for the future:

Are children to be consumed in the world of work, a technological environment and attainment targets? Can we not ask ourselves if there is more to schools than this? Aren't children people too? Can they not make a contribution to how they see their worlds and indeed their schools?

(Caul 1990: 202)

(8) The educational self-perceptions of children with Down Syndrome

AMANDA BEGLEY

In the past, children with Down Syndrome were unlikely to be asked for their views, even on issues that directly involved them, like school placement. Unfortunately, this failure to ask people with learning difficulties for their opinions continues to be common practice. However, since the 1980s and early 1990s trends in the integration of children with Down Syndrome have made it necessary to research the impact of school placement on these young people. It is not just teachers who are involved in collecting the views of children with Down Syndrome. For example, educational psychologists may need the views of children with Down Syndrome on their schooling, social workers may require children's views about their care context, doctors may need children to talk about their illnesses, and children may be required to act as witnesses in court cases. Therefore, knowing how to elicit the views of children with Down Syndrome should have implications for numerous professionals. Furthermore, since children with Down Syndrome experience a number of difficulties, the information provided in this chapter should help those working with children with limited language skills and/or attentional difficulties.

One area worthy of investigation when assessing children's views is the self-concept. The nature of a child's self-concept is likely to have a pervasive and long term effect on, for example, academic achievements, social interaction, personal satisfaction and self-worth.

Unfortunately, gaining an understanding of the self-concept of children with Down Syndrome is problematic. The specific difficulties that children with Down Syndrome encounter limit the applicability of many instruments used to measure the self-concept. There are two potential solutions to the problem of how to investigate the self-concept of children with Down Syndrome. One solution is to glean the information from the adults who are close to children with Down Syndrome, for example, parents and teachers. A major shortcoming with this option is that adults can provide information on how they presume a child should feel based only on their opinions about the child's abilities, strengths, weaknesses, personality, and so on.

However, if the research aim is to understand how children feel about themselves, the researcher should gather views directly from children. Furthermore, it is debatable whether the validity of a child's views should be established by comparing his/her views to adults' judgements about the child's 'real' self-concept. After all, it is how children feel about themselves that will directly affect their behaviour and happiness, not how others presume they should feel. It is useful to interview adults, as adults can provide very important factual and subjective information, that children may not be able to provide. However, one person's views must not be regarded as superior to those of another. Children and adults are entitled to have their opinions respected, regardless of how divergent these opinions may turn out to be.

Research questions addressed

The aim of the research was to assess the self-perceptions of pupils with Down Syndrome in three school related domains (academic competence, physical competence and social acceptance) and to see if any differences existed across sex, age group (8–10 years, 11–13 years and 14–16 years) and school placement (special schools for moderate learning difficulties and for severe learning difficulties and mainstream schools). With this research aim it was essential to find a sound means to elicit views from the children themselves.

Methods of data collection

Methodological and ethical issues

The selection of an appropriate measure for assessing the self-concept of pupils with Down Syndrome was determined by a number of fundamental methodological issues which are discussed in more detail elsewhere (Begley and Lewis 1998). The methodological issues considered were fourfold and surrounded the implications of doing research: with a relatively powerless group, with children, with children with a learning difficulty and with children with Down syndrome.

First, the method had to include strategies to reduce the unequal power distribution between the researcher and children with Down Syndrome. It was impossible to eliminate myself as the unequal power between the researcher and children with Down Syndrome because I am an adult, the research took place in school, the respondents had learning difficulties, and so on. All these factors are likely to reduce children's ability to exert their rights. In order to allow children more power over the research process, a number of strategies were employed; for example, the children decided whether they were willing to participate, they were allowed to withdraw their participation at any time, they were allowed to complete the tasks at their own pace, they were not stopped from talking during the task or carrying out other non-task-related activities. Furthermore, I explained that I was not a teacher, that the task was not a test, and there were no right and wrong answers.

The issues surrounding doing research with children, with children with learning difficulties and children with Down Syndrome affected the selection of the research techniques. There is an overlap in the methodological issues associated with doing research with children and children with learning disabilities. Both research groups have been found to demonstrate a number of response tendencies that may affect the validity of their responses, for example, acquiescence, socially desirable responding, giving 'don't know' responses or interpreting questions literally (Wylie 1974; Burns 1982, Lewis 1992). Due to their age and/or difficulties, both research groups may also experience difficulties with language comprehension and production and have difficulty sustaining attention. All of these features were taken into account when selecting an appropriate method. (See also Detheridge, Chapter 9, and Costley, Chapter 13, for discussion of research involving children with learning difficulties.)

The methodological issues associated with children with Down Syndrome relate to the specific difficulties encountered by these children. The four areas of specific difficulties considered were developmental delay which limited the selection to methods suitable for young children, language production and comprehension difficulties which limited the selection to methods requiring minimal language production and comprehension skills, difficulty with auditory/vocal processing which limited the selection to methods involving visual/manual processing, and the difficulty with sustaining and shifting attention which limited the selection to methods to likely to sustain attention. However, it is important to note that children with Down Syndrome are a heterogeneous group with much variation in individual attainment (Stratford and Gunn 1996). Therefore, not all children with Down Syndrome will encounter all the difficulties noted or will experience the same degrees of difficulty. The aim was to select a method that would allow as many children with Down Syndrome to participate regardless of the difficulties they encountered.

Finally, children with Down Syndrome are not likely to be familiar with people genuinely asking for their views. This problem can be reduced by changing the research process to help put children at ease, for example, conversing with children about activities familiar to them prior to administering the research task. The strangeness of the situation can also be reduced by choosing a method which is less threatening, more familiar and more fun. The chosen method in this research included a picture book and a postbox game.

Measures

On the basis of the above information, two techniques were chosen to assess the self-perceptions of children with Down Syndrome: the Pictorial Scale of Perceived Competence and Acceptance (Harter and Pike 1984) and a School Situations Grid. These were selected because they are designed for use with young children, they require minimal language comprehension as the stimuli is pictorial, and they require minimal language production skills because the response is manual. Furthermore, both techniques are likely to sustain attention because they have pictures for the children to look at and a manual response (pointing for the scale and posting pictures for the grid) to involve the children physically.

The Pictorial Scale of Perceived Competence and Acceptance (Harter and Pike 1984) has been used successfully by children with learning difficulties between the ages of 6.6 and 7.6 years (Priel and Leshem 1990) and children with Down Syndrome between the ages of 13 and 17 years (Cuskelly and de Jong 1996). The scale is available in a preschool/kindergarten (4- and 5-year-olds) version and a first grade/second grade (6- and 7-year-olds) version. The latter of these was chosen for use in this research because it contains items likely to be relevant to school aged pupils with Down Syndrome, for example, writing, reading, ball games, climbing, sitting with friends and being asked to play (for examples of the scale, see Appendix 1). This twenty-four item scale contains six questions on four domains (academic competence, physical competence, social acceptance and maternal acceptance). The maternal acceptance subscale was not used in this research as the aim was to assess self-perceptions in relation to school. The standard procedure requires the respondent to decide which of two types of children presented in pictorial format is most like him/her. One picture denotes a child with a high level of competence or acceptance and the other picture denotes a child with a low level of competence or acceptance. The respondent is then asked to indicate whether the chosen child is 'really like' or 'sort of like' him or her.

To reduce the language comprehension requirements further, some of the wording of the scale was modified or omitted during piloting. Changes were made to words thought likely to be unfamiliar to British children (e.g. pretty many) and/or unnecessary (e.g. very). So, for example, the original wording used in the Harter and Pike (1984) scale was: 'This girl isn't very good at bouncing the ball, and this girl is pretty good at bouncing the ball'. This was changed to 'This girl isn't good at bouncing the ball, and this girl is good at bouncing the ball'. The wording was also altered to ensure that consistent phrases were used throughout the scale and between the scale and the grid. Therefore, the standard four-point response format was replaced with a three-point response format using the phrases 'all of the time', 'some of the time' and 'none of the time'. So, for example, in the Harter and Pike (1984) scale, the original question put to children who selected the successful child was: 'Are you pretty good? Or are you really good at bouncing the ball?' This was changed to 'Are you good at bouncing the ball all of the time? Or some of the time?' The original question put to children who selected the unsuccessful child was: 'Are you not too good at bouncing the ball? Or sort of good?' This was changed to 'Are you good at bouncing the ball none of the time? Or some of the time?'

The School Situations Grid was derived from the Personal Construct Psychology approach (Kelly 1955) and adapted from a grid devised by Edwards (1988). The grid consists of nine school situations chosen to mirror those found in the scale and to represent experiences relevant to school aged pupils (see Appendix 2). There are three situations to represent each of the three self-domains (academic competence, physical competence and social acceptance). The instructions and wording used in the grid were chosen to be consistent with the scale.

The constructs were chosen from a list generated during the pilot study in which the repertory grid technique was used with a small group of pupils with Down Syndrome. Five constructs were chosen from the total pool on the basis of frequency and applicability to the school situations. The constructs were *good at*, *likes* doing, *happy* doing, finds *hard* and *naughty* when doing. Using constructs generated from children with Down Syndrome was felt to be more valid than using constructs that I had generated.

Three postboxes affixed with clock faces with graduated shading provided the three-point response format of 'all of the time', 'some of the time' and 'none of the time'. The response format was selected on the basis of the pilot study as the preferred and most easy to comprehend format. Published line drawings of male and female children involved in each of the nine situations were photocopied (with permission). These were used to make the task less abstract.

First, pupils were shown a picture of a situation (e.g. a child reading). They were asked whether they were good at the activity 'all of the time' (while the researcher points at the 'all of the time' box), 'some of the time' (pointing at the relevant box) or 'none of the time' (pointing at the relevant box). The same procedure was repeated for the same situation (e.g.

reading) with the remaining four constructs. The five constructs were then applied to each of the remaining eight situations. To control for order effects the orders of the three domains, five constructs and three responses were changed randomly.

The scale was completed once I felt that children were comfortable with me and I was familiar to them. The grid was administered about a week later, on the final visit. The consistency between the scale and the grid measures was expected to provide a measure of the reliability and consistency in the children's responses.

Methodological issues arising in relation to collecting children's views

Prior to research

The heterogeneity of children with Down Syndrome
It was anticipated that the sample would be heterogeneous in terms of children's capabilities, comprehension levels, language production skills and so on. This would be compounded by the large age range (8 to 16 years) and by the school placement types covered (special schools for pupils with severe learning difficulties or moderate learning difficulties and mainstream schools). This anticipated heterogeneity posed two potential problems. First, with such a wide ability spread it was difficult to select a method that would be suitable for all the children. This problem was dealt with by selecting a method that would allow the youngest and least able child to participate. Second, the heterogeneity posed a potential problem with having a standardized research approach. It was therefore decided to adopt a flexible research approach which included, for example, interviewing children where they and their teachers felt the children would be most comfortable (i.e. in or away from the classroom), repeating questions and/ or rephrasing wording if children did not appear to understand the wording used in the scale or grid.

Gaining access and informed consent
Before research can be carried out with children, the researcher must gain parental consent. School and teacher approval also had to be gained because this research was carried out in schools. Each child's consent was gained in order to give the children more power over the research process.

Initially the headteachers of a number of special schools throughout the English Midlands were contacted via telephone. Headteachers who showed an interest in the research were sent detailed information about the study along with some letters of parental consent to distribute among relevant parents. The children's consent to participate was gained on each school visit. Where possible children were always asked for consent privately and away from their class teacher, in the hope that this would give them more freedom to refuse if they did not wish to participate. Very few parents and no schools refused to allow me to work with their child or children. Unfortunately, the children of parents who did refuse could not be given the option to participate.

Accessing the mainstream sample was more difficult. Four sources of information were used. The Down's Syndrome Association kindly distributed a letter explaining the research among its members with a contact number to call if parents were willing for their child to participate. The special needs advisors in relevant local authorities were contacted and distributed letters among mainstream schools with children with Down Syndrome. Some headteachers of special schools I visited were able to inform me of children with Down Syndrome whom they knew to be integrated in mainstream schools. Finally, some of the schools already identified had other pupils with Down Syndrome with whom I was able to gain consent to work.

The method of gaining access to the sample was not uniform across special and mainstream schools, which added further differences between the two school types. The parents who contacted me after receiving the letter from the Down's Syndrome Association may have, for example, different views on the importance of schooling, of child rearing and so on, when compared to parents contacted via letters from their child's school. The different strategies employed to gain a mainstream sample were necessary in order to find as many children with Down Syndrome as possible in this type of school. However, the additional differences between the pupils in each school placement must be considered when analysing the results.

Gaining informed consent from persons with learning difficulties is problematic (e.g. Swain *et al.* 1998). The research was explained to children with Down Syndrome in simplified terms explaining that I wanted to write a book on children's views of themselves in school. However, it is unlikely that the children knew exactly to what they were consenting. Did they, for example, understand the whole research process, including the publications and presentations that have arisen from the research? Therefore, it is important to consider the information that children have a right to know and to consider their language limitations when deciding how best to communicate this information.

During the data collection

Working only with children with Down Syndrome
There were two problems related to how to explain, first, why only the children with Down Syndrome in each class were singled out for the research, and second, why none of the other children in the class were asked to participate. In general the teachers dealt with the problem by implying that

the children with Down Syndrome had been chosen because they were special. Teachers tended to say to the children with Down Syndrome that they had been chosen because they were, for example, so hard working, the most cooperative in the class, the most likely to be helpful, and so on.

This strategy is not ideal. By identifying children as helpful or cooperative, the teacher may have prompted the children into giving their consent to participate in the research. Children may wish to fulfil their teacher's expectations or may feel anxious about not cooperating after being specifically chosen. Therefore, children's right to exercise power freely over their participation may have been inadvertently affected. Furthermore, the teacher's explanation may have biased children's self-perceptions to correspond with the teacher's labelling of them as, for example, hardworking, cooperative or helpful.

Although this strategy was not honest or ideal, it did avoid the problem of identifying the children as different from their classmates because they have Down Syndrome. A number of parents, prior to giving their consent, expressed concern over their child being asked about 'having Down Syndrome'. The parents explained that their child did not understand what Down Syndrome was and they did not want their child being made aware of having Down Syndrome. Therefore, it was decided on the basis of teacher and parental wishes not to disclose to the children the real reason they had been selected, and instead to allow the teachers to deal with the problem as they saw fit.

One teacher adopted an ingenious strategy of asking pupils in the class to raise their hand if they wanted to have a break from the lesson to help me with my work. The teacher then looked around at the mass of raised hands and eventually chose the two children with Down Syndrome in the class. However, this requires the children in a class to be enthusiastic and willing to work with strangers.

Familiarization with the pupils

Due to the size of the sample (96 pupils) and time constraints, it was not possible to spend much time with each pupil prior to the interviews. Ideally, I would have met every pupil for a length of time at least once prior to administering the Pictorial Scale. The children would probably have felt more comfortable and at ease working with someone with whom they were familiar.

To help children feel more at ease, a brief conversation was carried out prior to beginning the scale and grid. The individual children were asked general questions about the lesson they had just attended, whether they liked the lesson, what lessons they liked best, and so on. After this, I explained that I was not a teacher, that I was visiting lots of children in different schools because I wanted to find out what children think about themselves and school. The children were then asked if they would mind helping me with my work. This initial conversation phase appeared to put the children at ease, and the length of the phase was determined by how relaxed each child appeared to be. Children were deemed to be relaxed when, for example, they were able to maintain eye contact, the level of their speech increased, their posture relaxed and they fidgeted less.

Heterogeneity of the sample

The children were heterogeneous in numerous ways, including their language comprehension and production skill, their attention span, their motivation levels, cooperation levels and their age. The heterogeneity was dealt with by adopting a flexible research approach. Unfortunately, this flexibility resulted in a lack of consistency in the data collection across the sample. The three major inconsistencies were the place where children were interviewed, whether they were interviewed in private or not, and whether the wording of the scale was changed.

The location of the interview was determined by where teachers thought that each child would feel most comfortable working. Interviewing all children either in or away from the classroom would have increased the robustness of any comparisons made across the sample. However, both locations have advantages and disadvantages attached to them. Some children may be more comfortable working with strangers in the familiar surroundings of their classroom with their teacher nearby, while other children may find it difficult to sustain their attention when in a busy classroom. Therefore, it was decided to choose the most suitable option for each child because children are more likely to concentrate on completing a task in a situation in which they feel at ease. When possible, children were asked if they agreed with the teacher's decision. Some schools gave me a room and the children were brought to me. Under these circumstances I never met the child's class teacher. Since the headteachers and teachers had allowed me to come into their schools, their preferred procedures were followed. Within the constraints of each school's procedures, I tried to give the pupils freedom to exert their own choices over the research process.

If a child had severe language production and comprehension difficulties, an assistant teacher was often present during the interviewing. The decision to have an assistant teacher was based on either the teacher's recommendation and/or because the child communicated using only sign language (of which I know very little). This meant that some children were not interviewed or asked for their consent in private. The presence of a teacher is likely to influence children's responses by making the situation more formal, increasing the unequal power distribution between the researcher and the children with Down Syndrome, reducing the children's freedom to exert their choice over participation and possibly biasing children's responses to conform to how they felt the teacher perceived them.

Working with a familiar adult may have also reduced the potential problem of socially desirable responding. Children may be more inclined to present themselves as unrealistically competent and accepted, when talking to a stranger who had no knowledge of their true competence and acceptance. However, the assistant teachers who had been present often informed me after the interviews, that they had disagreed with the child's perceptions of his or her competence and/or acceptance. Therefore, the presence of a familiar assistant teacher did not appear to have altered children's responses in a way that made them consistent with the views of the familiar teacher. This finding was important because the aim was to collect children's perceptions. This meant that any adults present during the data collection should not affect the children's responses. Since the children's responses did not appear to have been affected by the presence of a familiar adult, it is hoped that their responses were not unduly affected by being interviewed by an unfamiliar adult.

If a child had limited language comprehension skills, the instructions for the scale and grid were often repeated and the standard wording was altered to try to aid comprehension. This meant that the administration procedure and wording used in the scale and grid were not consistent across the sample.

The majority of the sample were able to complete the scale and grid using the standard research procedure. However, the flexibility of the research approach and the heterogeneity of the sample resulted in a lack of standardization in the method used. This lack of consistency is a disadvantage because it reduces the robustness of comparisons made across the sample. However, the choice had to be made between a flexible approach that enabled as many pupils as possible to participate, or a rigid approach that allowed more robust comparisons to be made. The former option was chosen because the results would not have been representative of children with Down Syndrome if only the most able children had participated. Furthermore, deviations from the method appeared quite random. No one sex, age group or school placement group were consistently having to be interviewed either in or away from the classroom, to be interviewed with an assistant teacher present, to have the instruction repeated or the wording changed. This randomness should help maintain the validity of any comparisons.

In relation to the age range covered, some of the items in the scale were not relevant to particular children because of their age and/or specific difficulties. The older children, for example, were asked how good they were at swinging. Children who were unable to read and write were asked, for example, how good they were at spelling. This is a problem with using a scale standardized on children without learning difficulties. However, all the children were asked all the questions on the scale. The responses were not discarded because the children's responses to seemingly irrelevant questions were found to be consistent with the rest of their responses. However, future researchers may wish to revise the scale by discarding items irrelevant to the specific age of their sample and adding more relevant items.

Incomplete or unreliable scales

In spite of the careful choice of techniques and the flexible approach, some children were unable to complete the scale (9 out of 96 pupils) and one-third of the children were unable to complete the grid (32 out of 96). In addition, two children refused to participate. Included in the non-completers were children whose response patterns suggested that they did not comprehend the scale and/or the grid, for example, children who constantly pointed to the left (or right) hand picture of the scale throughout, or children who posted all the pictures from the grid into the same response postbox.

The children who were unable to comprehend the scale even after repetition and word changes were the least able in terms of their language comprehension and production, and in their ability to sustain attention. Unfortunately the research method failed to allow these children to share their views. To gain an understanding of the self-perceptions of these children, a different and more individualized approach would need to be developed. These children may benefit from the researcher having more time to become familiar with each child or for an adult close to the child to gather the information. Someone more familiar with the child is likely to know the child's language comprehension and production difficulties, the child's personality, preferences and so on.

The children who did not complete the scale were never made to feel wrong for not wishing to participate or made to feel a failure for not comprehending the task. The two pupils who refused to participate were told that it was all right for them not to want to take part and they were thanked for their time. When a child was unable to complete the scale, I looked through the picture book with him or her and asked simple questions while pointing to the activities depicted, for example, do you like swinging? When a child was unable to complete the grid I gave the child the picture cards individually and asked simple questions about the activities depicted and then allowed the child to post the pictures in the boxes. At the end of the interview the children were always thanked for their help.

Interpretation of results

Socially desirable responding

As mentioned above, when asking children about their views, especially concerning how competent or accepted they are, there is a risk of them presenting themselves in a socially desirable and positive way. The validity of the results will be affected if children's responses reflect how they want to appear to others, rather than how they really perceive themselves. The scale and grid both adopted a graded response format of four and three points respectively, to control for socially desirable responding. Furthermore, very few children replied in a maximally positive way to all the items on the scale and/or grid. This lack of maximally positive responses suggests that the majority of pupils were not motivated to present themselves in an unrealistically positive manner, academically, physically or socially.

Validity of responses

In order to assess the validity of children's responses, researchers have tended to compare children's views to, say, parental and teacher ratings, academic grades and so on. However, because young children have been found to view themselves in an unrealistically positive manner, the ratings of parents and teachers are unlikely to provide suitable validity measures (Harter and Pike 1984; Harter 1990). Furthermore, the aim of this research was to establish how children with Down Syndrome perceive themselves. The aim was not to establish how precise their self-perceptions were in comparison to some 'objective' standard. It is children's conception of themselves that will affect their self-concept, regardless of how accurate their self-perceptions are.

Female children with Down Syndrome and older children with Down Syndrome (14–16 years) were found to have higher and, therefore, more positive self-perceptions. However, when interpreting the validity of these findings it is important to consider whether my sex (female) and age (closer to the 14–16 year age group) influenced the results. As the female and older pupils were more similar to myself, they differed from the sample for reasons other then their sex and age. To assess the effects of similarity with the researcher further research with researchers of a different age and sex is necessary.

The restrictions that the instruments placed on the children may also have affected the validity of the responses. There are a number of problems associated with forced choice instruments. The forced choice format on the scale did not allow me to ascertain whether a picture was chosen because a child preferred it to the alternative or because it was the only remaining picture to choose after the alternative had been rejected. Forced choice self-response instruments also constrict children's responses. The participation of children with Down Syndrome in the research process was limited by forcing them to respond to a set of predetermined categories. Using such instruments makes it especially important to try to reduce the power imbalance by giving children more power over the research process. For example, ensuring that they are able to give informed consent, allowing children to complete the instruments at their own pace, allowing children to refuse to participate at any time during the research, and so on. Furthermore, by using these forced choice instruments, it was not possible to establish whether the predetermined categories were salient in the lives of children with Down Syndrome. This has major implications for the children's self-concept because this is unlikely to be greatly affected by their self-perceptions in a domain they consider unimportant. However, because of the language limitations of children with Down Syndrome and because the aim was to ascertain self-perceptions within specific school related areas these instruments were deemed appropriate. However, it is important to remember Harter and Pike's (1981; 1984) cautions that the scale (and the grid) should 'not be viewed as an index of self-concept or self-esteem *per se*'.

Reliability of responses

To assess the reliability of self-perceptions of children with Down Syndrome, two techniques were employed. First, the internal consistency of the scale was assessed using Cronbach's Alpha. The internal reliabilities were found to be acceptably high: 0.80 for the academic domain, 0.72 for physical and 0.84 for social. The internal reliability of the grid was assessed using Wilcoxon Signed-Ranks test to examine the differences between the constructs. A significant difference was expected between certain construct pairs (i.e. between the positive constructs of *good, happy, likes* and the negative constructs of *hard, naughty*) and no significant difference was expected between other construct pairs (i.e. between pairs of positive and between pairs of negative constructs). Expected patterns were found for nine of the ten comparisons. An unexpected significant difference was found between the two negative constructs *hard* and *naughty*.

Second, some consistency was expected between the two scales, for example, if a child scored positively (or negatively) on a particular domain for the scale, the child should also score positively (or negatively) on the same domain for the grid. However, a significant correlation was found only between the two instruments for the academic domain. On closer inspection of the two instruments, it appears that the lack of correlation may be due to the instruments providing slightly different information on the three self domains. The scale measures only self-perceptions. The grid measures self-perceptions, but it also taps into children's preferences by asking questions about what they like and are happy doing. Therefore, only some correspondence should be expected between the two instruments.

Conclusion

With the instruments used and flexible response approach adopted, it was possible to obtain the views of 87 children with Down Syndrome out of a sample of 96. When working with children with Down Syndrome any professional should consider the specific difficulties that children with Down Syndrome encounter, such as limited language skills and their attention difficulties, their susceptibility to certain response biases, and their unfamiliarity with being asked for their views. From my research I learned two main considerations when working with children with Down Syndrome. These were the importance of having a flexible research approach to deal with the heterogeneity of the sample and the inclusion of safeguards into the research process to protect this vulnerable group from having their research rights neglected.

9 Research involving children with severe learning difficulties

TINA DETHERIDGE

This chapter is concerned with gathering the attitudes and responses of children with severe or profound learning disabilities. These children will have significant communication difficulties, may be non-speaking and are likely to have other disabilities which affect their freedom to respond to stimuli in their environments. The children who fall within this population show very different individual characteristics. This diversity of individual capability puts constraints on the choice of appropriate research methods. (See also Begley, Chapter 8, and Costley, Chapter 13, for discussion of research involving children with learning difficulties.)

The particular difficulties and unique communication patterns of these children pose specific challenges for the researcher. These can be loosely seen as concerning validity and reliability in data collection. Central to these issues is the nature of communication. Everything the researcher deduces about these children has passed through the medium of the communication. While this is true of any researcher–researched context, it is critical when the means of communication is complex, unusual and, through aiming to simplify, open to misinterpretation. In this research context, perhaps more than in any other, the researcher has, in order to communicate effectively, to understand the child's communication capabilities and to provide the mechanisms and framework in which communicative exchange can take place (Martinsen and von Tetzchner 1996).

A major concern of this chapter is fostering communication, in a research context, with the groups of children described earlier. In particular the chapter will look at the role that information and communications technology (ICT) can play in developing the child's understanding of communication and providing mechanisms for expression. (For the purposes of this chapter, 'child' will be used to indicate the disabled partner and 'adult' to signify the non-disabled communication partner.)

Issues relating to research method

The population of children with severe and profound learning difficulties cannot be considered a homogenous group. The very significant different and individual needs of this population precludes their treatment as a group. It also represents a very small population: the numbers of individuals in any area is very small in comparison to the total population, or even the total population of people with special educational needs. Recognition of these differences suggests that small scale interpretative approaches are likely to be more suitable than large scale, quantitative approaches. Peck and Furman (cited in Mertens and McLaughlin 1995: 47) observed that 'Qualitative research has enabled the development of professional interventions in special education that are responsive to cognitive and motivational interpretations of the world held by children, parents and professionals'. Such work has led to insights into interpersonal interactions that influence special educational practice.

Pupil behaviours can be studied in their natural environment or in clinical settings. The research on discrete interventions, such as ICT, is often carried out in clinical settings, where the pupil is removed to a separate area, if not to a different institution (Glenn and O'Brien 1994). However, removing pupils, whose understanding of the world is very limited, from their familiar environments can be very distressing. In unfamiliar environments, possibly surrounded by unfamiliar people, the reliability of the responses is likely to be poor and therefore an inadequate basis for drawing conclusions about treatments or methods relating to social or educational development.

The teacher is frequently the interpreter and mediator between the child and the surrounding world. As the responsible adult, the teacher has a duty to protect the child and to ensure that observation and intervention are not detrimental to the child's well-being. This requires the researcher to develop a good working relationship with the teacher and wherever possible for the teacher-carer to be the person who effects any intervention leaving the researcher to observe and record.

The double effect of working with very individual pupils and with teachers acting as intermediaries indicates that each pupil, in each situation, is likely to be very different from the next. Where the number of pupils being studied is small, and where the nature of their needs and environments in which they will respond naturally is variable, the most appropriate approach to gathering reliable data on educational behaviours will be through individual studies carried out in naturalistic settings.

Empowerment of children with learning difficulties in the research process

Through communication we are able to perceive and exercise power. Shotter (1973, cited in Harris 1994) indicated that part of 'being a person' was the ability to exercise personal power, which allows the individual to influence the world and to achieve desired outcomes. In the research context, part of empowering children with learning difficulties is ensuring that we develop and use the tools whereby they can communicate; thereby research respondents include these children. Some people with learning difficulties may have a tendency to acquiesce to the suggestions of others (Stalker 1998, Grove *et al.* in press). The freedom to communicate will depend not only on the availability of appropriate communication mechanisms and sensitive interpretation, but also on the power relationships in the exchange and attitudes established over time.

Ethical issues

Integrity of research, while being absolutely important in itself as well as important in relation to the individual study, may be hard to achieve for two reasons. First, researchers invest a great deal of time and effort into their research, and so there is a strong desire to see the work yield positive results (Golby 1994). Second, there is a natural desire for intervention to be beneficial. Pupils with profound disabilities, whose rate of development is very slow and whose progression is marked by exceedingly small steps, provide a challenge to those working with them, and with that challenge comes a great desire to see progress. It is imperative, therefore, that in every intervention any signs of progress are confirmed, so that teachers and researchers are quite sure that what they observe is genuinely occurring, and that it is attributable to the intervention or outcome under discussion. Teachers and carers can have a tendency to see a wish fulfilment. Researchers must ensure that they maintain an objective and professional stance.

It is unlikely that children with severe communication or intellectual impairments will be able to give permission for their involvement in a study. Stalker and Harris (1998) report that no examples were found in the literature of researchers finding ways to gain consent from people with a profound level of impairment. It would, therefore, on first appearance, seem correct therefore to seek permission from and involve the parents in the study. However, just as each teacher and carer working with profoundly handicapped children wants to see progression, so too do parents. The danger of any new initiative is that it can raise expectations which cannot be fulfilled. There is a responsibility on researchers using intervention strategies not to raise expectations, or to influence other people's perceptions of what does or might occur. For this reason consultation with parents needs care and sensitivity.

Reliability

In working with children with severe communication difficulties and where communicative gestures require interpretation, the researcher will need to take steps to check the inferences being made. The researcher needs to be sensitive to how communication is being interpreted and take steps to validate inferences (Grove *et al.* in press). Video recordings of interactions which can be independently analysed, the use of multiple data formats, including formal assessments as well as informal observation, will facilitate the interpretation of data.

One of the difficulties of working in naturalistic settings is that there will be a number of other influences taking place. Grove *et al.* (in press) cite the case of a young man being asked permission for an operation. Two carers, who believed that the operation would be beneficial, interpreted his eye gaze and facial gesture response as 'yes', while a third, less involved advocate interpreted it as 'no'. The judgement of the communication partner appeared to affect the interpretation.

The confidence of any findings concerns the degree to which they can be replicated. A high level of replicability assumes that similar results will be observed from equivalent experiments or sequences of events applied to other cases in the class. The replicability will relate to the homogeneity of the class. Although pupils with profound and multiple learning difficulties (PMLD) are classified under a single label, internally there are significant differences between individuals. This will affect the replicability of the findings of any single case study. Having said that, findings can be presented in a way that are recognizable to readers so that they 'will first, recognise the authenticity of the case studied' and 'will be able to investigate their own situations in-so-far as they are similar situations and (using the same techniques) come to similar results' (Golby 1994: 22).

Communication as part of the research process

Communication is interactive, demanding an exchange between two or more communicating partners (Kraat 1985). The communicator's receptive and expressive communication and cognitive capabilities affect this exchange, i.e. how well the child understands what is being communicated, how the child is able to process it, how well the child can express his or her own ideas and how well the partner can understand the meaning. When one partner has a severe communication disability, there is an onus on the non-disabled partner to facilitate and sustain communication so that meanings inferred are clarified or confirmed (Grove *et al.* in press). The process of interpretation has implications for the reliability of the communication exchange, and raises serious questions in gathering research data.

Assessment of communicative capability

The first step for the researcher in gathering the child's responses is to establish the communicative competence of the child. This might be done formally by the researcher or another professional. There are various formal assessment frameworks, such as the Affective Communication Assessment (Coupe *et al.* 1985) which can assist the researcher in identifying the child's response to stimuli and understanding of the communicative process. Assessment of communication skills will identify what the child is currently able to demonstrate. However, it is significantly more difficult to assess the extent or nature of ideas and wants that the child may have but which are not demonstrated. There may well be a gap between the child's ideas and wants and the capability of production to communicate them (Lahey 1988; Detheridge 1996). Many of the non-verbal cues used automatically by socially skilled people may be unusable by children with a physical disability (Light *et al.* 1986). A learning disability may mean that important non-verbal skills may not have been learned because, as the severity of the disability increases, less incidental learning takes place.

Adults, including researchers, may not recognize communication attempts and so may underestimate both the communication needs and the capabilities of the child. This in turn may affect the child's reason to communicate. For example, Jennifer, an adult in her late 40s, grew up in institutional care. Although Jennifer was able to vocalize and gesture, her social and environmental experiences had not led her to understand that others would respond to her communicative attempts, and so she did not acquire a reason to communicate. Despite her passivity, it would not, however, be safe to assume that she had nothing to say, or that she had no means of communicating.

Use of ICT in the research context to demonstrate communicative intent

ICT can provide tools with which the child can initiate actions that can in turn affect others and elicit responses (Glenn and O'Brien 1990; Detheridge 1996). In a research context this may, for example, involve the researcher gauging a child's preferences through activation of preferred on-screen action. Typical ICT activities which explore cause and effect use switches to control toys or simple computer programmes. A switch is the general term for a range of mechanisms which can send signals to control an electronic device. Its advantage is in producing immediate and unambiguous signals. In addition, a single physical action by the child, to press the switch, can trigger a range of different actions. The use of this is illustrated in the following extract from research involving case studies of individual pupils (Detheridge 1996):

Ben (aged 3 years) was blind, had no speech and had severe physical disabilities. The first time he was offered a switch it was set up to produce a piece of speech recorded by his teacher. As soon as he activated the switch and heard the message he showed, through facial gesture and head movement, that he was aware that it was his teacher's voice, and that it did not come from where he expected his teacher to be. He was plainly distressed by this outcome, demonstrating that he recognised the voice, knew where his teacher was, that the voice came from a different place, and that this was unusual. The observations were made by a non-participant observer, who was able to make detailed notes of Ben's responses. The use of supporting evidence, such as video, enabled the corroboration of observation. It was clear that Ben demonstrated contingency awareness which his teacher had not had the means of recognising before. Comparisons with other behaviours gave the researcher confidence in the interpretation of Ben's responses in this situation.

(Detheridge 1996)

Communicative purpose – a reason to communicate – is also important. The studies cited above showed that social contingencies are more motivating than non-social ones. They showed that pupils given switches to operate electronic devices to produce an effect demonstrated preferences and indicated the ability to make choices. Being able to produce a clear overt signal can indicate to the child and adult simultaneously that the child has made a communicative gesture. The feedback provided by the ICT mechanism can reduce instances of missed signals.

Amy (aged 4 years) had no speech and had severe physical disabilities. Prior to using an ICT device she was not able to interact with her peers in class, or to participate in group activities. She was given a switch, by which she learned that she could operate a favourite toy. It was observed, however, that her principal motivation was from the effect this had on the adults around her. When she had learned to control her switch she used it to activate a voice message. This message was used in a game in which she took turns with another child to play 'Simon says'. As well as showing that she could physically control the device, she showed pleasure in the activity, a high level of understanding of the subtleties of the game itself, and the ability to interact with another child. Amy learned that she could show and give pleasure with the help of her devices; that she could exercise power by controlling when she used her switch; and through all this demonstrated much greater cognitive skills than had previously been recognised.

(Detheridge 1996)

The effect of the environment in which the activity took place influenced Amy's motivation to respond. Clinical studies, in which the child is placed in isolated non-social settings, may be less productive in enabling demonstration of awareness because there seems to be less reason to communicate.

Aided means of communication

A child will normally understand utterances before being able to produce them (Dockrell and McShane 1993) and expressive communication may not, therefore, match the cognitive level or comprehension of the child. However, Bloom and Lacey (1978, cited in Musslewhite and St Louis 1982: 43) propose that 'the developmental gap between comprehension and speaking probably varies among different children, and at different times, and that the gap may be more apparent then real'. This gap may well be exacerbated by communication difficulties or severe physical disability because children lack the means of production (by speech or by the use of alternative or augmentative communication systems).

Aided communication is essentially more complex than direct speech. The communicator is generally required to translate between modes, for example between speech and graphics or speech and gesture (von Tetzchner *et al.* 1997). Total Communication uses a multimodal approach to communication, usually combining speech, signing (gesture) and graphics (symbols), allowing reinforcement of communication elements, with the intention of increasing the reliability. Children with poor speech, or without speech and unable to sign, may use communication boards or electronic communication aids. Communication boards often use a graphic representation to illustrate the ideas being communicated. Other communication aids may use synthesized or recorded speech. Messages are selected or built up by the user. The extent or complexity of the message are dependent upon the cognitive capability of the user, the flexibility of the device and the users ability to manipulate the selection. Although there are signing and symbol systems with full language capability, simplified systems are available for people with cognitive impairments. Children at a prelinguistic level of communication or who are at an early level of language development may use context based icons or actions.

The simplest electronic communication aid may be a device which will replay a single short recorded message. Ben used this in the illustration on p. 117. He was not able to choose the message, and so the communication was more about his choosing to play the message or not, than about the specific content. More complex devices have a number of prerecorded messages from which the user can select. This requires a different level of cognition and physical control. The flexibility of the communication will be determined by both the content of the individual messages and the context in which they are used. For example a device with just 'yes' and 'no' can give access to complex and extended conversations when used with a competent communication partner.

Communicative content
The flexibility and breadth of children's communication will depend upon the content at their disposal. This comprises the individual communicative elements and the number of elements. At the simplest level a single representation (object, gesture or graphic) will be an index, used to represent an entire communication – for example a cup used to signify that it is time for a drink, or as a request 'I want a drink'. The communication capability available to the child would thus depend on the number of indexes available and which were understood. At a second level the communication elements are iconic, standing for a single idea which can be used in sequence to express more complex meanings. The highest level of representation is that with grammatical structures (Smith 1996). No matter at what place a child may be along this progression, the important concern for the researcher is the reliability of the child's understanding of the referent and ability to use it to express ideas.

Indexed communication
As soon as there is a choice of elements from which to choose, we need to consider the reliability of the child's selection mechanism. Symbols, pictures or small objects on a board to which the child can indicate, by pointing or eye gaze, provide a simple communication aid. However, there may be times when the selection is ambiguous, or the indication insufficiently clear for it to be a definite selection. Also a board may have a physical limit to the number of messages it can display, appropriate to the child's vision and cognition. Computer programs exist which can offer a wider range of selectable items; once control has been gained over the switch or input device, they can give less ambiguous indications. The software can help children make these connections by breaking the process into smaller steps. For example, a computer program has a number of pictures displayed. These are highlighted in turn. As the highlighter moves over each picture the name of the picture is spoken. The child presses the switch when the highlighter is on the item wanted. If an error is made and the child presses the switch at the wrong moment, an alternative selection can be made before moving on to another set of items. So, for example, children can choose who they would like to sit next to at lunch. Sequences of choices

can be set up, enabling a longer interaction, without presenting too much information at once. The choice of display is set up by the researcher using digitized or scanned photographs or pictorial symbols to represent items. The choice made can be confirmed or reinforced by physically moving the selected item to another part of the screen, by additional speech, as well as by the feedback from the person sharing the conversation. Feedback to both the child and researcher may increase the reliability of interpretation of such communicative gestures.

Iconic communication
Pictorial symbols provide a step between indexed and grammatical communication. Each idea or concept is represented by a graphic. These can be sequenced to construct more flexible or more precise meaning. Pictorial symbol sets, such as Rebus, the Makaton Vocabulary or Picture Communication Symbols (PCS), contain some of the elements of language, but do not have the full capability to enable syntactically structured communication (van Balkom and Welle Donker-Gimbrere 1996). However, children with cognitive difficulties are learning to use these types of symbol sets to communicate quite complex ideas. Whichever level of communication element is being used the child must associate the representation with the referent and be able to indicate accurately a selection. There must be feedback from the selection and there must be a consequence.

Direct and indirect communication
There is one other aspect of communication which may affect researchers. This is whether the communication is conversational or 'direct', or whether it is indirect (non-interactive), for example through paper based materials. Direct communication is that which forms part of a conversational 'turn'. The normal modes used in direct communication are speaking and listening. Although the frequency and spontaneity of conversational turns may be affected by the means (such as communication aid) it is essentially dynamic. Some children, who take time to process information, may find the ephemeral nature of speech problematic. A supporting gesture, giving a visual image may help. Signing in support of speech is a common approach used with children who have severe learning difficulties. However, some children may find the use of more permanent symbolic icons, such as graphic symbols, helps to hold the elements in the communication whilst it is being processed. The success of direct communication will depend on the child's and adult's conversational skills in the modes available. Researchers who are not able to sign will be handicapped in their communication with a child using speech and sign together, but being with the child the researcher may pick up gestures and other indicators to supplement the formal system.

In contrast, indirect communication is that which is normally associated with reading and writing. It has a measure of permanence and is retrievable.

The 'writing' may be a collection of photographs or a sequence of symbols. The important feature is that the creator can revisit the writing and retrieve the original message. In addition, as a means of communicating, the reader should also be able to interpret the meaning. There are many children who are unable to read text and may use graphic symbols as a means of reading and writing (Detheridge and Detheridge 1997). The success of indirect communication will depend on the readers' and writers' literacy skills using the modes available. Indirect communication allows children to consider the information being presented to them, allows them time to consider their responses, possibly to discuss or seek help from a carer, and then to express their considered response. The reliability of this may depend on the support the child is given. Being able to reread and reflect upon input or output may contribute to reliability. Speech technology, which will read the writing back to the creator, helps children to check that their writing says what they intended.

Conclusion

Studies aimed at gathering the responses of children with severe or profound learning difficulties require the researcher to be clear about the child's communication capability, as well as the ability of any adult partners to understand and interact with the child. Steps must be taken to see that the child has a means of communication which is appropriate for the level of interpretation placed on responses. The very significant differences between individuals with severe or profound learning difficulties precludes treatment as a group, although comparisons between similar studies may allow inferences to be drawn where there are strong similarities of outcome.

Information and communications technology can support the communication of children with severe or profound learning difficulties. The nature of an electronic aid may enable signals to be more overt than entirely natural gestures. However, communicative gestures have to be interpreted and stringent steps are required to enhance the reliability of the interpretation, and the inferences made as a result. The environment in which communication takes place needs to be natural and familiar. Interventions or interactions may be more successful with familiar partners. It has also been shown that socially contingent situations are more motivating than non-social ones, and so may yield more fluent responses by the child. The power relationships between the child and the adults in the environment need to be such that the child feels free to communicate. Despite these difficulties, many studies have shown that children with even very profound disabilities have feelings and ideas to express, and successful attempts have been made to elicit their views.

(10) Let's do it properly: inviting children to be researchers

SIMON WARREN

When we ask children to participate as 'researchers' rather than as the objects of classroom investigations, what is the character of this social identity we ask children to take on? This is the question at the heart of this chapter. It takes the form of a critical reflection on my attempts to involve children as 'researchers' in the investigation of gender identities, and in particular the construction of masculine identities, in a primary school context. With this focus in mind, the chapter considers to what extent dominant ideas within social research, regarding both the role of the researcher and the relationship between methods and theory building, act to regulate both the boundaries of 'proper' research and the gendered nature of that research.

The first section of the chapter looks at my research focus, research questions and general methodological approach. I spend some time looking at the involvement of the children in the research process, and in particular the survey of gendered perceptions. I conclude this section with an outline of my conception of the methodological 'problem' the conduct of the survey appeared to present at that time. Next, I re-examine my reading of the 'problem', illustrating the assumptions about the character of research and the researcher embedded in this original understanding. I go on to discuss my unease with this original definition and the critique of it that I have latterly developed. Finally, I suggest alternative approaches I could have taken in involving children as researchers. While the main focus of my research was the way boys in a primary school class attempted to construct masculine identities, I refer to gender identities throughout this chapter. This is because the example I have used to explore the problematics of inviting children to participate as researchers, a survey of gender perceptions, involved all the children in my class.

In the beginning

While working as a primary school teacher in the early 1990s, I became conscious of a growing concern with the behaviours displayed by boys within the schools I taught. Talk of boys' behaviours dominated staff room discussion, focusing upon, for example, the disruption they caused in class and the playground, their seeming inability to attend to school work for any length of time and their captivation with the images and language of aggression. In sharing these concerns with my colleagues, a number of commonsense explanations presented themselves. Reference was made to boys' developmental lag in relation to that of girls, the 'male' hormone testosterone, the lack of positive male role models in fatherless families, and the violence depicted in popular children's entertainment. My personal and local concern found resonance in a slowly emerging media attention characterized by a *Times Educational Supplement* (TES 1993) editorial, entitled 'What about the boys?' This highlighted concern about working class boys' academic underachievement and the possible social consequences: 'It could be that the key educational issue of the 1990s will be how to handle underachieving working-class urban boys in a society which has suffered structural male unemployment for two decades.'

This editorial was opportune in its remarks, as it was soon followed by a plethora of popular reports, government statistics and latterly, official government pronouncements. These described a seeming displacement of young, predominantly working-class men, from a domestic labour market that was increasingly being 'feminized' under the pressure for Britain to compete in a global economy. This displacement can perhaps be overstated. While girls and women appear to be improving their performance in all educational sectors, this does not necessarily equate with improved chances in the labour market overall. Despite a higher number of women achieving first class honours degrees, male graduates, by and large, fill the more highly sought after and remunerated jobs (DfEE 1997b).

These popular, academic and official reports charted a troubling cartography. Where explanations were given, they tended to rely upon assumed causal relationships between either biological differences between males and females; abstract socializing processes, which were usually reducible to deficit theories of the family; or the product of a changing economic infrastructure. I found these as inadequate as the commonsense theories of my colleagues. This impelled me to look at the 'meaning-making practices' that the boys in my class were engaged in, in their projects of 'becoming somebody'. I wanted to explain how these projects emerged as being both produced by and productive of wider processes of masculine construction.

The research design

Initially, there were three questions that framed my research:

- What behaviours do boys display in different group contexts, and to what extent do these differ according to task and group composition?
- What connections might there be between these behaviours and learning performance, and the connections between these and group/task composition?
- What skills can be identified that encourage boys to engage in positive group work?

I was intent on mapping the patterns of interaction engaged in by the boys in my class. I was concerned, though, not only to record the boys' behaviours but also to describe and explain them, to gain insights into the meanings behind their actions in the particular setting of their primary classroom.

My initial research design had called for the use of interviews as the main means by which to gather the boys' perceptions of their classroom interactions. I share Connolly's (1998) view that primary school children are socially competent and able to give expression to complex experiences and concerns, that they should be heard as well as seen. Relationships between researchers and research participants are always influenced by contextual variables, such as race, gender, age, etc. Age was particularly pertinent. It became apparent, during the trialling of the methodological techniques, that my position as class teacher was having a reactive effect. It was impossible to determine whether the boys were producing answers they thought I wanted, or were cautious about revealing their true intentions lest this result in disciplinary measures being taken. I found it increasingly more difficult to break free from the social identity of 'teacher' that the boys were determined to locate me within. I had also planned to keep a detailed research diary of my daily observations. This, in combination with the interviews, would allow me to ground theory construction in the boys' own voices. The hurly-burly of daily classroom life meant that my notes were highly partial and fragmented. I needed something much more structured that would allow me to integrate both teaching and researching.

In order to compose a picture of the kinds of interactions the boys were involved in I needed to gather data in three different areas: pupil–pupil interactions, pupil–task interactions and pupil–teacher interactions. I produced a pupil observation record designed to provide a flexible structure for my observations. My intention was that it should be no more intrusive than a semi-structured interview. This record comprised both a checklist of different types of interactions and, where possible, a commentary on those interactions. Alongside these observational notes, I maintained complementary 'theoretical' and 'methodological' notes which related my observations to theoretical considerations of gender identity and group work, reflected on my methodological approach and suggested different avenues for data collection (see C. Hughes 1994 for a discussion of this approach to grounded theory).

Inviting 'them' in

Without direct access to the boys' voices, and the difficulties of sustaining a full-time job and doctoral research, I sought to integrate the research into the curricular practices of the class. Research strategies were embedded in the termly planning across as many subject areas as possible, most of which were aimed at eliciting the children's perceptions of gender. Among others, these involved structured diaries, self-perception inventories, friendship trees, circle time activities, group work reflection, narrative work, etc. In response to a suggestion by my (then) doctoral supervisor, I sought ways of involving the children in my research. This would involve them in the direct collection of data, and reflection on it as it was fed back into the curriculum, therefore contributing to its analysis. Mostly these were initiated by myself, while others were negotiated with the children. These ranged from the gender balance of air time given to different artists during breakfast radio, to preferences for male or female characters in books and films. This mode of involvement built on the children's experience of surveys conducted within curriculum topic work across the school.

How did the children perceive 'maleness' and 'femaleness'? I utilized an approach taken by Carrington and Short (1992) in their work on 'race' in predominantly white schools. The children in my class were set a task within a normal lesson where they were asked to respond to two open questions:

* What is good about being a girl?
* What is good about being a boy?

Girls and boys were required to answer both questions and so to provide some insights into how girls and boys saw themselves and each other. I was able to draw out a series of conceptulizations based upon the attributes that the children had assigned to the two genders and the frequency of statements applied to them (Figure 10.1).

The left hand column of Figure 10.1 provides the conceptual attributes derived from the children's descriptors in the right hand column. The

Figure 10.1   Examples of gendered perceptions elicitation exercise

Boys' concepts of femaleness

Attribute	Description
Appearance	'can wear more jewellery'; 'can do more with their hair'; 'can have long hair'; 'can wear better clothes'; 'can wear boys' clothes as well'.
Social networks and pursuits	'can go to Brownies'; 'can go to Girl Guides'; 'can have Barbies'; 'can have dolls'.
Physicality and action	'can play netball'; 'don't have to play football'; 'can play girls' games'.
Life trajectories	'can be a bride'; 'can have an easier life'; 'can pay the bills'.
Relations to school	'find it easier to learn'.

Boys' conception of maleness

Attribute	Description
Superiority (cognitive)	'draw better than girls'; 'have better ideas than girls'; 'can be very educated'.
Superiority (physicalness)	'run faster than girls'; 'play football better'; 'get to be stronger'.
Appearance	'can have short or long hair'; 'can wear nice clothes'; 'have nice shoes'; 'can do nice things with their hair'; 'can wear sportier clothes'.
Life trajectories	'can be famous'; 'can become a pop star'; 'can have more beer'; 'can play football on TV'.
Social networks and pursuits	'can go out with girls'; 'eat junk food'; 'boys get to ask girls out'.
Physicality and action	'have got a bigger opportunity to play football than girls'; 'boys can do lots of sports'.
Public/private realm	'don't have to do as much housework'.
Personality	'are nice'.

conceptual attributes are arranged hierarchically according to their frequency within the children's statements. A series of similar figures were produced detailing conceptual attributes and descriptors for 'Boys' conceptions of genderedness – femaleness'; 'Boys' conceptions of genderedness – maleness'; 'Girls' positive attributes of maleness'; 'Girls' negative attributes of maleness'; 'Girls' positive attributes of femaleness'; and 'Girls' negative attributes of femaleness'. These datasets described a world structured around notions of significant differences between girls and boys, attributing quite different values to maleness and femaleness. I produced a table of the children's own descriptors organized in four sections – 'What girls think of boys'; 'What girls think of girls'; 'What boys think of boys'; 'What boys think of girls' – in order to present it to the class as a focus for discussion and reflection. I chose not to introduce my conceptual attributes at this stage, wishing the children to see their own words. The ensuing discussion was located in my concern to see if the descriptors provided valid statements about the children's differentiated understandings of femaleness and maleness. The discussion did indeed show up the diversity of understandings held, even as certain patterns emerged. It was these patterns, rather than the individual differences, that the children gradually began to focus upon, raising questions about how these might be produced. Suggestions included the socialization of children into these ways of thinking, with parents playing the major socializing role.

Let's be researchers too

Within this mêlée, one of the boys asked if it was possible to undertake the same exercise with other children in the school. This was immediately seized upon and produced a debate about the feasibility of such a suggestion. Through posing questions about the practical nature of the various solutions presented, the idea of a survey, similar to those the children were used to conducting in their curriculum work, established itself as the way forward. I had not planned for this. Should I take this idea from the children, and bring it back as a properly planned activity, or go along with the energy and enthusiasm? I chose the latter. This seemed an opportunity to go beyond the passive participation of the children in data collection attempted so far, activities not dissimilar to 'school work', and to invite the children to take on the role of researcher, to design research tools, collect and analyse data. I knew that the enthusiasm could easily be dissipated by the afternoon, so the survey would have to be ready for use by lunchtime, in just over an hour. Because of timetabling reasons we would not meet together again as a class until lunchtime. I quickly appointed a small group of children to design a survey sheet, which the class would look at before going off for lunch.

It was decided that the children would work in pairs, a more able reader with a less able one. They could question only four children each, and they should not question anyone more than once. They would read out one descriptor at a time and ask the respondent to say whether they thought the statement referred to boys or girls. The answer would be recorded on the survey sheet. Once completed, the survey should have been able to tell us to what extent the understandings of maleness and femaleness, as demonstrated by this class, were shared by children across the school.

A problem in the making?

With the survey sheets returned to me, I set some time aside at the end of the school day to see what the range of responses were. What struck me, almost immediately, was not the tendency for these responses to fall into predictable patterns, but the seeming impossibility of reading the response sheets in any meaningful fashion. Despite my belief that the structure of the sheet was obvious, and that its style was similar to the many surveys carried out by the children before, there was no consistency in the recording of the data. I had expected that a number of the children might requestion some of those already approached. This was not of any great concern to me. The survey was not meant to produce hard quantitative information, simply to indicate similarities or differences in patterns of gendered perceptions between the children in my class and the wider school population.

My initial feeling was one of frustration directed at the children for not following what I regarded as simple instructions. The frustration was then relocated on to myself. I had not allowed enough time to consider the suggestion of a survey of all the children in the school. The basic idea was a good one, and I was pleased that this had been generated by one of the children. It seemed obvious that in order to involve the children in the research in any meaningful sense, time should have been dedicated to 'training' them in the techniques of survey collection. It also occurred to me that I had provided few, if any, safeguards against the reactive effects of certain pupil–pupil interactions: the effect of older children questioning younger children; how some girls might react to some of the more aggressive boys; and whether girls would tend to ask only girls, and boys ask only boys. I filed it away with the intention of coming back to it at a later date. However, before such an occasion arose, I left that school, and was unable to 'train' the children or conduct the survey again.

Re-examining the problem

The problem, as I perceived it then, was framed in terms of threats to the validity of the survey. My assertion was that if the children had been trained in the use of data gathering techniques, and safeguards were established against the threat of reactivity, then the data produced would have been valid. The use of a survey method itself was not under question. I thought I would be able to check the validity of my classroom observations against the information generated by the survey.

I had moved from seeing the problem as being that of the children's misunderstanding of the task, to how I had structured the research activity. What I was not reflecting on was my perception of what constituted proper research. Therefore, I want to re-examine my original analysis of the difficulties presented by the children's participation as researchers through a discussion of three problematics: participant observation, bounded systems and visibility.

Distance, objectivity and masculine detachment: the problematic of participant observation

A central character in the ethnographic tradition in educational research is that of the participant observer. Participant observation is, perhaps, best suited to the study of classroom interactions. Along with interviews, it appears to be uniquely able to illuminate the 'meaning making' practices of social actors in school contexts. It is also an obvious methodological choice for practitioner researchers. Participant observation suggests an 'insider-outsider' approach, implying different degrees of closeness and distance to the object of study. In being an insider, the practitioner is able to detail the specific happenings of particular locations and draw upon intuitive knowledges borne of the daily interactions of classroom life. As the outsider, the researcher can step back and locate these phenomena within wider systems of meaning.

It is the distance achieved by the outsider element of this relationship that appears to be fundamental to obtaining the necessary objectivity required for valid research claims. It is argued that without this objective distance research claims can be dismissed as subjective or biased (see Hammersley 1997). But where does this opposition between objectivity and subjectivity, and the subsequent linking of the former with 'truth' and the latter with 'falsehood', derive?

The scientific knowledges that now form much of our commonsense view of the world, and underpin much social science, emerged from the philosophical meditations of the Enlightenment. It marked a shift in European thinking from one based on religion and superstition to one founded on science. A particular kind of rationality came to be established, often associated with the philosopher René Descartes (1596–1650). This rationality was organized around a set of oppositional pairs, most notably that of the distinction between mind and body. The mind was understood as being the location of rational thought, of logic, that which makes humans superior to animals and the world of nature. Flowing from this primary distinction are a set of further binaries: rationality/irrationality; reason/ emotion; subject/object; objectivity/subjectivity; civilized/uncivilized; culture/nature; public/private; natural/unnatural; male/female. Historically, this rationality came to be associated with masculine traits, whereas femininity was associated with the body, subjectivity, nature, irrationality and emotion. Western masculinity has been largely constructed around a series of denials associated with the 'feminine' – the rejection of dependency, control of emotions, a projection into the public rather than the private and domestic, a privileging of the objective over subjective, and so on.

What bearing does this have on the children's participation in the research process? Like participant observation, the children's involvement in the survey, required them to be both insider and outsider, to be simultaneously passionately engaged in the precarious business of securing a gender identity (Davies 1989; Warren 1997), and yet somehow disengage themselves from that process in order to be observers and cataloguers of that gendered world. The research activity cannot itself be disengaged from the children's own projects of 'self-making'. We can see that if ethnography evokes objective distance and dispassionate analysis as the privileged goal, it links proper research with a particularly masculinist view of the world, that any research that does not secure for itself the necessary objective (masculine) distance, cannot make truthful claims about reality. Even where research models counsel us to take account of our influence as researchers on the research process, this often becomes little more than an autobiographical footnote, a reflection on the research. My argument is that the dominant modes of doing social research implicitly assume a primary dichotomy between the reality we research and the research process; that it is theoretically possible to achieve adequate critical distance between this reality and the research process, even when we recognize its impact upon that reality. I also argue that it is the conceptualization of objectivity as distance, embraced by an objective/subjective dualism that gives much research a masculinist imperative.

Collectable culture: the problematic of bounded systems

The ethnographer's approach to the real can sometimes resemble the collections of artifacts found in museums. These collections, whether they be in museums, in research theses or the peer reviewed texts of academic research, all embody particular notions of 'culture', how it can be understood and represented.

At the beginning of my research, I set myself the task of discerning the meaning-making practices engaged in by the boys that produced particular kinds of masculine identity. Built into this was an understanding that social action is produced by social actors, and comprehended through the meanings attributed to these actions by the actors, rather than as effects of external forces – determining structures of power or socialization processes. As with other educational ethnographies working within symbolic interactionist or critical theory traditions, my emphasis was on a bounded cultural system – a classroom. Scott (1996: 152) describes two underlying assumptions to this approach. First, institutions and smaller social units, such as classrooms, are populated by social actors who share common values and operate within 'systems of rules by which they can be identified'. Second, the categories we use allow us to study these identifiable areas of social life, extract elements from them, and discern the rules that govern behaviour in these holistic units.

Rosaldo (1993), however, argues against the idea that we live our lives by following rules, by fixed cultural expectations and norms, suggesting instead that we live with ambiguity and uncertainty, that we engage with the processes of 'self-making' in 'cultural borderlands' or 'zones of difference', those social spaces within which we improvise life, and deal with life's contingencies. Rosaldo is concerned that in assuming that culture is naturally made up of normative regulations, that social scientists may disregard the disconnections and discontinuities in their data since their 'seeing' assumes that reality is made up of patterns of connection and continuity. This brings to mind Thorne's (1993) work in US elementary schools. She focused not only on the ways children erected borders between the genders, and therefore defined maleness and femaleness, but also on the border crossings engaged in by different children. She described the ways that gender identities, and thus the borders, were full of ambiguity, how border maintenance had to be worked at and constantly redefined. This border work draws on cultural resources far beyond the walls of the classroom or the school or the individual children, calling on the gender work of families or the symbolic images of popular culture. In such instances, the frontiers of classroom, playground or school seem rather more permeable and shifting than the 'bounded system' approach allows for.

The establishment of schools as distinct buildings that house large numbers of children, subdivided into classrooms, is a historical phenomenon. The nature of classrooms and what occurs within them has, and continues, to change. They cannot be seen as bounded systems, as closed spaces of given definition. The social definitions of a school or a classroom undergo contestation and change. In putting together our ethnographic collections, then, we may be in danger of collecting highly selective items, and inferring from them bounded systems of continuity and wholeness.

The tyranny of observation: the problematic of visibility

We constantly trip over the detritus of the visual metaphor in educational research; I sought to 'illuminate' the children's gendered perceptions, that is shed light on them so as to 'see' them better, bring them into 'view'. Involved here is a sleight of hand conflating the seen with the known, making reality only that which can be recorded and measured in some form. The metaphor of observation invites us to conceive of the research process as being made up of two distinct realms of experience. On the one hand there is the world of brute facts, of data, of objective material reality. On the other, there is the world of interpretation, analysis and theory building. Even grounded theory conceives of this kind of distinction, positing the idea of a constant moving *between* the two worlds. But research, particularly ethnography, is seldom concerned with gross material reality. What we are concerned with are interpretations and meanings. Consequently, the reality we purport to seek is a reality mediated by interpretation. In fact, I would go further and suggest that the reality I was asking the children to observe was not only mediated by their act of observation, but was an already interpreted reality.

In attaining their gender identities, the children are already engaged in interpreting themselves and others. They do this through interpretative frameworks. These frameworks set out the boundaries of understanding that make possible not only certain ways of being male and female, but also the very desire of there being two distinct categories, and that you may have to be one *or* the other, but never both (Davies 1989). What is 'seen' then, is not the real, in the sense of an experience distinct from interpretation. The survey, as with interviewing, assumes that the observed behaviours or the direct account offer a unique insight into the reality of the children's gendered worlds. The behaviours I had observed formed the basis for the survey. But these behaviours were themselves acts of interpretation. They were attempts to construct meaningful ways of being 'somebody' in contexts that already attempted to constrain the different possibilities of 'becoming somebody'. But these interpretations, and the frameworks that made them possible in particular ways, were being changed by the very acts of constructing themselves as boys and girls. In this sense, reality is always a moving target, always in the process of becoming, always already interpreted.

The distinction between an envisioned and an interpreted reality no longer holds up. Yet, in involving children as researchers, we often attempt to invoke such a distinction. The frameworks that make possible this way of seeing are veiled, hidden, forced into the background.

Doing it differently

Almost everyone doing a doctoral thesis must come to a point where they say 'If I was to do that again, I would do it differently'. So, how would I do it differently? First, let me pose some rhetorical questions. Could not a drama be as powerful an inscription device as a structured survey? Could not a poem speak as resonantly of the reality of children's gendered worlds as tabulated statements and descriptors? Does not a journalistic report, with evocative photographs, involve the same processes of selection and abstraction of elements, as academic research? And could not such a report speak as truthfully about children's worlds?

Second, let me suggest just one alternative way of conducting my research (retrospectively) and how it meets the challenges posed above. I would need to start with a different set of questions, which might look something like this: how are the boundaries of maleness and femaleness defined through action in the classroom? How do some modes of maleness come to be dominant over others? How does this dominant mode of maleness regulate subordinate or alternative ways of being male? I would be seeking to engage the children, and particularly the boys, in reflecting on how they construct meaningful self-identities and why some appear to be more possible than others. Let us say I gave each child a disposable camera and asked the children to photograph places, people, objects and activities that were important to their sense of self. These could be used in a variety of ways. Collages could be produced, story lines sketched, relationships between images explained, personal diaries written. Whatever holding frame is chosen, the aim would be to encourage the children to reflect upon why they had chosen those images over others, what processes of choosing they had involved themselves in, what other images could have been chosen, how the meanings of the images change over time and in the context of doing the research. There would be a degree of challenge to these dialogues necessary for any reflective action.

While the collage and the story line would always have the danger of suggesting fixed identities, the images are always understood as partial and temporary. They become gateways into the meaning making practices of self-making. They constantly beg further questions, and possibly further images, constantly making reference to worlds outside of the classroom. The activity is engaging rather than distancing, yet also contains reflection and critique.

Conclusion

To speak of and do research differently is not to step beyond our interpretative understandings. Even an alternative research approach would define particular ways of knowing the world, and what that world was comprised of. It involves more than adopting different techniques, though these will surely evolve. It is to understand that all ways of 'seeing' involve the means by which we regulate what and how to see (Sheurich 1997). The activity above brings to the surface the process of selecting items and bringing them into the research gaze. In using any method, the assumptions it holds of what reality is and how it can be known, need to be brought to the surface. Therefore, as researchers, children need to engage, and critique, different ways of 'seeing'. This includes the difficult task of foregrounding their own interpretative frameworks, and how their different identities, including that of researcher, are always in the process of 'becoming'.

(11) Researching 8 to 13-year-olds' perspectives on their experience of religion

ELEANOR NESBITT

What are the most appropriate ways of researching children's perspectives on their experience of religion? This is the question that this chapter addresses. Sensitivity emerges as the single most important factor, and this chapter teases out what this may mean in practice. To illustrate the issues I shall draw on specific instances from field studies of young Christians, Hindus and Sikhs in Coventry that were based at the University of Warwick between 1986 and 1996 (Jackson and Nesbitt 1993). Central to these studies was the question: how is religious culture transmitted or how are children 'nurtured' in faith (Bushnell 1967; Hull 1984)? This entailed alertness to the relationship between religion and culture and to changes and continuities in individuals' relationship with their tradition, always with the research variables of the children's ethnicity, membership group, age and gender.

Anyone researching children's perspectives on religion needs to have clearly defined research questions and to subdivide these clearly. For example, subsidiary questions in the Warwick studies were: how do children identify themselves? How do they regard their involvement in religious activity? How do they regard religious experience – whether their own or another's? The identity question involved discovering with what terms children identified themselves and their religious tradition (Hindu, Punjabi, Orthodox, Ukrainian and so on) and the contexts in which they did so, as well as how they regarded this identity – with pride, relish, regret. Similarly, with regard to religious behaviour or activity, data were needed not only on children's degree of involvement (e.g. in congregational ritual) but also on their attitude to this. 'Religious experience' was used to refer to episodes of an intense awareness which transcends human institutions while being extremely personal. The term subsumes dreams, visions, conversion experiences and memorable sensations which the individual understands as encounters with the divine or with such agencies of a believed in supernatural order as angels. The diversity of children's experience and the variety of ways in which religion is conceptualized mean that there is abundant scope for potential research questions.

Towards an appropriate methodology: quantitative or qualitative?

Hyde (1990) provides a comprehensive, classified review of research on religion in childhood. Psychology provides the disciplinary framework for most of these studies and common to them is the concept of a sequence of developmental stages from infancy to adult maturity. The research is quantitative, using such tools as attitudinal scales. In Britain, Leslie Francis and colleagues have conducted extensive studies with this approach (listed by Hyde 1990). The scale of their many survey based studies makes it possible to detect both patterns which occur over a number of years and patterns evident at one point in time. These lend support to hypotheses which correlate attitudes, levels of information and cultic practice with personality (e.g. extroversion, neuroticism), age, gender, social class, type of school (primary/secondary, Roman Catholic, Church of England, county), religious denomination or geographic area. The theoretical considerations in thus measuring attitudes to religion are discussed by Hyde (1990: 391–6).

An alternative (or complementary) approach is ethnography: through research methods which owe more to anthropology that to psychology, individual children's voices can be relayed in their social context. The percentage based conclusions yielded by large scale surveys can be brought to life and indeed challenged by qualitative data and such data in turn suggest hypotheses for more quantitative testing. My aim in the Warwick studies was to present the individual child by means of 'thick description', in other words to be conscious of levels of interpretation inherent in reporting complex data (Geertz 1973). This entails not only recording individual voices at great length, but also situating these in the context of the speakers' observed behaviour and interactions in their families and other membership groups. The interpretative approach involves alertness to 'experience near' concepts and not confusing these with one's own 'experience distant' concepts (Geertz 1983: 58) or analytic terms (Spradley 1980).

'Religion' itself provides an example of a single term, used by both fieldworker and children, and designating related but not identical concepts.

(When a Hindu boy at primary school mentioned having 'English religion food' in his sandwiches the gap was especially clear.) Many Hindu and Sikh children used the terms 'language' and 'religion' interchangeably to refer to what I as fieldworker termed 'culture' or 'ethnic group'. Similarly they equated 'Hindu' and 'Sikh' (for me their 'religion') with 'Gujarati', 'Hindi' or 'Punjabi' (their community's language) (see Jackson and Nesbitt 1993: 29–31).

Issues in field studies of religion

Of the theoretical issues, with methodological implications for field studies of religion in the experience of children, five need to be raised. The first of these is the question of whether religion is a 'sensitive topic' and what the ethical implications of this are. The second is the matter of reflexivity. Related to this is the third issue – language. The fourth issue, and the only one which is not common to studies of adults' perspectives on religion, is age: whether and to what extent children differ from adults as subjects of ethnographic study. This entails discussion of gatekeepers and of reliability, authenticity and validity. We shall leave until last the dangers inherent in adopting a 'world religions' approach.

Is religion a sensitive topic?

First, should religion be deemed a 'sensitive topic' and, if so, what are the consequences? Certainly, religion 'deals with things sacred to those being studied that they do not wish profaned' (Renzetti and Lee 1993: 5–6). Consequently, the ethical and methodological implications have to be acknowledged. Moreover, researchers are likely to decide that children should not be prompted to answer questions which seem likely to cause embarrassment or pain (for instance required to give their views on death if it was known that they had recently been bereaved). Additionally, consideration of confidentiality suggests that any quotations published should not be attributed to individuals by name, and that their identity should not be given. The history of some communities makes confidentiality and anonymity especially important – for example the Jewish community's experience and fear of anti-Semitism.

Researching religion can also be sensitive in the further sense that some religious groups are controversial, with attendant difficulties in access, fieldwork and reporting (Barker 1983; Beckford 1985; Ayella 1993). Clearly, researching the perspectives of children – or their elders – in some new religious movements is more problematic than in less controversial, more established religious communities.

A sensitive approach is one which has clearly formulated the ethical implications for each stage of the research. For example, seeking the informed consent of religious leaders, parents and children, means explaining carefully the nature and purpose of the research. If data are published in, say, curriculum books, using names and photographs, this must be only after negotiation with the individual children concerned, their parents and consultants from within the faith community (Everington 1996a).

The ethical significance for fieldwork includes making it clear to interviewees that they may ask for the tape recorder to be turned off at any point. In the Warwick studies, this rarely happened, and when it did the child's sensitivity was not necessarily to do with religion. For instance, when one young Sikh from a locally controversial *gurdwara* asked me to stop recording, it was because he did not want anyone to know that he received extra tuition in mathematics.

If religion (in both controversial and non-controversial groupings) is conceived of as encompassing inherently sensitive areas of experience, the further question arises whether researching children's experience of religion, or at least their religious experience, calls for that empathy arising from personal experience on the part of the researcher which E. M. Forster invoked when, in *The Hill of Devi*, he wrote of the Maharajah: 'His religion was the deepest thing in him. It ought to be studied neither by the psychologist nor by the mythologist but by an individual who has experienced similar promptings' (1953: 175).

This sentiment sidesteps the implications of any cultural difference between the ethnographer and the faith community. As Jackson (1997) cautions:

> Sensitivity is a necessary but not a sufficient condition for understanding . . . I would suggest that one's capacity for empathy develops after grasping the grammar of someone else's discourse, otherwise there is a real danger that the interpreter might project his or her own concepts, feelings or attitudes on the situation being studied.
>
> (Jackson 1997: 24)

Forster's suggestion clouds considerations of unconscious bias and encourages overeasy equations between the fieldworker's and the child's experience and understandings of it.

Reflexivity

This interplay, often subconscious, between researcher and researched constitutes the second concern: reflexivity. At every stage of the research it is necessary to be aware of the effect that the fieldworker's presence and people's perceptions of him or her may have upon the field and on the nature of the children's replies to questions. In the Warwick studies this included being aware of how many non-English terms young Sikhs and Hindus used, as compared to the frequency in their exchanges with parents, siblings, peers and teachers, and why this might be (see next section). Fieldworkers need to be vigilant in examining what influence their presuppositions may have upon the questions they pose and upon how they interpret the answers. Thus, on occasion my presence made an obvious impact, as when their teacher exhorted a class of young Sikhs learning Punjabi in the *gurdwara*: 'A distinguished visitor, Eleanor Nesbitt, is studying your attitudes: show your good aspect!' Impact may be longer term too: nine years after his initial period of involvement in a field study of young Hindus a young Gujarati man mentioned the research as having increased his interest in Hinduism (Nesbitt 1998). This issue of reflexivity was especially important in the Warwick studies as many of the children had met me as a temporary participant in their community's acts of worship, and had formed an impression of my likely level of familiarity with activities and with languages of which they assumed 'outsiders' (non-Asians, non-Cypriots, etc.) to be ignorant.

Language

For many children the language of interviews is not their only or first language. Interviewers of monolingual speakers of the relevant language must also pay careful attention to their own use of language. Hence our third concern: what is the effect of the interviewer's use of language and perceived and actual linguistic proficiency on the design and conduct of research?

If a decision is taken to employ English with a group of children which includes those with minimal or no competence in English, the researcher may decide that competence in English is a criterion for selecting interviewees. This needs to be recognized and made explicit when reporting. Otherwise the data may be read as reflecting the perspectives of a wider group of children than is actually represented. Conversely, if the interviewer is multilingual and interviews in several languages, a high degree of linguistic awareness will be necessary when analysing the data, since questions in different languages carry different connotations. The use of interpreters can distance the fieldworker from the children's expression of their experience in multiple ways and complicate analysis.

The fieldworker needs to recognize the very uneven nature of 'bilingualism' in children. When I played a few sentences of a Punjabi story to Sikh children and asked them to retell it to me in English, some departed significantly from what they had heard, but without indicating that they had had difficulty in following it (Nesbitt and Jackson 1994). Had I not understood the Punjabi I would not have recognized the range of comprehension, as well as ability to articulate this in English, in the group.

One must also take into account the interviewees' perceptions of the interviewer's linguistic competence. In the course of the Warwick studies the Punjabis and Gujaratis frequently used words from Indian languages in speaking to me in English, whereas neither the Cypriots nor the Ukrainians used mother tongue in this way. It was necessary to consider the fact that English provided equivalent terms for words arising in European Christian cultural contexts (such as the Orthodox Church) but not for the language associated with Sikh and Hindu practice. But also to be considered in such circumstances is the extent to which one's own – however minimal – awareness of other languages affects conversational exchanges in English, for example the extent to which one uses words from these languages in questions and prompts. Even limited access to the child's community language(s) makes it possible to initiate and extend conversation, even if (as with almost all my interviewees) the children use English (or any other language selected for interviewing) with confidence.

Also at issue is whether speaking about religion particularly predisposes children to 'switch codes', in the case of English-medium interviews, embedding elements of their mother tongue in English sentences (Romaine 1989). This seems likely since, as Mills and Mills (1993: 64) have pointed out, 'certain settings appear particularly to encourage use of mother-tongue'. It is in the least ambiguously religious domains of their experience, such as corporate worship, that mother tongue (e.g. Gujarati) or a 'quasi-lect', an older cognate language such as Hebrew, Sanskrit or the Greek of the Orthodox liturgy (see Glinert 1993), is most likely to oust English.

However, it may be children's perception of the interviewer, at least as much as the subject matter, which is decisive in the level of code switching. During fieldwork with very young Punjabi children, Spann (1988) noted that switching occurs more between minor contacts, whereas good friends and complete strangers preferred the use of one language. Certainly, children's use of terms, whether as monolingual, bilingual or multilingual speakers of English, raises particular questions regarding the possible influence of the interview situation. For example, when in the Warwick studies a Baptist girl referred to the minister as 'vicar' and a Sikh girl referred to the *granthi* as 'priest', consideration of the reasons for this included discerning whether the speaker was allowing her assumptions about the interviewer to decide her choice of terms. Triangulation – for example considering the response of, respectively, a child and an adult from the same family or congregation in conjunction with literature about and by the 'membership group' – was useful in interpreting vocabulary. In this instance, checking revealed that while the Baptist was departing from Baptist practice in her choice of word, older Sikhs frequently used the word priest to translate '*granthi*'.

As far as possible the interviewer needs to avoid introducing group specific terminology and idiom, such as 'minister' or 'mass'. By using more general terms or circumlocutions (like 'the person taking the service'), one leaves the child the opportunity to demonstrate active knowledge by initiating the use of distinctive language.

Age

Does researching children's perspectives call for different methods of data gathering and interpretation? Powney and Watts (1987: 21) state unambivalently that 'in addition to the normal difficulties experienced by interviewers, there are extra problems when working with children'. With the exception of one longitudinal study, all the Warwick studies focused exclusively upon 8 to 13-year-olds. The factors which arise with children below the age of 8 (the subject of Hull 1991) will not be discussed here – they have already received scholarly attention. For example, Lewis (1992) provides references for discussions of such tendencies as distractability, readiness to be dishonest and their linguistic limitations. Here I am raising such questions as the extent to which and the age at which children can articulate a perspective on religion, and to what degree they are able to articulate a perspective other than that learned from parents and influential elders. Moreover, is a child's response more strongly conditioned by the interview situation than an older person's and how can researchers both minimize such conditioning and maximize their awareness of it?

Certainly, teacher-researchers conducting research into religion among their own pupils, and in a school setting, have sensitively to address the inherent imbalance of power, the children's and their own presuppositions about the relationship and factors which inhibit communication. Teachers have to learn to speak less than they would as teachers, 'to let the child talk freely, without ever checking or side tracking his utterance' (Piaget 1929: 10), to prompt in a less directive way than when teaching and to avoid correcting 'wrong' answers.

Children's age means that the range of possible gatekeepers includes not only religious leaders such as imams or temple committees, but also parents, guardians, teachers and LEAs. At an early stage in each of the Warwick studies, contact was made with religious organizations and the nature and purpose of the research was discussed with an authority figure (the priest or minister, for example, or the president of a temple committee) and the organizer of activities for children (e.g. in the Salvation Army, the young people's sergeant major). Potential children for interview were identified (with these gatekeepers' permission) by observing youth activities (such as Sunday school, youth club or Gujarati classes). The children who volunteered for interview gave me the name of their day school, and I sought the headteacher's permission to proceed. A letter which I had drafted was sent by the school to the children's parents for their formal consent.

Flexibility is necessary at this stage, because of different structural relationships between faith communities and the education system. The Warwick studies involved pupils at both Church of England and Roman Catholic schools. Unlike children in all the other denominations, the Roman Catholic children received their instruction in the faith and their preparation for life cycle rites (first communion and confirmation) in the school rather than the church. Gatekeepers may show their own criteria for recommending or sanctioning individuals – at least if they expect their community to be represented in publications on the basis of the research. A Sunday school teacher in an Anglican church enquired if I wanted only the 'Christians', whom he then defined as those individuals who had asked Jesus into their lives. An office bearer on a *gurdwara* committee insisted that I should not point the camera at 'clean shaven children' – in other words young Sikhs who featured in any photographs must be *keshdhari* (long haired), so conforming with 'the Sikh look'.

Of course the role of gatekeepers and the process of selecting children raises the issues of reliability, authenticity and validity. As an ethnographer, using qualitative methods, I am not employing the term reliability precisely as it is used in quantitative contexts. What can be achieved is transparency, so that imperfections, compromises and variables beyond the researcher's control are made explicit. Adherence to this basic principle results in data which can be of value in constructing hypotheses for testing in larger scale studies.

Paradigm of religions

The nature of religion throws up another fundamental issue – the effect that any conceptualization of religious traditions has on the criteria for selecting children and on collecting and analysing data. By this I mean that the 'world religions' approach, which is a paradigm for religious studies and religious education, is not value free, nor is it the only paradigm. Geaves (1998) has contested the assumption that individuals belong unproblematic-ally to one of a limited number of discrete communities of faith such as Islam. Anyone studying children's perspectives on their experience of religion must tackle the problematic nature of boundaries and the complexity and pluralism of identity, spirituality and allegiance in the global village of 'secular', broken, 'uncommitted' and 'mixed faith' families. Alertness to the risks of pigeon holing and stereotyping are crucial throughout the design of field studies and the collection and reporting of data. Partly because of decisions about the ultimate production of curriculum materials the Warwick studies were strongly influenced by a world religions approach. However, to take the example of the Punjabi children, not all attended places of worship that were incontrovertibly either Hindu or Sikh. More-over, even our 'committed' children were clearly influenced by more than just this one world religion or denomination. This is clear, for example, in children's overlapping, plural views of what happens after death (Nesbitt 1993a).

Interviews

Contribution of participant observation

Semi-structured interviews allow greater flexibility than fully structured ones, while also facilitating comparison. If these interviews are conducted in the context of participant observation in children's homes, schools, places of worship and supplementary classes the interviewer's flexibility can be grounded in observation and incipient insights from the field. Thus, for the Warwick studies, observation in places of worship, usually during corporate acts of worship, plus conversation (and semi-structured interviews) with key adults preceded and continued in parallel with the interviews with the children. This initial fieldwork can provide the pool of potential interviewees, shape the criteria for selecting them and the questions for the semi-structured interviews with them, and enables deeper understanding of the children's responses. Photographs taken in, for example, their places of worship provide visual stimuli to children's responses. If children meet the fieldworker on their home ground, in their churches or temples or religious classes, this can ease the relationship between interviewer and interviewee. Children know that in-group language and many community activities and details of ritual practice are unfamiliar to outsiders. The fieldworker's attendance, repeatedly where possible, encourages children's confidence in speaking about these areas of their experience.

Designing the schedule

The interview needs to be designed so that it progresses from initial enquiries with brief factual answers (such as 'Remind me of your full name') to questions which require more thought or a more trusting relationship with the interviewer, such as 'Tell me about any time when you have had a feeling that God was near you.' The opening questions relax the interviewee and build confidence. Any questions which risk causing any anxiety or embarrassment should be included (if at all) only towards the end.

The language of the question schedule must be pitched at an appropriate level in terms of vocabulary and sentence structure, neither condescendingly simple nor bafflingly complex. At the same time, in-group terms need to be kept to a minimum, until introduced by the child. If interviews are semi-structured or informal, the interviewer's language will be more spontaneous and variable from one interview to another, and so it will be additionally important to have the interviewers' cues on tape to facilitate analysis of the data. Transcripts which indicate pauses, intonation, emotion and similar detail are likely to require too much time to be feasible.

In the Warwick studies the basis of the initial interviews for children was the schedule devised by Knott (1992) for use with (older) young people in Leeds. (See Appendix 3 for the version that was used with Sikhs.)

Questions 9 and 10 invited the young person to 'talk about what an average weekday in term time might be like for you from the first moment someone gets up in your house' and 'How do weekends differ from weekdays?' These provided a wealth of insight into the children's lives as such topics as private devotion and congregational worship arose in the context of narrating their families' day-to-day experience.

In devising the question schedule, attention needs to be paid to including questions directed at all the areas one wishes to explore, to framing each question unthreateningly and unambiguously and to posing open questions ('How . . . ?'; 'Tell me about . . .') rather than closed ones with yes/no answers. Follow up questions/prompts needed to be thought of, especially for the most open questions ('Tell me what you do on an ordinary weekday').

Visual stimuli

Visual images are invaluable in the course of interviewing. In the case of the Warwick studies, the homes of all except Christian families from some denominations afforded visual stimuli for questions and answers. These were religious pictures (e.g. Hindu trade calendars featuring deities). Slides taken during participant observation linked this phase of the fieldwork with the interviews. Slides that are recent and local attract children's attention and stimulate animated conversation. In the Warwick studies the use of a piece of equipment previously unfamiliar to the children, but easy for them to operate, introduced activity into a session which was otherwise interview dominated and shifted the focus from the child to the image. Pictures that are incomplete can be of particular value to interviews as children demonstrate their knowledge by pointing out what is missing. So it was thanks to overexposed transparencies of images in a Hindu temple that I realized the detail and depth of two children's acquaintance with this shrine and its iconography.

Of course, sensitivity is vital when using photographs of religious activity as a research tool (Nesbitt 1993b). For example any temptation to photograph acts of worship must be resisted unless permission has been granted by a gatekeeper such as the secretary of the temple committee or the vicar of a church. This permission will depend upon factors such as the cultural norms of the congregation and the perceived aims (e.g. education) of the photography. For example Hindus tend readily to accept being photographed during worship but might withhold permission if they feared that pictures including the deities would be treated disrespectfully.

Diaries

Inviting children to keep diaries can be particularly valuable in individualizing and deepening subsequent interviews, by drawing out respondents' feelings and impressions. I explained to the children who were subjects of case studies that I was interested in their accounts of anything that they wished to write about either on a daily basis or less frequently, and that anything associated with their religion and 'community' would be of particular interest.

Venue and privacy

There are advantages in interviewing children individually. Using the school as the venue for initial interviews increased the likelihood of ensuring privacy. The respondents' homes provided the venue for follow up interviews. Any marked difference between a child's readiness to speak in the first and subsequent interviews correlated with whether others were within earshot on any occasion, and not with venue *per se*. The assumption that they would speak more readily alone was borne out by interviews in which another person was present. A teacher was in the same room as a Hindu boy who gave mostly monosyllabic answers, apart from the statement that 'religion's the most private thing'. Father was present in an interview with a Sikh girl who (though forthcoming in an earlier interview on her own) became almost mute, letting him answer the questions. Another Sikh girl spoke seriously and at length in her individual interview, but with her older sister present she did little other than giggle.

However, when interviewing children at home about their religion, it is also important to reassure parents by allowing others to be present if they wish. As a guest in others' houses, courtesy requires one to defer to parental preference and to fit into family life. In turn there are observable benefits for the collection of data as one notes interactions, glimpses joint family living and hears the ways in which other relatives brief the interviewee. Moreover discussions develop between siblings or between parents/ grandparents and children, and these impromptu 'group interviews' provide valuable insights.

Listening

Of paramount importance throughout – from first visit to the field to final analysis and respondent validation – is being 'a good listener' who is not 'trapped by his or her own ideologies or preconceptions' but 'sensitive and responsive to contradictory evidence' (Yin 1994: 56).

Listening was vital not only in the interview but also when reviewing the tape recordings and transcripts. Listening to the tapes confirmed that the pace of the interviews differed from, say, a radio interview. Pauses intersperse the dialogue and the fieldworker avoids coming in quickly on the tail of a child's attempt to articulate something of his or her experience of religion. The interviewer's tone is generally low and tentative, as non-threatening as possible. The children are encouraged to feel that there is time for them to think aloud. Prompts such as 'ah', 'really' or 'right' reassure the child that the interviewer is paying attention, without steering the child with more explicit cues.

Listening carries with it the responsibility to convey the emotion of children's statements when reporting their perspectives: for example an Irish Roman Catholic boy's sense of responsibility as a trusted server, the reverence of some young Sikh girls for a Baba, the excitement of a Baptist at asking Jesus into her life, and the isolation which a Quaker felt amid jingoistic peers and teachers during the Gulf War.

Emotion can be the key to detecting individual (as distinct from parental) perspectives. Such a glimpse is evident in a Gujarati Hindu girls' emphatic account of a conflict of interest when her mother wanted to listen to tape recordings of a celebrated Hindu preacher-singer and to take her along to hear him on the days when he was performing to vast audiences in Britain, whereas she herself just wanted to watch television (Jackson and Nesbitt 1993: 139).

Listening also exposes patterns of idiom within and between interviews. It throws up group specific language, such as the black Pentecostals' 'being filled' (for 'being filled with the Holy Spirit', a state which manifests itself in such distinctive behaviour as glossalalia) and concerns, such as (for the Orthodox and the Pentecostal churches) the Devil. Attention to the children's use of language provided such insights as the probable equivalence of young Sikhs' use of the word 'God' to the Punjabi term 'Baba', which encompasses the scriptures and spiritual masters including the ten Gurus (Nesbitt and Jackson 1995). It also reveals similes and analogies: a Hindu likening a coconut to a christingle or speaking of being a 'bridesmaid' and Sikhs describing their naming ceremony as 'christening'. Reflection confirms that, instinctively, children are 'building bridges' between their faith community's practices and those (such as christening) known to them from the wider, English speaking, Christianity moulded society to which they assume I belong.

The listening, attentive quality of the data analysis requires a disciplined procedural framework. In the Warwick studies analysis used coding to identify themes together with the computer search facility. Data from interviews, once transcribed, could be sorted by the child's group, by interview question and by theme.

Listening is also vital to the final stage – of respondent validation – when the interviewee offers feedback on the ethnographer's account. In the case of children it is inappropriate to seek their feedback (rather than their elders') on academic text, but their feedback on drafts of curriculum books can be illuminating. For example 12-year-old Anita's reaction to being named in a curriculum book was one of concern lest this be bad for her ego.

Researching continuities and discontinuities

As young adults, some Hindus reflected on an ethnographic report of their lives as children (Jackson and Nesbitt 1993). This occurred during the follow up phase (nine years after the previous fieldwork) of a longitudinal study of young British Hindus' perceptions of their religious tradition. Such a study makes it possible to identify changes and continuities in the young people's perspectives upon their experience of religion and allows them to comment upon this as well, for instance in reaction to seeing the transcript from an interview nine years previously. In this Warwick study, data analysis reveals striking resonances – in some cases almost verbatim – between individuals' comments nine years apart. Changes and continuities in their perspectives require the researcher to reflect upon contributory factors such as peer pressure, the media, involvement in supplementary classes or a *sampradaya* (sectarian group), or the impact of a visiting charismatic leader, or indeed the effect of involvement in the research itself (Nesbitt 1999a, 1999b, 1999c).

Most longitudinal studies of religion in children's lives have examined successive cohorts rather than following the same individuals. The Warwick study suggests the value of longitudinal studies, not only for plotting continuity and change but also for deeper understanding of the significance of childhood experience. This longitudinal study has highlighted methodological issues which arise: the optimum interval between studies and the relationship between the question schedules. Comparability requires common questions, but intervening events and the increased maturity of the respondents has to be accommodated.

Why research children's perspectives on religion?

Children's experience of religion is arguably as wide as their experience of life itself, even if one does not include 'implicit religion' (Bailey 1998), a term used for, among other things, 'some kind of inherent religiosity' in such areas of 'secular life' as football matches or political rallies. Certainly, religion can mean many things, as the diversity of scholarly models suggests. For Smart (1968, 1971) religion exists in 'six dimensions': the doctrinal, mythological, ethical, ritual, experiential and social. Jackson's (1997) theoretical work foregrounds the levels of 'individual', 'membership group' and 'faith tradition'. The width of religion's embrace is a powerful reason for wishing to understand children's perspectives on it.

The need for teachers to be aware of children's perspectives on their experience of religion, if meaningful communication is to occur, was fundamental to the curriculum materials (the Warwick RE Project) which were informed by the field studies.[1] It can be the very children who are members of a faith community who apparently make the most basic factual mistakes when assessed according to what the curriculum books tell us about their belief and practice. So, for example, research among Sikh children (and their parents) sheds light on the discrepancy between their statement that 'we have ten gods' (the Gurus) and the presentation of Sikhism as emphatically monotheistic practice (Nesbitt and Jackson 1995).

More generally, teachers cannot treat all children 'equally' if they assume that, for example, their birthday parties conform to one (western, non-religious) model (Nesbitt 1995). Birthdays are marked with ritual and this may (in some South Asian families at least) be the worship distinctive of a particular faith community.

Not only teachers but also social workers may require an awareness of children's experience of religion and their perspectives on this (e.g. Crompton 1996). Or, to take an example from the legal profession, matrimonial cases in which religion plays a part – as in custody cases involving the partners in mixed faith marriages – increasingly necessitate 'expert' advice based on knowledge of religion in children's lives.

Children's perspectives on religion are also of concern to the wider study of religion, since – as Hyde points out – it is during their childhood and adolescence that people's

traditional beliefs are learned and individual beliefs formulated, individual and group religious practices and rituals meaningfully established, feelings such as awareness, trust and awe developed, relevant religious knowledge acquired, and the individual and social effects of religious commitment worked out.

(Hyde 1990: 350)

Despite this fact, most of the numerous psychological studies of religious experience – at least in Britain – have involved adult subjects (sometimes recalling and interpreting their childhood experiences): children's perspectives are needed to supplement these studies.

Conclusion

Whether or not a child's religion is a sensitive topic, sensitivity – expressed in a listening approach – is crucially important at each stage of research into children's perspectives on their experiences of religion. This is no substitute for rigorous attention to other methodological principles. Sensitivity must be grounded systematically in the researcher's strategic and on the spot decisions in diverse cultural contexts. These require an ever growing resource of data, deliberate attention to the detail of young people's faith traditions and awareness of the necessarily interpretative nature of ethnography.

Some of the best insights into children's perspectives come unexpectedly, stimulated not by the question designed with that aspect of experience in mind but by a visual cue or by some other question. Qualitative research provides the opportunity for this to happen as well as a depth and detail which valuably supplement quantitative data. The Warwick studies suggest the value of a methodology in which interviewing and participant observation continuously interact. The data analysis requires that same attentive listening mode which encourages children to be forthcoming during interviews. Longitudinal study additionally allows for a retrospective view of change and continuity of individuals' perspectives through childhood and early adulthood and confirms our recognition of the reflexive character of research, and the responsibility which this lays on anyone investigating children's experience of religion.

Note

1 The Warwick RE Project (Heinemann) consists of two series: *Bridges to Religions* (Key Stages 1 and 2) see Jackson *et al.* 1994, Barratt and Price 1996 and Everington 1996b, and *Interpreting Religions* (Key Stage 3) e.g. Wayne *et al.* 1996. The intention was that pupils learn about faith traditions through reading about young people's involvement, via 'membership groups' such as a Christian denomination. This learning entails pupils 'building bridges' between these young people's experience and their own and being 'edified' by this encounter and reflection (Jackson 1997: 111–12).

(12) A 'risky' business: researching the health beliefs of children and young people

ALAN FRANCE, GILL BENDELOW AND SIMON WILLIAMS

This chapter arises from research conducted for the National Health Executive under the South Thames Mother and Child Health Programme. Fieldwork was conducted over six months in three different LEA comprehensive schools in the English West Midlands (Bendelow *et al.* 1998). The schools involved were located in different geographical areas with students from Year 7 (11- and 12-year-olds) and Year 10 (14- and 15-year-olds).

In the first section of this chapter, we outline the major practical and ethical issues that researchers need to consider if a more grounded approach to researching children and young people is to be implemented. In the second section we discuss these issues in the light of our own experience, highlighting some of the difficulties and dilemmas such an approach can raise in the process of doing child or young person centred fieldwork. In the third section we draw out the implications of our experience for the development of child or young person centred approaches to doing research.

Understanding childhood and youth: the importance of 'grounded theory'

Since the late 1980s there has been a growing recognition that children and young people can make a major contribution to our understanding of childhood and youth. Children (O'Brien *et al.* 1996) and young people (Willis *et al.* 1990) are being seen as 'creators' and social actors who are active in creating themselves in different social contexts. As James and Prout (1996) suggest, this is a shift away from an emphasis on structure to that of agency where children are recognized as people in their 'own right'. Children are therefore seen as having a perception and experience of childhood that greatly enhances our understanding, in late modernity, of childhood. This is not to deny the importance of structure or biology but to suggest that childhood is a negotiated process where children are active in constructing their own social worlds, and reflecting upon and understanding its meaning and significance to their own personal lives.

This 'new' approach to understanding childhood and youth also requires a methodology that puts the child or young person at the centre of focus – one that recognizes their social relationships and cultures as 'worthy of study in their own right' (James and Prout 1990). Mayall (1996), for example, argues that this approach needs to have three major components. First, it has to conceptualize and accept children as competent reporters of their own experiences, recognizing that they are capable of reflexivity. Second, giving children a voice means taking them seriously and putting their views at the centre of analysis. Third, the aim of research should be to work *for* children rather than *on* them and to describe their social worlds with a view of influencing social change. Such a methodology also requires a grounded approach to developing theory. Again as Mayall (1996) argues:

> The construction of an argument needs to be sensitive to its quality of fit – a theory has to be measured against the experiences of those it purports to describe. There needs to be an interaction between theory and the experience, each building on and refining the other.
>
> (Mayall 1996: 12–13)

Theory, in other words, should not be the driving force to conceptualizing the lives of children and young people; rather it should *emerge* from the data under investigation. Such an approach is clearly influenced by the writings of Glaser and Strauss (1967) and their work on 'grounded theory'. They argue that theory should be generated from the 'empirical world' ensuring that the theoretical model that evolves from the data 'must fit the situation being researched' (Glaser and Strauss 1967: 3). Theoretical models should not be imposed as a final result but they should emerge from the data in the process of analysis. Such an approach has been challenged because of its problems of theoretical modelling (Mason 1998) and the difficulties associated with turning it into practice (Bulmer 1979; Hammersley and Atkinson 1984; Roseneil 1993; Bryman and Burgess 1994) yet as a method it is recognized as offering an effective approach to understanding social phenonoma (Burgess 1982; Hammersley and Atkinson 1984; Bryman and Burgess 1994; Coffey and Atkinson 1996).

Constructing a child or young person centred approach: principles and practice

Developing a method that is grounded in the views and experiences of children and young people does not differ from other forms of research practice. Yet, this is not to say that the methodology required does not recognize 'difference'. Researching children and young people needs to recognize a number of factors. First, there are inherent tensions that exist between adults and youth which may well create difficulties for the social researcher (Davies 1982). Age differences between the researched and the researcher therefore may well create a gap that needs to be addressed (Pollard 1987). Second, traditional approaches of engaging research subjects may not be the best suited methods for creating opportunities for children and young people to express their views (Hazel 1996). Third, researching children and young people has an ethical dimension that is specific to this age group. Questions of consent and confidentiality, for example, raise a number of issues the researcher needs to consider in designing a research methodology that is child or young person centred (Alderson 1995).

'Bridging the gap': age and research

Getting access to, and understanding, the complexities of children's worlds can be greatly influenced by age. Pollard (1987) has argued that researchers need to think carefully about their identity, suggesting that how they are perceived by participants is an essential component of 'bridging the gap' between researcher and researched. He suggests that being someone they can trust or someone that is fun to be around can aid the process. Being seen not as a 'proper adult' is therefore crucial to getting young people's involvement. Butler and Williamson (1994: 39) go further, however, arguing that the identity the researcher creates must not be an attempt to 'go native':

> Age inevitably, unavoidably, creates its barriers and divisions and no child or young person wants to talk to any adult who is patently falsely projecting too youthful an image or persona or self consciously letting fly with contemporary street *argot*.
>
> (Butler and Williamson 1994: 39)

Butler and Williamson argue that 'bridging the gap' involves more than just constructing an identity that is acceptable. They believe that four key factors are important to consider if bridges are to be built effectively. First, researchers need to engage with young people in a role of 'naive curiosity' which is honest, open and empathetic. This must not stray on to the condescending or patronizing. Second, judgemental attitudes about young people's beliefs and behaviours should be avoided. Research is concerned with unravelling why young people might have views that are challenging or different from others. Third, the researcher has a responsibility to nurture young people's curiosity and provide opportunities for them to present their own views and to explore the complexity of issues under examination. Finally, the researcher needs to be creative and flexible. If the bridge is to be built then the research framework needs to recognize participants' experience and, of course, their lack of it. Dealing with young people's desire to talk about other issues or to express little interest requires the researcher to develop methods that are more engaging and challenging.

Engaging the young in research

Such an approach paradoxically suggests, therefore, that on the one hand, we recognize children and young people as no different from other research participants yet, on the other hand, as in some senses 'different'. This also relates to how we get children and young people to report their own views and experiences. Traditional methods of engaging research participants revolve around the questionnaire and interview, but these processes can, for certain groups of young people, be alienating. Researchers therefore have to devise and construct research methods that open opportunities to involve young people and children in different ways (Hazel 1996). One such approach is the 'draw and write' technique. This method involves inviting young people or children to draw a response to the question under consideration and then to write a short explanation of what is happening and who is involved. Such a method has since been developed to include 'labels' thus aiming to eliminate any uncertainty about meaning. Evidence concerning the success of this approach is now strengthening suggesting that it is a powerful tool for exploring children's and young people's perceptions and experiences (A. Oakley *et al.* 1995; Pridmore and Bendelow 1995).

Another approach has been suggested by Hazel (1996), who argues that if communication between adults and young people is to be increased and improved, methods need to build on young people's experiences and interests. Vignettes, for example, allow young participants opportunities to explore their own perceptions and beliefs about a given situation. They can be valuable tools as 'ice breakers' (Finch 1987) and for building young people's confidence (Hazel 1996). Vignettes are also valuable to the researcher, enabling the discussion to move from a more abstract to focused level and providing opportunities for participants to be to more reflective of their wider and personal experience. Other similar tools can aid participation. For example, photographs and popular culture offer opportunities for researchers to locate discussions about particular issues. Soap operas and TV documentaries are important aspects of young people's lives which may offer a topic for discussion and debate (A. Oakley *et al.* 1995; Hazel 1996).

Considering ethical questions

Interest in ethics and social research has a long established history, one that has influenced how and on whom research should be undertaken (Burgess 1982; Punch 1986; Homan 1991). Ethics as a subject of inquiry arose from philosophies concerned about moral action. As Homan (1991: 1) suggests, 'Ethics is the science of morality; those who engage in it determine values for the regulation of human behaviour'. On one side are ethical absolutists, who are guided by Kantian legislative reason and appeals to duty, and on the other, there are those who adopt a more relativist stance. One area where this has had a strong influence is in medicine, where an ethical code of practice has been central to the professional control of standards and practices. Developments in the social sciences have seen attempts by academic communities to emulate the medical profession by constructing and implementing codes of conduct for researchers (see Lindsay, Chapter 1 in this book). For example, the British Sociological Association published its statement of ethical practice in 1993, laying down key principles that researchers should adhere to in the practice of social research (BSA 1993). Three main areas were highlighted: professional integrity; relationships with and responsibilities towards research participants; and relations with and responsibilities towards sponsors and/or funders. Within this document sociologists are told that they have a responsibility to participants to ensure they are not harmed by the research, that consent to participate is freely given, and that confidentiality and anonymity is respected. While such documents have limitations, in that they are only guidelines (but see Chapter 1), they aim to set down clear criteria and codes of practice that ensure professional standards are maintained and implemented by the social researcher community.

When it comes to research with children and young people, the BSA document offers little help in clarifying what our practice should look like. This is not surprising in that the history of ethics and research with children and young people has been marginalized or limited to discussions about ethical considerations in doing medical research (Alderson 1995). What has been written in this area focuses on two issues; informed consent and confidentiality and anonymity (Alderson 1995; Butler and Williamson 1994; I. Shaw 1996).

Alderson (1995), for example, highlights the importance of 'consent' as a guiding principle to practice. In her discussion on ethical research on children, she argues that informed consent is central. Children, she proposes should be consulted at all stages of the work, allowing them opportunities to change their minds and to refuse further involvement. Part of this process requires them to be well informed and to have the correct knowledge on which to make their decisions. This includes being clear about the costs and benefits to themselves about participation. Others support such a position. Pollard (1987), for example, argues that ethical research with young people requires the researcher to be open and honest about the process and proposed outcomes. To make informed decisions young people need all the relevant information.

At one level this issue seems unproblematic, yet there is much uncertainty about who should be consulted for consent. For example, 16 to 18-year-olds are seen as young adults and entitled to make decisions for themselves but when it comes to younger children issues of competence and rights are raised. There is a long running debate about children's rights in decision making processes which remains unresolved. Questions about the need to consult parents and gain permission for children and young people to participate remains unresolved. Alderson (1995: 22) suggests that 'the safest course, though it can also be repressive, is to ask parental consent and also ask for children's consent, when they are able to understand'. While Hudson (1996: 6) has argued that consent from parents should be gained the overriding consideration should be the child's consent: 'I told students that although I was sending a letter home about parental consent . . . it was the individual student's choice whether or not to be interviewed.' This, however, still does not resolve the difficulty of the child who wants to participate but is refused permission by parents. Butler and Williamson (1994) suggest that in such circumstances the will of the parents must be respected.

The second issue relates to issues of confidentiality and anonymity. Alderson (1995), while giving limited attention to such issues, suggests that children and young people should clearly be consulted about how the data are to be collected and how confidentiality and anonymity are to be assured. Difficulties surrounding issues of confidentiality can and do arise, however, suggesting that 'No one has an absolute right to confidentiality' (Alderson 1995: 19). Such a position is supported by writers such as Fine and Sandstrom (1988: 27), who argue that 'Children can place themselves in danger. In that event, an adult participant has a moral obligation to assist them in way that is "protective".'

What these 'dangers' are remain ill defined, although Alderson (1995) suggests that if a breach of confidentiality is necessary, it should be undertaken in full consultation with the young person. Again no solution is offered here to the possibility that the child or young person might refuse permission to disclosure. Others take a more 'absolute' position towards the breaking of confidentiality. Hudson (1996) argues that confidentiality must not be broken. If trust and respect are to be gained, the researcher must protect the confidentiality at all costs.

Hudson herself admits, however, that this position can and does come under pressure, especially in relation to behaviour that she sees as problematic.

In many cases, for example, it is pragmatic to avoid situations rather than deal with them, therefore, regarding places where risk taking and illegal activities take place it is easier to 'steer well clear' (Hudson 1996: 11). Butler and Williamson (1994) take a similar line to confidentiality, arguing that if young people disclose something that is of concern then the obligation of the researcher is to negotiate and discuss possible action with the young person. But as they argue, this has to be conducted with the 'security of complete confidentiality – meaning that further action will only be taken with the full consent and knowledge of the child' (Butler and Williamson 1994: 42). Confidentiality should therefore be absolute for Butler and Williamson.

Ethical dilemmas and tensions in practice

Having argued for the importance and centrality of these practices and ethics to child and young person centred research, we now turn attention to our attempts to implement them into our fieldwork. In the discussion that follows we intend to highlight the tensions and difficulties that arise from trying to develop a fully working practice of child and youth centred research methods in the field of health and risk taking.

The fieldwork

The fieldwork was located in three separate schools. All young people, from Years 7 and 10, undertook structured activities in personal and social education (PSE) lessons. First, they completed a 'write and draw' exercise where they were asked to draw someone taking a 'risk' or doing something 'risky'. Once drawn, they were asked to label it, outlining what the risk was, why it was risky and if they would take the risk. The second exercise was a questionnaire, designed to collect aggregate data on young people's beliefs about health, lifestyle and risk taking. It was constructed so that the majority of young people could read it while also having a strong emphasis on being 'open ended', therefore encouraging young people to define the issues for themselves. The fieldwork also involved focus groups, which have become recognized as a good method of gaining a group's views about particular issues. They are also seen as a successful method of getting a more in-depth understanding of social phenomema.

Young people were invited to volunteer their participation. Four sessions were organized for each group covering four distinct themes: young people's lifestyle; definitions of risk and risk taking; definitions of health and risk taking; young people's experience of health promotion and education. Within these discussions vignettes were used to get young people to explore key issues surrounding decisions about health and beliefs about risk and risk taking. For example, at the time of the research the BBC television soap *EastEnders* was running a story line on one of its young characters (Joe) who was suffering a mental illness. Participants in our study were encouraged to outline the story and discuss how emotional health and illness were being portrayed and how their own views agreed or conflicted with such a representation.

Bridging the gap: beyond identity

Getting young people to volunteer for the focus group work was essential but this involved building up their trust in both the researcher and the research. This was especially relevant because we wished to explore questions of 'risk' and 'risk taking'. Having such an agenda could clearly have created difficulties, in that young people may well have thought questioning would be too personal and would have required them to reveal details about their own risk taking behaviour. Relationship building and retaining young people's trust required many visits to the school where the researcher needed to hang about at breaktimes and before and after school. It was important that the researcher interacted with young people outside the classroom and tried to be accepted as a non-adult. Hanging about is a well known research activity (Whyte 1943) and one that allows the researcher to get to know participants in more informal ways. Being there, joining in conversations and asking questions about everyday events helped to build relationships. Initially, such behaviour, by an adult, was viewed by young people as strange or weird but eventually, after much questioning and the discussion, it was seen as a normal part of the day. Trust was gained through the researcher being accepted and someone that showed interest in what they had to say. This led to young people showing signs of trust. For example, at one site the researcher was used as a go-between, taking notes and passing on personal messages between friends. Young people recognized that this information did not get passed on to the teaching staff (or other young people), neither were they confronted with moral judgements from the researcher.

Creating a distance from the teaching staff was also important. Young people have limited trust of teachers, therefore being seen not only as a non-adult but also as a non-teacher was important if young people were to feel at ease with the fieldwork. Locating the research within the library and not the staff room, dressing less formally and differently from teachers, and also encouraging young people to use the researcher's first name, all helped to bridge the gap between the researcher and young people. One clear advantage that researchers have over teachers is that discipline is not the researcher's responsibility, therefore boundaries are there to be crossed. At one level this approach clearly worked in that we had over 65 young people involved in the focus groups.

Such an approach, like all others, also has its limits. Clearly, many young people remained cautious, keeping back details of their personal feelings and lives. Letting a stranger in was something many resisted. Gaining young people's trust and being accepted was never totally successful. The gap between the adult researcher and young person can be bridged only in short steps; the researcher's involvement is only a small part of a young person's life and, in most cases, insignificant to the everyday order of events. There is no advantage or gain for the young person in having the bridge crossed. In fact such a relationship with a stranger over a short period of time, may itself be risky in that they will feel vulnerable to any such adult interest and interference. Such a relationship therefore benefits the researcher rather then the young person.

Who gains from research was also an issue raised in other discussions with young people. Some groups were unwilling to get involved, rejecting requests to volunteer. These young people displayed a cynical and uninterested approach to the research, suggesting that they saw little value or reason for getting involved. They continually asked the question 'What was in it for them?' At one level we did not have the response that would convince them. Usually, we argued that their contribution would give us a better understanding of what it means to be young, which *could* then shape future policy around health education and access to information. But none of this would benefit them directly; instead it would have greater impact for generations that followed. Many young people thought that this was enough, but others thought that unless it had more direct or immediate benefits, they were not willing to get involved. These young people suggested that adults continually demand their participation in activities that promote the 'common good' but little is given back in return. Young people are expected to be 'good citizens' but little attention is given to their own needs as citizens (France 1996).

Informed consent and questions of confidentiality

As previously discussed, informed consent is an important aspect of young person centred approaches, but within the context of schools such a principle is difficult to implement. First, getting consent from young people involved a lengthy negotiation between guardians and stakeholders. Local authority officials, headteachers, parents and teachers were all involved in the process of gaining access to the views and beliefs of young people. Participation and consent by young people is not simply under their control. Decisions about their participation can be made before they are even aware that a request has been made for their involvement.

A second difficulty regarding consent arose in discussions with headteachers and teachers. Having recognized the problems that our strategy of 'giving young people a choice' raised, we decided to implement our principles in the classroom work with young people. Teachers were consulted about offering young people the option of not taking part in the classroom work. We suggested that, in the research introduction, we would inform young people they had a right to withdraw, and that alternative provision would be available. Offering such a choice raised three key issues. First, offering young people choices to opt out of classes went against the ethos and culture of schools. Teachers saw choice as a limited option, and one not to be encouraged within the school setting. Second, discussions with teachers focused on the practical application of this process, and their desire not to reward opting out. They generally suggested that the alternative should be school work and learning tasks. In other words young people were not to be rewarded but isolated and made to do school work for deciding against participation. Third, we felt uneasy about challenging teachers. Not only did we hold strong principles on this matter, but also we were concerned that large numbers of young people opting out would affect our ability to fulfil our research obligations to the funder, and would also have created anxieties and concerns about meeting our objectives. Offering choice was, therefore, a 'risky' business for us.

Implementing the practice of absolute confidentiality within the research also had its problems. Two key issues brought this question to the fore. First, we quickly became aware that 'confidentiality' could have different meanings to different people. In our introductions, to teachers and staff, we explained the importance of this for our work and asked for their cooperation to maintain confidentiality within the research process. No teacher questioned this principle or asked for clarification or explanation. It was assumed, by us, that teachers had the same understanding of what confidentiality meant, but we soon discovered that this was not necessarily the case. Some teachers saw themselves as having *in loco parentis* responsibilities that gave them the right to know what students were doing and, in some cases, what they were saying. Clearly, teachers and schools do have certain responsibilities which mirror those of parents, but how far these extend into knowing *everything* about the actions and behaviour of young people under their charge is questionable. In many cases this view was also underpinned by beliefs that schools cannot be private or have spaces and places that teachers are refused access to. Part of this arises because of concerns about discipline but it also relates to teachers' rights to know.

Two examples make the point. In all the schools we set up focus groups to run at lunchtime. Classroom space was negotiated and young people informed that this, while the focus group was running, was 'their space' but it soon became clear that teachers did not recognize such a position. Teachers would continually enter the room without knocking and ask the group to ignore their presence. Teachers would want to stay, suggesting that they would 'not get in the way'. The reason for being there usually related to their having to prepare lessons or catch up on marking, which is quite understandable, yet they had difficulty in seeing how this was a problem for confidentiality. A second example relates to the implementation of the questionnaire. Teachers were informed that their role was to hand out the questionnaires and arrange collection after completion. Guidance notes were prepared giving teachers information on how they should respond to certain questions. Throughout this short document teachers were asked to 'create an atmosphere where young people felt confident that confidentiality would be maintained'. Such demands are difficult to implement within classrooms but it was also the case that some teachers did not see themselves included in this request. It was not unusual for the members of the research team to visit classrooms and find teachers looking over the shoulders of students while they wrote. In one case, a teacher was found reading a completed questionnaire and discussing the contents with the student concerned. Such actions clearly undermined our attempts to convince young people that confidentiality was an important principle to our practice.

A second problem with the notion of absolute confidentiality arose over issues of child protection. In our opening discussions with schools, the question was raised over what our response was to be if there was a disclosure of sexual abuse. As a response to the Children Act 1989, schools have been developing their internal policies about responding to disclosure. It was therefore a reasonable request and expectation that we would have considered how we would deal with such an issue. It was also the case that our work was concerned with 'risk' and 'risk taking'. We were a group of strangers who would, when our work was completed, leave the area. We were offering young people a confidential space to talk about risk and, although we were interested in their beliefs about 'risk' and 'risk taking in health', the agenda focus may well have been seen by a young person, who was being abused, as an opportunity to talk about their own abuse. In constructing the research, our initial approach was to protect and maintain this absolute position. In other words if young people did disclose to us, then we would discuss with them further action they wanted to take allowing them autonomy and control. In consequence if they decided not to report it or take it further we would respect their views. But was such a position justifiable?

After much discussion with colleagues we decided that as adults we had other obligations that challenged our position of ethical absolutism. First, at a pragmatic level, researchers do not have the power to claim confidential status. In a court of law, claiming similar rights as lawyers and doctors to confidentiality would not be accepted. Social researchers do not have special privilege and would be forced by a court of law to reveal sources. Also under the Children Act 1989, all adults who work with young people have a legal responsibility to report sexual abuse to the appropriate authority. Social researchers are not exempt from such a legal requirement. Second, as adults (and researchers) we have a *moral* obligation to protect young people 'at risk' or 'in danger'. To suggest that if, after much discussion and persuasion, a young person decides not to take further action, we would allow the abuse to carry on, is to ignore our moral responsibilities to vulnerable individuals. This is not, of course, to say that we should not try to support and guide young people in their decision making process, but it is to recognize that we have other moral obligations that override, in certain circumstances, our responsibilities to the notion of 'absolute confidentiality and anonymity'.

The recognition of these legal and moral obligations resulted in us changing our research practice. In line with the notion of informed consent, we decided that we had an obligation to inform young people what our policy on confidentiality was. In our introduction we therefore announced that 'we offered complete confidentiality although if any disclosure of sexual abuse was made then we had an obligation to take appropriate action'. Our rationale for this statement was that those who may have considered disclosure would be clearly informed of what our ultimate response would be, therefore allowing them to make an informed decision about disclosure themselves. It was not our intention to discourage disclosure, only to provide young people with the relevant information they needed to make such a decision.

Conclusion

In this chapter we have tried to show why and how a youth or child centred focused approach should underpin research with young people and children. We have also drawn upon our own fieldwork experiences to show how the principles of such an approach are tested and challenged by the context of implementing the process within schools. Having a commitment and practice that encourages participation is essential but clearly other factors need to shape and influence any such approach.

In this chapter, three issues have been raised. First, if we are to gain a greater understanding of young people and children's social worlds, we clearly have to develop an approach that builds trust between the researcher and the researched as an *active*, ongoing process. Having an identity that is non-threatening or non-adult like is important, but this 'gap' is not just a symbolic space between generations. It is also built on hierarchical power relationships and adult expectations of the responsibilities of the young. Being able to explore their social worlds therefore needs researchers to concentrate upon not only image and identity, but also the nature of the relationship in terms of who gains what, when, where and how.

Second, achieving informed consent within a school setting is not without its problems. Not only does it reflect young people or children's experience of their relationships with adults, but also it highlights the lack of control they have over making decisions about their lives. Challenging this within the school setting, as we have seen, is difficult, especially as such an approach may bring researchers into conflict with teachers who make decisions about access. This is not made any easier by the pressures we, as researchers, feel under because of our responsibilities to funders. It is not, however, to say that researchers should trade creation of opportunities to participants to be *actively* involved in decisions about their participation. In constructing research with children and young people, how precisely this practice is to be implemented should be a central concern within debates on access.

Finally, we have to recognize that the notion of absolute confidentiality is not morally or pragmatically defensible. Social researchers have legal and moral obligations that require them to take action if a young person is 'at risk' or 'in danger'. Such an issue should not, however, be a major problem to gaining young people's trust and involvement. Being honest, open and truthful about why such issues are important and engaging young people in discussions which treat them as individuals who have feelings, views and experiences to share and the ability to make decisions for *themselves*, all of which supports the notion of young person and child centred approaches. By not being honest, we reinforce the gap between generations and relegate their views and opinions to one of 'incompetent child'.

(13) Collecting the views of young people with moderate learning difficulties

DEBRA COSTLEY

There are over 87,000 children with statements of special educational need who attend segregated special schools in England and Wales. That is just under half of all those who have statemented special needs (DfE 1994b). Of those over 50 per cent attend special schools for pupils with moderate learning difficulties (MLD) (Audit Commission 1992). Many of these are small schools catering for the full range of pupils from 5 to 16 years old.

Young people labelled as having moderate learning difficulties are a diffuse group with a variety of individual learning needs. However, there are characteristics which many of them share, including low self-esteem and self-confidence; difficulty with basic skills such as literacy and numeracy; and underdeveloped personal and social skills. The Warnock Committee (Department of Education and Science (DES) 1978), who first introduced the term, defined MLD as those difficulties which may stem from a variety or combination of causes. 'These often include mild and multiple physical and sensory disabilities, an impoverished or adverse social or educational background, specific learning difficulties and limited general ability' (DES 1978: 219).

Bell (1998) agrees that it is difficult to define precisely what constitutes moderate to severe learning difficulties but suggests that most pupils will, to a lesser or greater extent, have difficulty in, among other things: gaining access to the curriculum through normal teaching and learning approaches, acquiring concepts and achieving the standards expected in terms of National

Curriculum level descriptors; processing language and instructions; expressing their own ideas; retaining and applying previous learning. In addition young people with moderate learning difficulties may exhibit emotional and/or behavioural difficulties. Behaviours include attention seeking, difficulties with concentration, lack of motivation, disruption, displays of frustration and temper and even violence. The interplay of difficulties with learning, social and emotional or behavioural problems combine in an infinite variety of ways to make the characteristics of young people with moderate learning difficulties extremely varied and challenging. This has implications for conducting research with this group of pupils.

Any definition of MLD is contentious and open to subjective interpretation. Tomlinson (1982) suggested that it would be more difficult to achieve normative agreement on what constitutes MLD than it would be to reach consensus on the normative status of visual impairment, for example. The arguments about labelling are well rehearsed. However, in the present system of education the emphasis is still on the difficulties of the individual, rather than the system (*Code of Practice on the Identification and Assessment of Special Educational Needs*: DfE 1994a; DfEE 1997a).

Considering the numbers of children and teachers involved in special education, focusing on moderate learning difficulties, there is very little literature describing their experiences. The Education Reform Act 1988 brought in legislation that made significant changes to the content and organization of school curricula. Teachers working in MLD special schools had no research and knowledge base on which to structure their interpretation and implementation of the National Curriculum. Nevertheless, teachers welcomed the equality and entitlement of the National Curriculum and began planning for maximum access for all pupils (Her Majesty's Inspectorate (HMI) 1991). The challenge in MLD schools was to make sure that the National Curriculum met the statemented needs of their pupils, by reconciling individual needs with the opportunity to have access to the same learning experiences as their peers. (See also Begley, Chapter 8, and Detheridge, Chapter 9, for discussion of research involving children with learning difficulties.)

Scope of the research

I was working as a teacher in a special school when the National Curriculum was first introduced. I was responsible for Key Stage 4 and all activities relevant to Years 10 and 11 (14 to 16-year-olds). As more and more subjects came on stream and accreditation began to evolve, I became increasingly concerned that we were no longer able to spend as much time on the leavers' curriculum. Aspects of personal and social education, college links, careers and work experience were crucial to young people with moderate learning difficulties about to leave school. The young people I was teaching noticed the changes in the curriculum and missed some of the opportunities that they knew previous groups had experienced. In 1993 I felt that I was no longer able to do what I felt was right for the pupils. I was keen to see how other education authorities had responded to the initiative of the National Curriculum (NC) so I applied to study for a PhD. The case study research described in this chapter formed part of that research, which also included a large scale postal questionnaire.

During 1994–5 I spent one term in each of three special schools for MLD pupils. This was five years after the introduction of the NC. Each school was a focus for a detailed case study that aimed to evaluate the impact of the NC on individual schools and to document the reaction of staff to that initiative. The three schools were all in the same LEA so had received the same training and support for the introduction of the NC, but each had evolved different strategies for coping with it in practice. Two schools were all age special schools (5 to 16-year-olds) and the third was secondary age only. Of the two all age schools, one had adopted a subject based curriculum to cope with the NC, while the second school had adopted a cross-curricular approach to teaching at Key Stage 4. Both maintained a primary model of school organization with class teachers taking a majority of lessons with their class group of pupils. The secondary age special school was run like a mainstream secondary with subject specialists and specialist teaching rooms.

Time was spent in each school getting to know the staff and the pupils involved in Key Stage 4 work. This involved spending time in classrooms and sometimes helping pupils with work. It also involved talking informally to all staff, teaching and non-teaching, to build up a picture of the school and its ethos. Semi-structured interviews were conducted with the headteacher, deputy head and the Key Stage 4 teachers in each school. Documents were collected and lessons observed. The pupil interviews formed part of this data collection. The research focused on the impact of the subject curriculum on the whole curriculum experienced by pupils at Key Stage 4. The views of pupils in Years 10 and 11 were considered crucial for a complete analysis of the impact of the NC on the curriculums experienced by pupils. All three schools had made changes to curricular organization, teaching and learning methods and assessment of learning. The pupils were aware of the changes and (to a certain extent) of what had brought them about. Therefore, this was an important time in their education, involving changes, and about which they would have thoughts and feelings. They after all are the consumers of education, which makes their views important, and often illuminating.

Research questions

There were four research questions which formed the basis of data collection tools for the research conducted in three MLD special schools. These questions concerned the commonality of the aims of education, the ensuing implications at the planning and implementation stages, assessment and record keeping, and opportunities post-16. The pupil interview schedules were devised with reference to these questions, corresponding to areas of pupils' experience.

Methods of data collection

Familiarization

Time was spent with pupils in their classrooms in order to build a good relationship with each group and so make the interview process more comfortable for the pupils as well as help to elicit valid and reliable information from pupils. Individual interviews put a lot of pressure on pupils to respond to questions and, in the school situation, may be more often used for measuring progress or judging a pupil's potential. Examples of this type of interview are discussions with senior teachers about behaviour or attainment, preparing targets and recording achievements with teachers, and interviews with educational psychologists or other adult support workers.

I decided to interview pupils in small groups. This related to the more natural method of classroom discussion with which pupils were likely to be familiar. Group interviewing encourages pupils to relax and to feel at ease with people they know in a situation they can identify with (M. Watts and Ebutt 1987). This was particularly important given the learning difficulties of these pupils and the associated lack of confidence one might expect to find. In the group situation pupils had the support of friends who would encourage each other to take part and to discuss issues.

Group interviews are moderated by the interviewer but allow a discussion to be developed which may elicit a wide range of responses (Powney and Watts 1987; Lewis 1992). The responses provided may be different from those which could be gathered through individual interviews; but, in consideration of the factors outlined above, the response to the pilot interview and my knowledge of the pupils, it was felt that group interviews would be the most successful tool.

Pilot: pupil group interview

A group of pupils from Year 9 in one of the study schools was asked to pilot the interview process. The class teacher selected older or more mature pupils from the year group and asked them if they would be involved. Four pupils formed the group (two boys and two girls). I knew them personally and rapport already existed between us. The purpose of the pilot was to test the questions for ease of comprehension and to see if they elicited the required information. Also, given the relationship of trust that existed between myself and the pupils, I felt that they could be asked to comment on the form of the questions and the applicability of the process to other groups of pupils.

The purpose of the research was explained to the pupils to try to allay any feelings of apprehension they may have had. The four pupils were eager to help with the research. The opportunity was taken to try an introductory activity which it was felt might put pupils at ease. An activity was selected that had been used successfully, as an 'ice breaker', with pupils as a precursor to more personal self-esteem activities. The 'Honesty' card game that was used gave each group member the chance to speak and prompted some discussion (for further discussion of this game see Sinclair Taylor and Costley 1995: 34–5). The card game involved each person selecting a card and reading out the beginning of a sentence that they had to complete. The 'honesty' in the game implies that the young people are encouraged to complete the sentences in a truthful and individual way, as opposed to saying what they think is expected of them by friends and the researcher. Most cards were written in simple language but one or two contained words which the pupils helped each other to work out. The card game activity helped pupils to relax and encouraged them to take part in the interview and discussion.

The pupils were first asked to identify themselves on the tape to get them used to the tape recorder and to aid transcription. The format adopted appeared to work well and all four pupils contributed. Once all the questions had been tested the group were asked to comment on the process and to give their views on how successful it would be with pupils who had not known me as a teacher. The response was positive and the pupils thought that children in other schools would be more relaxed and willing to talk if they were in groups with their peers. It was calculated that 10 minutes would be the optimum time for the 'Honesty' card game, followed by a 30-minute interview. Some minor alterations were made to the interview questions to make them clearer for pupils to understand. Areas where explanation might be needed were also highlighted, for example, a description of the National Curriculum might be needed before pupils could answer questions about it.

Interview/discussion group organization

I devised a schedule of lead questions that I used to moderate the discussions and to provide points of comparison across the groups within each school (see Appendix 4). The questions were intended to stimulate discussion and not to gather individual responses. The question order was flexible and could be changed to follow the flow of the discussion.

I decided that I would try to interview all pupils in Years 10 and 11 in each school in an attempt to overcome any issues of bias in selection either by myself or by the class teachers. This was possible in relatively small special schools. Wherever possible, in consultation with class teachers, pupils were allowed to choose to work in groups with which they felt comfortable. This meant that in some situations the groups were of mixed sex, while in other schools the pupils elected to work in single sex groups. The optimum number of pupils in each group was four, but owing to various circumstances this was not always possible. It was felt that fewer than four in a group could put too much emphasis on the views of a few pupils and several more than four could be difficult to control and keep on track. The composition of the groups altered the pattern of interaction and the data collected.

Example: effect of group composition on conversation

On one occasion the Year 10 pupils from an all age special school had elected to be interviewed together (three boys and three girls). I was concerned that their teacher, who was trying to accommodate the research in his busy timetable, might have influenced the decision. However, I continued with the arrangement, feeling that the teacher knew his pupils better than I did. The discussion was arranged to follow the afternoon break and the girls arrived in the room first. We began talking and the girls were all interested in the research and keen to offer their views on the school, teachers and subjects taught. I noticed that two of the girls who were usually very quiet in class were contributing equally to the discussion. The boys joined the group quite late, having been involved in some trouble at breaktime, and were noisy and disruptive. I managed to settle them and proceeded with the discussion. The girls appeared reluctant to speak and the two very shy girls hardly said another word. In this instance I did not feel that I had a full picture of the views of the Year 10 pupils. In hindsight the single sex groups seemed to work better, giving everyone an opportunity to speak and be listened to. In the other schools where single sex groups were used, the discussions were much more balanced and free ranging. Pupils seemed more relaxed and confident in articulating their ideas.

This may be a factor of the age of the pupils concerned, of particular group dynamics, or of the learning difficulties experienced by these pupils. My feeling is that the different reaction of mixed and single sex groups is related to relationships between the sexes rather than ability of pupils.

The interview process

At the beginning of each interview and discussion the purpose of the research was explained to the pupils to try to allay any feelings of apprehension they may have had. There are obvious difficulties when an adult is questioning children, including issues of status and position, perception of what the interviewer wants to hear, and peer group pressure (see Crozier, Chapter 14, for an alternative approach to tackling these issues). Children should always be extended the same courtesies as adults (Powney and Watts 1987).

Each group was encouraged to take part in an ice-breaking activity prior to the interview. This served to open communications and gave me some idea of the pupils who might try to dominate the discussion and those who would need to be encouraged to take part. The card game activity helped pupils to relax and encouraged them to take part in the interview. I decided that it was a very successful tool that I would use again when interviewing children.

The interview questions took the form of suggested lead questions for group discussion and were organized within the four areas of experience: the aims and purposes of education; the implementation of the National Curriculum; assessment; and opportunities after school. The tape recorder was switched on immediately the children entered the room so that all interactions were recorded and there would not be an artificial break in the conversation to switch on the machine. It was hoped that this would make the tape recorder less obtrusive and would encourage natural interaction and responses.

Transcribing and analysing data

I listened to the tapes on the way home from each discussion to fix the voices and interactions in my mind. I then took notes from each tape as soon as possible afterwards, while individual pupils' voices were still re-membered, and the context of the discussions could be added. This was a difficult task and would have been practically impossible for someone who was not part of the discussion. There are always difficulties when trying to record group discussions because of the limits of the technology (most microphones do not have a sufficient range to pick up all interactions clearly at a distance), the acoustics of most rooms and the natural inclina-tion for people to speak at the same time.

The initial analysis was content based and identified responses to par-ticular questions and the amount of group consensus on an issue. I made notes of the main subjects covered in the discussion relating to each of the four key areas of pupils' experience. For example, when talking about what pupils liked about their school, I noted that in most of the groups the emphasis was on small class sizes; supportive and friendly staff; under-standing and sympathetic peers; extra help with work; and support to achieve. This consensus across groups and across schools enabled me to conclude, with some degree of certainty, that these were among the factors that pupils' perceived as 'special' about their experience of special school.

At this stage some specific comments by individuals were recorded verbatim for purposes of illumination. The aim was to obtain a group viewpoint, not to ascribe views to individuals, which would have implications for protecting confidentiality. The results are a study of one group's dynamics and as such are not generalizable across the whole population of one school or between schools. In this situation 'each interview was a record of a social interaction' (Powney and Watts 1987: 15).

Methodological considerations when interviewing young people with learning difficulties

Ethical issues

Ethical issues need to be considered in case study research which uses the lived experiences of individuals as evidence from which to draw conclusions about that experience. In each school studied pupils were asked for their cooperation and none refused to take part in the research. However, the nature of the power relations between teachers and pupils must be considered, as Denscombe and Aubrook (1992: 129) highlighted: 'in the school context, young people are something of a captive audience'. They rarely feel able to say no to researchers and often see the research process as just another piece of school work. I was aware that it was important to ensure that pupils knew what I would do with the results of the discussion and who else would hear what they said. With these older pupils this was particularly important as it may have influenced what they said and how much they revealed about the school and their education. (See Chapter 14 for a pupil's perspective on this point.)

The vulnerability of interviewees had to be considered especially in the situation of an adult questioning children. Where group consensus existed it was valuable to document this but it was equally valuable to acknowledge each child and to report individual responses if they highlighted a particular issue for some pupils.

Practical considerations

When setting up the groups in each school, I was aware of the importance of group composition, number of children in the group, the organization of the room and the school context. I have already discussed the effect of group composition. It was equally important to consider where the children sat in relation to me and to each other. I was always careful to arrange the chairs in a circle so that no one was dominant in the group and everyone had an equal place. Also, I made sure that I sat as one of the group and did not appear to be 'interviewing' the group by sitting above them or behind a desk. The relationship that I had built up with the children and my previous experience as a teacher in a special school were very important to the breadth of information gathered from pupils. In a shared situation certain things can be regarded as common knowledge and may be taken for granted in the discussion. Sometimes interviewers from outside the situation can gather more information from interviewees because they do not have any preconceptions and, therefore, are more likely to make problematic issues that insiders might think they understand.

Considering the special needs of the pupils to be interviewed, their lack of confidence and self-esteem, it was particularly important to have spent time with the pupils prior to the interview and discussion to put them at their ease. Many of them were immature in their thinking and tended to use teachers or other adults for consent or confirmation of information. As the moderator of the discussion I had to relate to pupils and to draw them all into the discussion, and be careful not allow a dominant pupil to take over the discussion. It would have been useful sometimes to have had an observer in the group who could have noted the frequency and types of interaction between myself and pupils, interactions between individual pupils, and non-verbal behaviour.

With some groups I was able to extend the questioning and pupils' reasoning to purposes of education and segregated special schooling. The group situation seemed to encourage most pupils to speak and pupils responded to the views of others to extend the discussion of some topics. When the discussion went beyond what I had envisaged it was important to encourage pupils to think through and to articulate ideas. I was pleasantly surprised on one or two occasions when pupils showed that they had thought about issues and could express opinions that I would not have expected. This highlighted to me that as a researcher I needed to be aware of my preconceptions about the abilities of pupils with special needs and to be open to challenge by them.

Validity, reliability and authenticity

The ethical, methodological and practical considerations described here can be applied more widely to research with children and to interviewing with groups in other situations. The guidelines for well organized and structured qualitative research are likely to be similar whatever the research questions or specific methods used (see Appendix 5).

When interviewing young people described as having moderate learning difficulties it was particularly important to ensure the interview questions were well framed and that the process was clearly thought through. There were some difficulties with this method of interviewing, particularly with recording data. It would have been difficult, and possibly intrusive or disruptive, to take fieldnotes. However, the recording might have been difficult to transcribe unless pupils were encouraged to listen to each other and not all talk at once. Every attempt was made to ensure validity and authenticity at the time of the interviews as it was anticipated that verification of interview transcripts with pupils would be very difficult. This was because some of the pupils would have left school and others may not remember what they said or may have a different viewpoint on a different day. This is a particular concern when interviewing pupils with learning difficulties.

I found that being able to talk about my recent experience of teaching in a special school like theirs put pupils at their ease and established a common bond. Pupils may be tempted to try to please an adult by saying what they think the adult wants to hear. Using similar questions at different points in the discussion may help to increase internal validity by making sure pupils give similar answers each time. It was helpful to discuss some ground rules at the beginning of the session; these covered the importance of individual views and of listening to what other people think. Reliability is more difficult to achieve as questions are bound to be framed differently depending on the responses of the pupils to previous questions and the importance of the development of a 'natural' discussion.

Conclusion

Taking the time to ask young people their views on education was both illuminating and challenging. They offered an insight and depth of understanding that was unexpected and challenged my assumptions about their abilities. The group interaction was interesting and the consensus of opinions added both depth and validity to the case studies. We would not think of constructing a case study without collecting the opinions of the adults involved in a situation, so why should we ignore the views of the consumers of education – the children?

(14) Falling out of school: a young woman's reflections on her chequered experience of schooling

JO CROZIER AND TRACEY

The authors of this chapter were teacher and pupil in an alternative school unit, located in a community centre, catering for pupils aged 15 to 16 in their last year of school who had for various reasons fallen out of, and fallen out with, mainstream school. The relationship that enables Tracey to tell her story in this way rests on each of our responses to the rather irregular sort of schooling in which we were both involved. The nature of the alternative school and the relationships between the staff and students were not those of traditional teacher–pupil; the chance to work together on the chapter reflects the more egalitarian style that underpinned the ideology and processes of the unit. (An account of the unit can be found in Shotton 1993.)

Tracey is now a woman in her mid-20s, living in a settled partnership, in steady employment and enjoying a good relationship with her parents and siblings. She went on being fairly wild for a couple of years after leaving education altogether, then settled down and committed herself to a job, a relationship and shared care of children. Jo went on to a different sort of work with young people with emotional and behavioural difficulties and then to university to teach teachers and do research in the area of pupil disaffection. Partly thanks to Tracey, Jo retained an interest in girls' experience of disaffection and did some research with a school colleague exploring this (Crozier and Anstiss 1995). We have kept in touch loosely, we live in the same area and bump into each other and each other's families from time to time. We have considerable regard for each other and view the year we spent together in the alternative school unit as important for both of us. When Jo rang Tracey to arrange the interviews her response was positive but also 'I'm only doing it because it's you' – an entirely mutual sentiment.

Methodological issues

There has been increasing and overdue interest in hearing the voices of young people themselves about their educational experiences. While there may be issues about the reliability of information, pupils' perspectives are of particular value. As consumers of the educational process they have points of view about what works well or badly for them that providers of education need to take into account. In relation to pupils whose disaffection has undermined their education, it is even more important to try to understand what has gone wrong. It is not always easy to get access to former pupils. Lloyd-Smith and Davies (1995: 11) discuss some of the difficulties in this sort of research: 'The subjects are often resentful, defensive, alienated and, in some cases, disturbed. Their educational careers have invariably involved individual and family stress and invitations to discuss them are not always welcomed'.

Unsuccessful pupils, those who fail in or are failed by the education system, are, as a group, in a marginal position. In an era of league tables their contribution to schools is either negligible or negative. This low status excludes them from participation (Garner 1995). It is in this context of negative experience of schooling and marginalization in terms of participation that it is especially important to treat people's accounts of their experience with sensitivity, and in the case of this study to leave a significant measure of control of the material with the focus, who chooses to be known by only her first name, Tracey.

The aim in this chapter is to explore a process of enabling Tracey to give her account, to have time to reflect on what she has said and modify it in the light of her reflections, to select what she wishes to include or leave out and to check the accuracy of the representation of her thoughts. The process we used was to tape record an interview loosely structured by questions and prompts, meet subsequently to discuss thoughts and memories that had been stirred up, look at the transcript and raise new areas or emphases from reflections on the material.

Thus we take a life history approach to the gathering of the story and also to the telling. Through a series of interviews we explored the story of Tracey's experience of schooling, from her earliest memories to the stage where it started going wrong for her. The process invited her to look at her reflections about herself and her contemporaries and her aspirations for the children in her family. The aim was to construct a way of telling that is committed to accessible language and ways of thinking and avoids a professionalized 'researcher' or 'theorist' stance as opposed to the 'subject'. Here the person whose story is the focus participates in the evolving discussion and the task of making sense of the story, a process of 'co-creation' (Huberman 1995: 139).

In selecting and organizing the material to write about we draw on a case study approach described by Denny 1978 (cited in Goodson and Walker 1995: 186) as 'seeking to describe (or to portray) rather than to analyse and explain'. Because we want to focus on telling Tracey's story rather than attempting to analyse it, we do not organize the material into topics. We want to be faithful to the story and the telling of it and to identify points of focus would be to manipulate the material into categories of interest to only one of us as researcher.

We offer no prescriptions for other young people who may, like Tracey, fall foul of school. We assume that each has a particular experience and his or her own story to tell. Some of the wider issues that Tracey's experience connects with are discussed as themes and issues, but Tracey is not a type of person, a genre of school pupil, rather she is particular and her perspective is her own. She is willing to tell her story, and to tell it to Jo, because she is concerned about what sense to make of her experience, what implications it may have in thinking about children who are going through school now, and because she is curious and finds it interesting to look back and reflect.

As one of us was a teacher there are issues of status and power that may inform the interview process, not least Tracey's selection from her memories. 'There is a tendency to reinvent one's past in order to give meaning to one's present . . . People are revisionist historians of their pasts' (Huberman 1995: 137). Acknowledging our different standpoints we are able to identify what we share: we each in our separate lives have a critical perspective on traditional relationships of power; we each respect each other's freedom to select from the story as it develops what is to be included and what is to remain private; and we both are committed to preserve the anonymity of other characters as they appear.

There are obvious problems in terms of accuracy, reliability, reconstruction of memory over time, and the desire to please the listener: these we all experience in telling our stories. These limitations are the price for the chance to develop 'personal' meaning, to check the validity by review and reflection. We attempt to challenge and diminish the status differential common in the relationship between the researcher and the subject of the research, no less in accounts of pupils with troubled schooling or lives than in other areas of research. As Goodson and Walker (1995: 193) point out, researchers 'have to learn to be accountable to those we research at all stages of the enterprise' in the interests of giving up some of our control over information and expertise.

Development of interest in understanding pupils' perspectives raises discussion of the layers of distance between researcher and subject, teacher and pupil, adult and child. Doherty (1997) warns of the risk of exploiting young people whom he calls 'on the margins'. If research is designed about young people rather than with them researchers take possession of the young people's views and make use of them as part of professional development. In sharing the responsibility for this piece of work, Tracey and Jo seek to avoid that.

The fact that we had shared experiences to some extent, albeit from different perspectives, expressed itself in the nature of the dialogue, in the ways in which responses were accepted or challenged, in what was seen as funny, in what was embargoed as unsuitable (see Huberman 1995: 139). Between interviews Jo looked at the material and sought links with some themes in the literature, while Tracey found that she thought about her schooldays and got involved in conversations with colleagues at work comparing experiences and with her parents about her own schooling. She also found that she was reflecting on the links between her experience and that of her partner's children, who at 10 and 11 years old were facing the transition to secondary school, an event that plays a significant part in Tracey's story.

The first part of the story is to do with Tracey's schooling before we met. Then there is some account of the year we spent as teacher and pupil in a shared context but with different perspectives. The extracts show some of the further reflection that was stimulated by talking and thinking about the story. The process we have described created the opportunity to draw on this evolving material. The outcome, the worked over telling of the story, enables Tracey's experiences to speak to an audience who may be interested in the experience of disaffection and who may value hearing young people's articulation of their own journey through school and the sense they make of it. She welcomes the chance to have a voice in this way.

Themes and issues

As the material from the interviews took shape in the form of transcripts, some threads emerged which were raised for discussion during the second and subsequent visits and these are identified here.

Tracey's schooling spans the period from 1975 to 1986, starting earlier if nursery is included. A theme emerged associated with change and upheaval accompanying moves from one school phase to another – nursery to first school, first to middle, and finally and most disastrously middle to secondary. These are vulnerable times, illustrated in Measor and Woods' (1984) study of the experience of pupils moving from middle to secondary school. The study demonstrates the profound threats posed to pupils' identities as they left behind securities and faced the uncertain future: 'The comfortable, homely environments they have known hitherto, where they have been looked after, will be exchanged for a brash, impersonal, more cosmopolitan and bureaucratic institution where they must find their own solutions' (Measor and Woods 1984: 9).

Tracey's struggle with these dilemmas culminated in her withdrawal from the field. Most of her secondary schooling is characterized by truancy. From Year 8, the year of entry (aged 12) to secondary school from middle school, until Year 11 when we met, her school career was increasingly interrupted by her refusal to attend and truancy emerged from the interviews as an important dimension of her experience.

A third strong theme is to do with siblings, in Tracey's case following a diligent and successful sister through school, and in turn being followed up the system by a younger brother. Measor and Woods (1984: 35) found that the part played by older siblings was on the whole helpful but for Tracey her perceptions of the contrast between her sister's abilities and her own, and the burden of teachers' expectations that she should be like her sister, demonstrate some negative aspects of following a sibling. Tracey's understanding of this experience shows her as desperate for attention at the middle school stage and lacking in confidence at secondary school.

Gender also comes out as a formative issue. Tracey's experience is of being a 'strong' girl, of being 'well hard', of preferring the company of boys and having more time for men teachers, of steering well clear of the feminine agenda offered by school and peers. Llewellyn (1980) draws attention to the gendered nature of the roles played at school. In her study a high status, low stream girl, Sandy, seen as troublesome by staff and a source of amusement and diversion to fellow pupils in the classroom, was isolated in the school and outside it because of behaviour which in a boy would have been socially successful. Llewellyn (1980: 48) argues that she was isolated because of deviating from 'accepted definitions of appropriate feminine behaviour'. Similarly Davies (1978) describes a girl called Janie exceeding the bounds by making cheeky remarks out loud, overstepping the range of permitted behaviour for girls and moving into the preserve of the boys (cited in Measor and Woods 1984: 117).

Tracey's self-identity was as a tough, hard young woman and this may have contributed to her isolation at secondary school. By the time we met, when she was 15, she was known as 'Fred' and enjoyed a tough image. She made good friends with the boys in the unit but also had a strong alliance with another young woman, who was more attached to a feminine image but reckless and fearless in many ways and a good companion in adventures. Tracey had found much solidarity and support, as well as freedom to explore her identity, first in a girls' group and later, in the period that we worked together, in connection with a Women's Room where feminist issues of the day informed the atmosphere and there was satisfaction

– sometimes triumph – in having a space where boys and men were not allowed. Feminism offered permission to invent ways of being a woman and acceptance of young women challenging gender stereotypes.

Tracey's story

Tracey's schooling started with attendance at nursery school. Her mother, as far as she remembers, has always worked. Her brother, four years younger, would have been born during this time, shortly before she started her first proper school. Tracey saw a connection between her nursery experience and the transition to first school:

> I suppose being at a nursery you can do what you want without any restrictions really, and I suppose being so young and going to school having been to the nursery perhaps I just expected school to be like the nursery was, you did what you wanted to do.

First school, for 5 to 8-year-olds, was a Roman Catholic school and Tracey's memories of it are at first vague as she begins to think about that period:

> It was run by nuns, that was fine, I can't remember too much about it, it's been a few years now.

However, she remembers it being strict. Tracey and another pupil, a boy, used to get into trouble together, and she recalls 'hands on your head and standing in the corner'. The friend and Tracey would meet early at school – there was a pond they played around.

> We used to go early in the morning and catch the tadpoles and kill them . . . we fished them out and threw them on the floor.

It seemed to be breaktimes when the dinner staff were supervising that Tracey and her ally would be 'boisterous and noisy':

> We would play up the dinner ladies, as you do.

As Tracey's memories were awakened she recalled the headteacher as being 'very stern'. She vividly remembered the stairs that led to the head's office. Going up them was a frightening experience: 'you were shaking'. Later Tracey remembered the physical punishment that probably lay in wait at the top of the stairs:

> I recalled today getting the slipper, you used to get the slipper there. It was quite funny, I was at work and we were talking about schools and they were going on about getting the cane and it flew back into my mind, back to getting the slipper across my hand, the palm of my hand. That was a frightening experience. For what I can't remember

but I do remember getting the slipper across the palm of my hand. It was a black plimsoll and I used to get that across the palm of my hand.

Learning was of little interest. Tracey can remember reading lessons:

> Yes the ABC book – we would read with a ruler under each line and you move it down as you read your line . . . If you had done well with a book, this was when the headmistress was feeling nice, you would go and read to her and you would get a lolly for it if you had read well.

The next school, a Roman Catholic middle school, was altogether a more positive experience for Tracey. She enjoyed learning more – remembers science and music in particular as interesting and enjoyable, netball and rounders and cookery were welcome opportunities. Relationships with teachers were quite good:

> I got on with the teachers OK. It was a bigger school so it was I think at first see how far I could push the teachers and once I knew where I stood it was like enough was enough, they took control and I realized I couldn't get away with things.

However, she also describes playing up teachers whom she did not like, mocking what they said, pushing them as far as she could: she still remembers hating the French teacher.

In relation to her peers, Tracey sees herself as somewhat the leader of a group of children, mainly boys she thinks but there are girls' names too in her account, who saw her and themselves as a group as 'well hard'. She liked the role of leader, of being looked up to. They smoked in the fields surrounding the school:

> I think it was just to be big, yes definitely just to show off.

They laughed a lot, 'took the mickey out of each other', threw water bags out of a window at people below and got into trouble, earning themselves detentions. Tracey's home was a distance from the school, and getting home meant catching the school bus. This was an advantage in relation to punishments. On the whole Tracey avoided the hated after-school detentions because of the problem of missing the bus. Lunchtime detentions were not nearly such a burden.

On reflection Tracey described her role as leader of the gang in more complicated ways. Being 'tough' was crucial to the role but she sees it as hiding a lot of insecurity. The first school experience had been hard. The school population dispersed to two Roman Catholic middle schools at opposite extremities of the town and she was isolated from her first school friends on entry to middle school, while other children had come up in groups and seemed to be more socially secure. Tracey also saw them as having had a better time at their first schools. She was determined not to replicate the first school experience:

> Knowing what I had gone through in first school I wasn't going to take it in middle school.

'Toughness' went along with relating better to boys whom Tracey saw as able to get away with much more, especially in relation to predominantly women teachers:

> Yes looking back then you probably thought, yes, boys are tough and teachers aren't going to challenge them and when you are young that's probably how your mind thinks or how mine did anyway. If they push it they are going to get away with it, whereas if you are a girl, woman to woman or woman to girl, well the woman is going to show who is boss to the girl. Whereas a boy, they might not think of messing with him. As a child that's probably how I thought, it's not how I see it now.

Reflecting on her school and talking with her mother, Tracey developed the view that by the time she was at middle school following a sister who, fours year ahead of her, was successful at school, she was burdened with comparisons:

> Because she was older than me and she was a good pupil, she was excellent and I think the school was just expecting me to follow suit, you know like teachers expected off me what they expected off my sister. What they got off her they expected off me and obviously you can't tar two children with the same brush and my mum seems to think that was a lot of my problems with middle school and second-ary school. Because my sister was always above me and she was excellent at everything obviously they expected the same from me and my capabilities weren't the same as hers.

This sibling factor, Tracey says, probably affected all her school career from the beginning. Her sister was very good at concentrating and getting on with her work, whereas Tracey would wander off the work if she found it boring. The comparisons became explicit when Tracey followed her sister to secondary school and found she had the same form tutor. The problems started on the first day and Tracey quickly got involved in truanting.

> I think a lot of my problems started when I went to secondary school. From day one I didn't like my year tutor that was in the first year I was there.

On further reflection Tracey says she was put off by the tutor's voice and her attitude:

She was very...I felt as if she was very hoity-toity, she was like looking down on you all the time and her attitude was just 'well you can do as I say and if you don't like it tough', that's the way she came across to me and that put me off straight away.

Tracey's response was immediate, she knew at once that the relationship with the tutor was problematic and felt that the antipathy was mutual:

You know from the minute you see someone whether you are going to take to them or not and I think with her there was an immediate click that there was going to be nothing there and I wasn't going to give her the time and she wasn't going to give me the time.

Tracey had chosen to go to the same school as her sister, again leaving behind her friends. Many from the Roman Catholic middle school went on to either Roman Catholic secondary school or a neighbourhood school near the middle school. As well as social isolation Tracey felt very insecure in relation to the work:

I just felt I couldn't cope in a lot of the lessons and I didn't have the ability, I felt, to cope with the work.

Many of the teachers had taught Tracey's sister and she felt the burden of that acutely:

From the day you started it was all 'I remember your sister and she did well' and I just didn't feel comfortable and I knew I was never going to be as good as her and I think that was when the mistake was made with my confidence being knocked. I just thought there was no point trying.

Her response was to truant, leaving after registration, then taking whole days off and taking in forged sick notes from her parents when she returned. Older friends had flats and were glad of Tracey's company so passing the time was easy. Through these friends she got interested in CB (Citizens' Band) radio, which she found fascinating. It took quite a while for Tracey's parents to find out.

The truanting officer, when I actually did get found out, the truanting officer was at my mum and dad's when I came in supposedly from school and she was sat there. I remember my mum asking me if I had had a good day at school and I said yes. Then this truanting officer said well according to our records you haven't been in school for so many days, so many weeks, and if I had been it was on an unbalanced schedule, it was in one day, out one day and so on and so forth.

The school's attempts to encourage Tracey to attend school regularly back-fired. She was assessed by an educational psychologist and found the tests humiliating:

I just felt as if my intelligence was insulted . . . it was like stars, it was like kids you know, those blocks that you put . . . like squares, you know what I mean.

People in the school knew that she was seeing the psychologist, which confirmed her view that not only was she stupid but also everyone would know. She has no memory of having any feedback from the testing, so she remained for a long time convinced that their purpose was to prove that she was 'thick'.

The school system was one in which the tutor went up the school with the group. Relations did not improve and what Tracey saw as a 'clash of personalities' continued. After a couple of years of erratic schooling, Tracey brought things to a head by throwing a chair at the tutor in a heated argument about her truanting. She was suspended for a period and the tutor visited her to encourage her to return to school. By coincidence Tracey had broken her leg so the proposal was that she should return in a wheelchair, a prospect that Tracey found unthinkable. For Tracey that marked the end of it: from then on she refused to go to school at all.

Strong feelings remain (at the time of writing these events were more than ten years ago) but Tracey still feels anger for the year tutor and about the wasted opportunities that now limit her choices. The only aspect of secondary school that she can recall with any pleasure is sport, but the negative feelings predominate. She occasionally sees a girl whom she used to sit with and she still remembers her sense of inadequacy alongside her more successful companion.

Tracey and Jo's shared part of the story

In due course Tracey was referred to a unit catering for disaffected fifth years (Year 11) offering a programme for their final year of schooling and the opportunity to take a few exams. By the time she entered the unit she had formed a strong friendship with another prospective pupil and together they were having a wild time.

Well we were just out for a laugh. She liked doing the things I liked doing, which was drinking, smoking, going to blues parties . . . yes we got on really well, she was definitely a good laugh.

While her social life was hectic and sometimes got her into trouble, Tracey's memories of schooling at the unit are positive. It was important for her that no one knew her and in particular no one knew her sister, so she could carve her own path.

It was like great, you could smoke, you could cheek the teachers and get away with it all and I think I felt comfortable and I then started to realize that it was good – I am going to end up as thick as two short planks if I don't start sorting myself out . . . it was the friendly atmosphere. The teachers had the time to spend with you and because there wasn't so many people in the group there was more attention paid . . . I think probably because I knew there were people in the same situation as me and I wasn't . . . I didn't feel below anyone. Obviously probably we all had the same difficulties and the same problems.

The initial picture that Tracey painted of her time in the unit seemed a little rosy. The perspective from Jo's standpoint as her teacher was somewhat different. We discussed the experience further and Tracey agreed that she explored the boundaries of tolerance in the unit and the community centre in which it was located with some vigour! From Jo's perspective Tracey had made her mark right from the beginning of the year. All the pupils spent the whole of their last school year in the unit, starting in September. Previously pupils went through a relatively calm settling in period in the early stages before they felt sufficiently confident to demonstrate their full range of behaviours. Tracey and her friend started off with a bang. They had been excited about their referral to the unit and had spent the summer hanging around the community centre getting to know everyone. By the time term started they were well past any honeymoon period and into full-on testing, usually goodhumouredly but establishing a leading role in the group and accelerating the rate of participation of all the members.

It was new and it was like going in and showing people where you stand . . . we knew we were starting something new and it was like we will show them who is boss.

The community activities created opportunities for pupils in the unit to participate beyond the confines of the school. Sitting around in the community centre coffee bar, sometimes taking a turn at serving, was not unlike the times Tracey had spent in friends' flats instead of at school. The playgroup was happy to have her help with the children whom she was getting to know as they passed through the coffee bar. It felt to Tracey that her school attendance was good because she was in the community centre building.

I actually restrained from truanting. I remember [a friend] often coming down for me to take the afternoon off and I enjoyed it so much that I wouldn't do it.

From Jo's viewpoint as teacher responsible for the conduct of the young people in the unit, the atmosphere had been highly volatile. Previous involvement in the community centre made her aware that the community centre both welcomed the young people attending the unit and sometimes experienced their behaviour as challenging. Located in the entrance to the building, the coffee bar and its users witnessed all the rushing in and out, excitements and dramas of the school group and often of their friends who would come to the centre to join in the action. Tracey recalled the peer pressures she felt within the unit where she was one of ten or twelve young people who had all fallen out with school. There were times when the young people behaved badly and the pressure to conform was considerable:

> I couldn't say 'Oh I can't' because I would have been called all the wimps under the sun.

Exploring some of these memories and our different perspectives on them, Tracey remains positive about her experience at the unit. She remembers it as being a happy experience and an environment where she 'settled in'. The relationships with people in the coffee bar, women in the Women's Room and youth workers who were attached to the project remained an important resource for Tracey in the period after leaving school.

Tracey feels that she would never have been able to fit in with the size and structure of a mainstream secondary school. She feels that she needed more attention than was available; it was too easy to pay no attention to instructions:

> I felt I didn't have to try, you know what I mean, you know nobody is going to know if I am not listening or paying attention.

When it came to doing the work at school, she was stuck because she had not taken in the necessary information or instructions. She thinks that she would inevitably have clashed with the discipline systems of a secondary school and that it was all too formal for her. She is also painfully aware of the extent to which her choices are curtailed by her limited qualifications. There is much she would like to do, including working with young people in similar difficulties, but she lacks the qualifications to embark on training and the confidence in her abilities to study and qualify.

Sensitive to her own experiences and the impact on her life chances, Tracey is concerned for the children she shares a home with, about to face the transitions that were so difficult for her. She senses acutely the vulnerability of the older one, a girl on the brink of starting secondary school and already anxious about the girls on the bus who make hostile remarks. Her concerns for the younger draw on her experience of following an older sibling, and she wonders whether the strong pull to send both to the same school is wise.

Conclusion

Tracey's story offers one young woman's perspectives on her schooling. The problems arising from transitions, from lack of confidence, from competing with siblings, from lack of sufficient attention available to meet a young person's needs, illustrate issues familiar in the literature about pupil disaffection. Perspectives drawing on self-esteem point to the importance of effective pastoral support and positive feedback to support vulnerable pupils (see e.g. Gurney 1990). The ecosystemic approach to developing an understanding of the processes that may contribute to disaffection (Cooper *et al.* 1994) seeks to take into account the perceptions of various parties to the interactions involved in schooling. These perceptions will differ but need to be accommodated into an understanding of the system in which teachers and pupils seek to negotiate the business of schooling. Crucial to this approach is listening to young people's own version of what is happening to them in school. The way forward lies in teachers' ability to be sensitive to the experience of pupils and the significance of their behaviour towards young people.

Gender and the development of an identity as a strong woman plays a part in Tracey's tussles with school. The role of her early woman headteacher, remembered as frightening as well as sometimes the source of approval, seemed to set an agenda as Tracey went up the school system and adopted a stance as a 'hard' girl. There is scope here for further exploration in terms of gender and power.

Burgess (1995) argues that gathering pupils' perspectives of schooling must include the 'accounts of disruptive pupils' and those who have least voice within the school system, so that we can understand their perspectives and the ways in which they experience school (Burgess 1995: 156). In order for Tracey's story of her schooling to be as accurate as possible in terms of her own understanding, each stage of the development of this account has been discussed between us and the discussion used as the basis for moving forward in constructing this narrative.

Tracey fared badly in the formal framework of traditional authority relations in mainstream school, and better in the more tolerant and egalitarian climate of an alternative school. In parallel the process of gathering and telling Tracey's story has sought to avoid reproducing the more formal researcher–subject relationship and reflect the latter style. There were of course inherent contradictions in our earlier relationship as sort-of-teacher and sort-of-pupil that in turn are reflected in our search for roles that sit more comfortably than researcher and subject. What we shared as teacher and pupil and share here as collaborators is an attraction to subverting traditional postures and roles, partly on principle and perhaps partly out of a sense of being 'on the margins' and not able to get the formally constructed roles right. However we do, whatever style we adopt, have different standpoints in status, life chances and risks and we seek to respect those differences.

Our comfortable relationship, affection and respect for each other have been fundamental to the process. Meeting up together, conducting the interviews, reflecting on the experiences described, looking together at the transcripts and developing the discussion was pleasurable and included emotional resonances for each of us. As a methodology the process of interviewing had the character of a social event, revisiting old memories rather like poring over old photographs (Blaxter *et al.* 1996). Tracey has found her thoughts stirred about her education, engendering conversations with friends, family and colleagues and shaping thoughts about the education of the children she lives with. Jo has a better idea of the educational path that Tracey took before arriving in the unit and some of the pressures she had been feeling. She has had to re-evaluate what was to her quite a hard year in the school unit and think differently about how it added up. Tracey's positive evaluation of that time was discussed in terms of getting some education. She felt that she attended reasonably well and learnt something during that final year of compulsory schooling, after a very long gap. Other teachers in similar contexts may, like Jo, lose sight of that significant advance in the hectic round of daily crises. A strong dimension for Jo was and remains the strong, warm, courageous character of a particular young woman taking on the roles and systems that construct girls' schooling and shaking her fist at them. There are many others out there to listen to in order to develop a more sensitive and effective school experience.

There it is, Tracey's story is told. We hope that it adds a voice to other voices of pupils articulating their school experience.

Acknowledgements

Thanks are due to Loraine Blaxter, who supported the work in the school unit and is still supporting now in relation to the process of reflecting on that period, and to Margaret Handy, who transcribed the tapes and felt involved with Tracey's story.

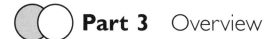

Part 3 Overview

 Emerging issues

ANN LEWIS AND GEOFF LINDSAY

The chapters in this book make the point that researching children's perspectives is a reasonable and worthwhile preoccupation. This position contrasts with that reflected in writing in the early part of this century. William McDougall (1921: 98), for example, concluded that 'a child or a savage [may] accept almost any extravagant proposition with primitive credulity'. Now we may be less inclined to believe in children's primitive credulity and researchers are concerned about exploring a range of valid and reliable ways in which to elicit children's views.

Research questions and methods

How should we decide which methods to use in researching children's perspectives? It is important to note that decisions about methods are only one of a number of decisions necessary when conducting research. Robson (1993), for example, suggests at least nine aspects of carrying out a research inquiry. These include deciding the focus, developing the research questions and strategy, selecting the method(s), collecting data, conducting the analyses and writing up.

The focus of the enterprise will underpin these matters. This focus may be driven by a practical issue in the professional life of, say, a teacher. Alternatively it may be part of a continuing research interest of those for whom research is a major aspect of their work. For example, we have been interested in children's perspectives as school teachers, educational psychologists and university researchers and teachers.

Choosing a research method may be considered a rational activity, logically following from the research questions, but this is not necessarily the case. We suggest five main bases for choice.

Preference

Researchers may prefer to carry out a particular method because they know or feel more comfortable with it. Interviewing children may be preferred to administering a questionnaire, for example, because the researcher likes to get to know the children and to understand their worlds more fully. This may not matter if either method is appropriate but being more time consuming may be a constraint.

Practicality

Practical considerations may be important. For example, there may be only a narrow time period during which data collection is possible, so limiting the opportunity for lengthy methods. If total time available is severely limited, depth of analysis will be constrained. Use of methods which depend upon information technology for data collection or analysis may be impractical as the researcher may not command the necessary skills or have the required access to ICT.

View of research or ideology

Some researchers will conduct only studies that use methods which they consider to meet the standards deriving from their view of the world. For example, while some might consider the use of questionnaires acceptable, even though they do not engage the child in a meaningful discussion about the project, others would refuse to do so. Rowan (1998) has argued this case in a contribution to a continuing debate among psychologists over the relative merits of quantitative versus qualitative methods. He sets out five reasons why 'treating people as things' is wrong. He is critical, for example, of a view of research which suggests that we build up knowledge by establishing facts: Rowan argues that this is a false view of human science. Rowan (1998: 578) also argues that 'using people as subjects (objects) denies their humanity'. To study 'the realm of the mind' (e.g. logic, imagination) adequately we need to experience them. Such views lead many researchers to reject quantitative methods and so make use only of qualitative, interpretative approaches.

Ethical considerations

Although a method may be desirable and practical from the perspective of gaining necessary information, there may be ethical reasons for rejecting this. Research ethics have been considered several times in this book, specifically in Chapter 1 as well as examples of ethical considerations in practice in other chapters. This exemplifies the importance we place on the topic. There are research studies which would be inconceivable now (e.g. see the Landis study, p. 13) but as Lindsay (Chapter 1) argued there are many instances in which ethical behaviour is less clear cut and researchers face dilemmas concerning action. Ethical codes are important guides but are not sufficient.

Following from the research questions

Methods may derive directly from research questions. For example, to explore children's views of bereavement may require children to be at ease, and the development of their contribution over a period of time while being gently led and feeling safe with a potentially distressing activity. An interview may be the approach of choice, with a skilled researcher able to ensure the approach is acceptable and gets at the experience of the child, which can be communicated to others. The use of stories or pictures, for example, allowing the child to depersonalize, to stand back and project, may also be successful.

Reconciling methods with purpose

Our view is that methods should be determined by the research questions, strongly influenced by ethical considerations. It would be helpful if the latter were clear cut, and so provided a bottom line below which research was unacceptable, but this is not always the case. At the time of writing, there is a report that the stories of the two boys convicted of the murder of the toddler James Bulger would be an important addition to our understanding of those who perpetrate such crimes (and presumably that such evidence might aid prevention or treatment). However, many may feel that this would be unacceptable and repugnant, especially if the perpetrators made money from the enterprise.

We recognize the need to take full account of practical considerations and preferences, but these should not *determine* the method, although they may determine the research focus and hence the questions. Such an approach is justified whenever the topic lends itself to the preferred or practical choice, but not otherwise. Also, while this degree of influence on the research questions is acceptable in individual cases (for example, the professional in any of the fields represented in this book, when undertaking a higher degree) it is also important to acknowledge how a summation of such studies builds to a corpus which may distort the field. This is one of the interesting elements of the reviews of educational research undertaken recently (Hillage *et al.* 1998; Tooley and Darby 1998; see also responses in *Times Higher Education Supplement*, e.g. 4 December 1998).

We do not argue for qualitative *or* quantitative methods. We are sympathetic to the concerns of Rowan (1998) outlined above, and the many researchers who have argued the case for qualitative approaches, including a large body of work in the feminist tradition. These are important voices questioning the dominance of quantitative methods, and have aided a redefinition of 'science', but our view is that these arguments do not preclude quantitative approaches. Rather, we return to the nature of the question. The answers derived must be shown to be valid. This does not *necessarily* require that the same answers be replicated with a new sample, a standard often sought in the physical sciences, but it does require that the *study* could be replicated. Also, the nature of the methods will determine the type of interpretation which is proper.

For example, a study which uses a single school as a 'case' (e.g. Warren, Chapter 10) cannot be assumed to provide evidence which is necessarily generalizable to others, but that is not its purpose. The perceptions of the boys in the sample provide a rich source of material to challenge current ideas, and further replications could explore the generalizability of the findings. Replication, therefore, has two meanings: others should be able to undertake the same study, and the generalizability of the findings may be discovered by repetition. This is an important distinction. In other cases, the findings may not be generalizable at all as they are of unique or very rare events, but careful study may provide not only insights into that case but also offer indications of information which is generalisable to others.

The researcher, therefore, must determine method(s) by reference to the research question and ethical considerations first, and by practical considerations second. Choice of method will be influenced by the view of research held by the researcher but we consider ideology as more relevant to the choice of research study than to choice of method. In the next section we explore methods more fully.

Commonality of method

In this book we have brought together researchers from a number of disciplines studying children's perspectives. It is interesting to note the similarity of method, with interviews being particularly common. In contrast, when we collated the references for the book we found that there was virtually no overlap between sources used by the different writers despite the common and relatively narrow methodological focus. Hence, there is an overlap of methods but separation of disciplinary and professional bases.

One interpretation of this commonality is that the researchers have been methodologically 'safe' in the means whereby they researched children's perspectives. If valid, this may reflect the context in which the research was conducted. All except one (Crozier, Chapter 14) were funded research projects or doctoral research. Arguably, neither context is one in which innovation in methodology is encouraged. The stakes are too high to risk not getting 'good' (in conventional terms) data. More broadly, the current climate of research activity may discourage innovative methods.

It is noteworthy that quantitative methods are relatively out of favour for researching children's perspectives, as is the use of approaches such as the repertory grid technique which, although lending itself to quantitative analysis, is fundamentally grounded in interpretative methodology. This reflects the field as we know it. For example, one of us recently noted when examining dissertations for a Masters programme that all used essentially the same methodology (interviews and participant observation, in particular). As psychologists brought up in the quantitative tradition, with heavy emphasis on experimental method and inferential statistics, we have for a number of years been active supporters of 'new paradigm' research, that is research which stresses interpretation and qualitative methods, as an important approach better suited to other research questions. Our approach as university teachers and researchers, based in universities or the LEA and schools, has been to stress the benefit of 'mixed methods', that is both qualitative and quantitative methods, as providing complementary opportunities to produce valid, interesting and useful findings.

Indirect measures of children's perspectives

Indirect techniques used to research children's perspectives encompass a wide range of methods including drawings, photographs, models, observation, analyses of talk, diaries and other written records (see e.g. Jones and Tannock, Chapter 7). Many of these techniques require a high degree of inference. The more that a child's perspective is inferred indirectly, the greater the danger of misinterpreting or overinterpreting what children present (see Dockrell, Lewis and Lindsay, Chapter 4). Hence researchers using these methods tend, rightly, to be concerned with validity and so to use a combination of methods of data collection. For example, dislike or fear of disabled classmates by non-disabled children might be inferred from avoidance of disabled children in the playground. However, the same behaviour may have an alternative explanation (e.g. fostering relations with a best friend) so the researcher might try to allow for this by tapping attitudes in a range of ways. Analyses of talk between the children would help to build up the picture (e.g. noting who introduces conversational topics, the nature and extent of reformulations, length of episodes) but here again alternative explanations may account for the pattern and nature of the talk. These difficulties apply to research with adults but will be heightened with children.

There are important differences in researching children compared with most research on adults. This is particularly related to children's developmental status plus the psychological and legal implications arising (see Chapters 3 and 4). This is not to regard children simply as 'deficient' adults (see Chapter 5 for a critique). However, taking a child rights position (see Chapter 2) does not absolve researchers from conducting research which is appropriate to the children's developmental and power status. Age, but also intellectual, communicative and sensory impairments should be important factors in determining research topic and method (see e.g. Chapters 4, 8, 9 and 13), as should sensitivity to cultural and religious issues (Chapter 11).

Direct measures of children's perspectives

This book has described direct measures of children's perspectives, hence interviews feature prominently. This focus is valuable as interviews with children have often been neglected in methodology texts. For example, Breakwell (1990) in her review of interviewing includes only a brief chapter on interviewing children and its sole focus is on 'hazards', i.e. threats to validity and reliability. Robson (1993) in an otherwise comprehensive text has little to say about researching children's perspectives.

The use of questionnaires with children seems to have received little attention in methodology texts. In contrast, teen magazines make frequent and apparently popular use of informal self-report questionnaires. There may be concerns about the reliability of children's and young people's responses to questionnaires. Surveys of adolescent drug taking or sexual behaviour, for example, are notoriously unreliable. Survey methods (encompassing questionnaires and attitude scales) merge with interviews. Some interviews may be little more than a face to face version of a written questionnaire or scale. This is particularly so when the respondents are children as the researcher may talk through a questionnaire with the child rather than leave the child to complete the form independently and encounter reading or concentration difficulties. The child might be encouraged to depict responses with a drawing rather than talk through the response. In this way a questionnaire may be a support to structured or semi-structured interviews with a child.

Concerns with validity and reliability

Another concern, which applies to all methods, is to ensure that the information obtained is valid in that it represents the perspective of the child, whether of a particular time, or a more permanent attitude. This can be limited by poorly worded questionnaires which inhibit or truncate the child's full and necessary expression, or by using a sound method but without adaptation for the children concerned, taking account of their developmental status, for example. The same issue applies to the use of interviews, drawing and other qualitative measures. In the case of the former, the interviewer is a key component in the production of the child's perspectives. Done well, the role is facilitative and non-intrusive.

Preparation for and opening of the interview

When children are interviewed they may need props or alternative signing systems through which to communicate their views. This is particularly so for children with severe or profound learning difficulties or children with speech and language difficulties. Alternative means of communication may be empowering (as discussed by Detheridge, Chapter 9) but may also constrain responses. If the child does not know the sign to convey a particular meaning then the expressive language limitations operating for some non-disabled children will apply. Use of researchers with signing skills will clearly be needed and this may have repercussions for research costs. This may also be the case when the research involves children for whom English is not the community language.

In the case of children with specific speech and language difficulties (SSLD), it is also important to ensure that the impaired communication is enhanced or bypassed to allow the child's true 'voice' to emerge. These children do not have an intellectual impairment. Only a minority of younger children will use signing, and the use of pictures and symbols may be appropriate. For example in a study of 8-year-olds with SSLD, self-esteem was assessed in the children by the use of a scale (Harter and Pike 1984) which required the children to point to one of four faces in response to questions (Lindsay and Dockrell, in preparation).

Many of the contributors to this book have referred to ways of building rapport with children and establishing a sense of trust. The child's perception of the adult's role will be important and some of the contributors were conducting research in a professional context with known children. This may have helped to establish rapport but will also have led to certain assumptions being made by the children (see Chapters 7, 10, 11 and 14). Putting children at ease was also raised in various ways, sometimes using small groups of peers to provide a supportive environment and elsewhere developing a friendship between the researcher and the researched.

Body of the interview

Validity and reliability may be particularly pertinent in a forensic rather than research situation, where a child may be interviewed as an eye witness. Great care is needed to ensure that the questions used are related to the child's developmental status. There is evidence to show that children with learning disabilities are similar in some respects to children of the same age, but not in others, particularly responses to questions designed to 'catch out', to children of comparable mental age (Henry and Gudjohnson 1998). Also in such cases, the beliefs of the interviewer (whether doubt or certainty of the child's witness testimony, or support for children's perceived opinions in a research study) must not confound children's own views, if these are what are sought. Chapter 14 by Jo Crozier and Tracey is an interesting example of how to address these issues, where both interviewer and interviewee contribute, check and finalize – but note that Tracey did this as an adult.

Closing the interview and giving feedback

Interpretations must be checked against the child's views. The danger here is that the views of the child are lost by the actions of the interviewer, whose own views take over. While it is possible that different researchers will produce different outcomes in such interviews, it is not reasonable to regard this as an unproblematic positive characteristic of such research.

Using children, particularly children with disabilities, as research respondents may create particular challenges in attempting to validate responses. Most researchers now regard as conventional good practice giving transcripts of interviews, or other feedback, to those involved in the research (see Chapters 10 and 14). When children have been involved the researcher may feel that this 'respondent' validation should be directed to a parent or caregiver. However, such a move negates any promise of confidentiality (see Chapter 8). If feedback is given to the children then this may require careful handling if it is not to be misunderstood, for example, seen as an indication that 'wrong' answers have been given. M. Moore *et al.* (1998) reflect on similar dilemmas in relation to research involving young deaf people; they were particularly concerned about these young people's views to the gatekeepers (service providers). If such views are critical of the gatekeepers, any doubts about the validity of the process of data collection may be seized on in order to discredit the views expressed.

Conclusion

In our view, researching children's perspectives is both a fascinating and rewarding task. It is also one that is underdeveloped, but important as a means of ensuring that children's voices are heard, whether in respect of their schooling, family or any other element of their lives. The contributors to this book have, in seeking the views of children and young people, given a voice to groups often neglected in these contexts (for example, the views of disabled children and views about religion, gender, disaffection, bereavement, health or legal procedures). The challenges to obtaining children's views are considerable but, as Robert Burgess noted in the Foreword, need to be addressed in developing innovative research practice.

Many adults decide what is 'best' for children, and that is proper: parents and professionals including teachers and care workers have important responsibilities. But children have rights, and they also have perspectives which are unique to themselves. It is our task as researchers, from both practical and ethical considerations, to ensure that we ask the right questions in our studies, those which are important, and that we conduct our research in a manner that optimizes the opportunity for children's perspectives to be listened to – and heard.

 **Appendices**

Appendix I Modification of Pictorial Scale of Perceived Competence and Acceptance

This appendix links with Chapter 8.

The following three questions represent academic (Item 1), social (Item 2) and physical (Item 3) questions taken from the first and second grades version of the Pictorial Scale of Perceived Competence and Acceptance (Harter and Pike 1981). The examples are only of the left hand page, which contains the written material available to researchers. Pupils are shown the right hand page, which depicts two pictures relevant to the item questions. The examples on the following page are taken from the booklet appropriate for male pupils. The booklet appropriate for female pupils contains the same questions but the word 'boy' is replaced by 'girl'.

Item 1

This boy isn't very good at
numbers.
Are you:

This boy is pretty good at
numbers.
Are you:

Not too good OR Sort of good
at numbers

Pretty good OR Really good at
                    numbers

1   2   3   4

Item 2

This boy has lots of friends to play
with.
Do you have:

This boy doesn't have a lot of
friends to play with.
Do you have:

A whole lot of OR Pretty many
friends

A few   OR Hardly any
                        friends

1   2   3   4

Item 3

This boy isn't very good at
swinging by himself.
Are you:

This boy is very good at swinging
by himself.
Are you:

Not too good OR Sort of good
at swinging
by yourself

Pretty good OR Really good
                    at swinging
                    by yourself

1   2   3   4

Appendix 2 Schedule used for scoring the School Situations Grid

This appendix links with Chapter 8.

Name ....

Age .... Sex ....

Class/Grade ....

Teacher ....

School ....

Test Date ....

	Good at	Hard work	Happy	Likes	Naughty
Writing					
Reading					
Maths					
On my own					
With lots of friends					
With my teacher					
Running					
Swimming					
Playing ball games					

Appendix 3 Interview schedule for Sikh children

This chapter links with Chapter 11 and is based on Knott (1992: 53–6).

Session One (in schools)

1 Hello. What is your name? Do you know what mine is? I'm Eleanor Nesbitt. I used to teach in Coventry. At the moment I work in the university in the department where people learn how to teach RE. You can help us by talking about yourself and your religion.

2 Some names have meanings. Do you know if your names have any meaning in English?

3 How were your names chosen?

4 Do you mind if I tape record our conversation today?

5 How old are you? Can you tell me your date of birth?

6 What year/class/tutor group are you in here in school?

7 What language do you speak at home? Do you or your parents ever speak any other languages? Can you tell me what these tapes are about?

[Play short section of two tapes: Guru Nanak's birth, Elephant and Mouse] Can you read these? [Show graded examples of Gurmukhi] Can you tell me what they mean in English?

8 The next thing I want to ask you about is your home and family, your parents, brothers and sisters. How many people live in your house? What do your mum and dad do?

9 Now let's talk about what an average weekday in term time might be like for you from the first moment someone gets up in your house.

Meals and food, food customs and taboos
Language (proportion of English:Punjabi)
Dress, normal and ceremonial including hair (Are parents *keshdhari*?)

What are the five Ks? How do you know? Which do you have? Why? Why not? Always? Does anyone in your family have all these? Does anyone in your family have more of these than you? Fewer than you? Are they important? Why?

Religious practice in the home – prayers/reading any holy book? *Akhand path*? Who? When? Where? Together? Alone?

Going to school or work
What other members of the family do
Relations with family during day/evening
The school day – lessons, meals, activities
Friends
Going home

Evening activities – sport, homework, clubs, supplementary classes, nightlife
Family attitudes to going out

TV and video – favourites
Independence
Privacy
What newspapers, magazines do you take in the house?
Any religious papers?
What comics do you read?
What do your parents buy for you to read?

10 How do weekends differ from weekdays? [prompt as above] (*gurdwara*, language classes, weddings). Can you talk me through your normal weekend?

11 Can you tell me anything about these:

Picture of Guru Nanak
Ik om kar
Kara

12 What kind of occasions do you enjoy most?
Festivals? Marriages? Trips out? Holidays? Visits to relatives? School events?

13 Can you tell me about some of the things you like most? And some you dislike?
Is there anything you are really afraid of?
Anything else?

14 What do you feel about smoking? Why? Is it worse for Sikhs to smoke?
What do you feel about alcohol? Why?
What do you feel about taking drugs? Why?

15 What do your parents feel are the most important qualities for you to have?
Would your parents agree about them?

16 What do you think you'll be like when you're 20? Do you have any pictures in your mind of what you might be like and what you might be doing?

College?
Employment? Is there anything you can't do because of your religion?
Marriage?
Material prosperity
Happiness
Family responsibilities – parents, children, etc.

17 How do you feel about being married one day?
Have you an ideal age in mind when it would be good to be married?
How do you think you'll meet the person you marry?
Who do you think will choose? (Do you mind this?)
What kind of a person do you hope to marry?
Would you marry a non-Sikh?
Have any of your brothers or sisters got married?
Does that make you more or less keen to get married?

18 Thinking further into the future, do you ever think about death?
What do think and feel about it?
What do you think will happen to you when you die?

Do you believe in ghosts?
Any other sort of life after death?
Has anyone you know died recently?
How did this affect you?
Tell me what you did?

19 Is religion important to you?
Why/why not?
What would you miss in a non-Sikh household?
[Probe and follow up whatever is mentioned, plus God and spiritual experience]

20 Is religion important to your parents?
Why/why not?
In what ways? Beliefs? Practices?
Do they practise at home or in a place of worship?
[Explore any differences between parents and children or any shared views]
Why are your views different from/so close to theirs?

21 Have you or any member of your family taken part in a special ceremony that made you into a Sikh or into a better Sikh? What was this called? How old were you? Can you describe it? Tell me how you felt/how you think you will feel.

22 Which of these do you identify with/are you?
European, British, African, Sikh, Asian, English, Indian, Punjabi, any other.
What makes you feel like this?
Are you happy about this or do you have any problems?

23 Do you think about [any country other than UK which child mentions]? Tell me your thoughts about it.
Have you ever been there? Would you like to go?
If so why, and for how long? Permanently? If not, why not?
Do you ever think about whether you are (e.g. Indian) or British?
Are there any advantages or disadvantages related to this? [Explore complexities of identity, language, parental traditions, schoolwork, friends, etc.]

24 What name would you give to your religion?
What makes you think of yourself as a Sikh? Would you say that you belong to any particular group within Sikhism?

25 What do you think is special/different about being a Sikh?

26 Which *gurdwara* do you have links with? What sort of connection?
What is its address?
Does anyone in particular look after the *gurdwara*?
Would you like to do this?
How often do you go?
For how long have you been going?
Do you look forward to going?

27 Finish this sentence: I would know more about my religion if . . .
How do you think you have learned most about your religion?
From the *gurdwara*? How?

> Extra classes?
> Home?
> Grandparents?
> Parents?
> Other relatives? Which?
> Any special person?
> Visiting India?
> Books?
> Videos?
> School?
> RE lessons?
> Friends?

> In any other way?

28 Would your parents mind if I came to your house with some more
questions? What is your telephone number?

Thank you very much.

Session Two (with subjects of case studies at home)

29 Do you study religion at school?
Does it include Sikhism?
Can you tell me something about it?
Do you enjoy it?
In what ways?

30 What do you think about people who belong to religions other than
your own? Islam, Hinduism, Christianity, Judaism . . .
What do you think about people who belong to different *gurdwaras*?

31 Do you think your life is planned for you in advance, that is, sort of written down somewhere? (role of God, of own behaviour in this or previous lives, fate, etc.)
Do people have power to make personal choices about what they do?

32 Do you think it is possible to know what will happen to you in future?
Is it right to try to find out?
Have you ever had your fortune told? By what method?
Has it ever come true?
Do you read your stars? What do you think of them? True/false? Helpful/unhelpful?

33 Is there anything which you particularly remember from the past?

34 Do you think you've changed as you've got older?

35 Do you think you'll be like your parents are when you are older? Why/why not? In what ways?

36 Who makes decisions about the important things in your life, e.g. the school you attend?
What other people influence what you do? (parents, teachers, government, religious leaders, anyone else)

37 Can you tell me three things which inspire you? Make you feel great, switch you on?

38 Do home, school (friends and teachers), people who speak in the *gurdwara*, all encourage you to behave in the same way, to believe the same things?

39 Here is a piece of paper with a list of personal qualities in alphabetical order. Would you circle those you think describe yourself and underline those you would like other people to use to describe you?

Bad-tempered Competitive Conformist Cooperative Cruel
Generous Hardworking Honest Humble Humorous Kind
Lazy Mean Optimistic Original Patient Pessimistic
Self-confident Selfish Self-sacrificing Serious

Now reread the circled items. What makes you say that? Is it your parents – are they like that? Or your day school or the extra classes you attend?

40 Tell me what happens when you go to the *gurdwaras*.

41 Tell me about any extra language or religion or music classes that you attend.

42 Tell me about any youth club.

43 How often do you read your holy book or hear passages from it? Is the holy book different from other books? How? Would you treat it any differently? Are there any other books which are almost as (different, holy, special)?

44 Have you ever been called names or treated badly or unkindly? Can you describe your experiences? Why do you think you were treated as you were?

45 Do you ever call other people names or bully them? Why? Why not?

46 What do you think are really cruel or wicked things to do?
   What happens to people who do things like these? Before they die/after they die? In every case?

47 Do you think there is a hell? What is it like? Why do you think that? What do you think about reincarnation? Do you think people are born again as human beings or in any other form?
   What can you tell me about the devil/evil?

48 Can you give me some examples of what you think are very good deeds? What happens to people who do these? Always?

49 Is there a heaven? Why do you think so? What is it like?

50 Why do some people suffer a lot? Why do you think this?

51 Some people refuse to fight. They say that war is always wrong. What do you think?

52 Do girls and boys usually like the same sort of things? Are girls or boys better at some things? Which?
   Do you like cooking? Do your brother/sisters do more cooking than you do? Is that as it should be? Do you think girls and boys should be able to do the same jobs when they leave school?

Session Three (with subjects of case studies at home)

53 What makes someone a Sikh? Birth? An experience? Teaching? Environment? How can you tell if someone is a Sikh? How they treat others?

54 What would you miss most if you were to live in a non-Sikh household? What would a non-Sikh notice especially in your home?

55 How should Sikhs behave towards people who are not Sikhs? Can Sikhs learn anything from non-Sikhs? Can they share anything special with them?

56 Tell me about any discussion which you have had with friends on a religious subject.

57 Does prayer play any part in your life? Can you tell me when you would pray, where, what sort of words you'd use, who you address your prayers to, how long you've been praying?

58 Do you ever say grace before meals? When? Where? What words do you use?

59 Are there any places which are important for Sikhs? For you? Have you been to any of them? Describe what they are like. If you've not been how do you know what they are like?

60 Are there any pictures or pieces of music which mean a lot to you? Are any of these religious?

61 What are your favourite hymns? At what age did you learn them and from whom?

62 What are your favourite prayers? At what age did you learn them and from whom?

63 What are your favourite stories about the Gurus and Sikh history. Which people in these do you like best?

64 Do you have any favourite saints? Any favourite stories of saints? Tell me about them. How did you hear about them?

65 Do you watch any religious videos? TV programmes? Have these affected what you believe or taught you anything? What?

66 Tell me your idea of God. Where? (Shape/qualities) What names do you use for God?

67 Tell me what these words mean to you:

Guru, Guru Nanak, Guru Gobind Singh, Gurbani, nam.

68 What is your favourite festival? What do you do?

69 What other festivals do you keep? Tell me about them.

70 Are there any days when you are expected to go without particular foods? Which? Why?

71 Are there any days when you are expected to be sad?

72 Is there anything you'd like to say about being a Sikh?

73 What do you think about church schools? Should there be Sikh schools?

74 Tell me about these pictures [show series of slides taken during the fieldwork].

Appendix 4 Issues to consider when interviewing young people with moderate learning difficulties

This appendix links with Chapter 13.

Setting the scene
- Importance of familiarization with the environment.
- Establishment of relationships with the pupils to be interviewed.
- Be prepared to ask critical or 'obvious' questions in shared situations.
- Be prepared to be challenged by pupils who may respond to the interview and discussion in ways you could not imagine.
- Be aware of your preconceptions about pupils' special needs.

Question design
- Formulate key questions or areas of interest to be explored.
- Establish the link between main research questions and key questions for interviews.
- Determine what it is you want to find out and what sort of response you need.
- What data are the questions designed to elicit?
- Draw up a list of questions that will allow you to explore those areas of pupils' experience.
- Be prepared to be flexible in how questions are framed and in the order in which they are addressed.

Piloting

- Always try to pilot the questions and process to be used with a similar group of pupils.
- Take note of difficulties pupils may have with terminology or forms of questions.
- Make sure they understand the process of discussion.
- If appropriate set down some ground rules about speaking, listening and respecting the views of others.
- Test all aspects of the process e.g. if using an introductory activity.
- Ask pupils for their views on the questions and process.
- Make a note of the time taken for each element of the process.

Organization of interviews

- Familiarize yourself with the space available for interviews.
- Make sure the room is free for as long as you need it.
- Check power supply if using a tape recorder.
- Check arrangement of seating and change if necessary.
- If possible allow pupils to select the groups they will work with.

Conducting interviews

- Explain what you are trying to find out.
- Treat the pupils with the same respect you would accord to adults.
- Consider using an introductory ice breaker.
- Try to make the discussion relaxed.
- If using a tape recorder make it as unobtrusive as possible but ensure that pupils know it is being used.
- Be aware of group dynamics, especially if someone else has selected the group.
- Ensure everyone is involved in the discussion.
- Try to facilitate discussion rather than lead or dominate.

Recording and transcribing

- If using a tape recorder it is important that pupils introduce themselves first so that you can identify their voices clearly.
- Encourage pupils to listen to each other so that you will be able to hear individual voices on the tape.
- Listen to the tape recording as soon as possible after the event to fix pupils' voices in your mind.
- Transcribe the discussion in full to aid validity and authenticity.
- Where appropriate take note of individual responses verbatim to illuminate the findings.
- Make a note of the context for the discussion and any key events that were not picked up by the recording.
- If taking notes use a form with the questions printed and room for notes based on key words.
- Write up full notes directly after the discussion.

Analysing data

- When using group interviews note should be taken of the group consensus on key issues.
- In the context described in Chapter 13 the main analysis was of content.
- It is important to note where pupils are able to extend the discussion by the group interacting.
- If possible check responses with pupils for reliability.
- If a reliability check is not possible be clear about authenticity of pupils' views and accuracy of note taking.
- Relate the content of discussion transcriptions to the original research questions.

Appendix 5 Schedule of suggested lead questions for pupil group discussions

This appendix links with Chapter 13.

The purpose of these questions is to frame group discussions with pupils in Years 10 and 11 (Key Stage 4), in an attempt to gain some insight into their perceptions of school. The questions are grouped according to their links with the basic research questions applied to all aspects of the case study. It is hoped that by including the pupils' perspective a fuller picture of the effect of the National Curriculum in each case study school will be drawn up.

It is hoped that all pupils from these year groups, who are present at the time of the discussions, will take part. This will avoid the need for selection which would introduce a number of variables with possibilities of bias and unreliability.

The purpose of the research should be explained to pupils and they should be offered the same confidentiality as adults in the research. To break the ice all pupils should be asked to introduce themselves and give their age (to get them all used to speaking, particularly in the presence of a tape recorder). If there is time an introductory game could be introduced.

Implementation of the National Curriculum
In this section I hope to get some idea of pupils' general views of school in relation to curriculum. Also, whether they are conscious of similarities and differences between themselves and peers at local comprehensive schools.

1 What do you like about this school, in general, not just lessons?
2 Is there anything you do not like about school?
3 Is school different now you are in this class?
4 What subjects do you like? Why?
5 Are there any subjects you do not like? Why?
6 What do you feel you spend most time on at school?
7 Is there anything they do at [*name of local comprehensive school*] that you wish you could do here?

Aims of education

These questions are aimed at discovering the extent of pupils' knowledge of the National Curriculum and any feelings that they may have about it.

8 What do you think teachers are trying to help you do when you are in this class?
9 Who do you think decides what you learn in school?
10 Do you think the government has any thing to do with schools?
11 Have you heard of the National Curriculum? [*If yes*] What does it mean? [*Interviewer may have to give a brief explanation here.*]
12 Do you think it is a good or a bad idea for all schools to have the same curriculum? Why?

Assessment

This section aims to discover pupils' views on assessment, both within their own school and in mainstream secondary, including the purpose of and uses for it.

13 Do you have to do any tests or exams before you leave school?
14 If so, why do you do these? If not, would you like to?
15 How do people outside school know what you have achieved while you have been here? For example, when you go for a job or to college.
16 Which things that you have done in school will help you when you leave?

Options post-16

Following from the previous questions, this section will elicit data on possible avenues for pupils as well as probable ones. It may include knowledge of last year's leavers as well as any careers input they may have had.

17 What sort of things could you do when you leave school?
18 What do you think you will do? [*Ask each member of the group to comment*]
19 Who will help you when you leave school?

 References

Adler, Patricia A. and Adler, Peter (1993) Ethical issues in self-censorship: ethnographic research on sensitive topics, in C. M. Renzetti and R. M. Lee (eds) *Researching Sensitive Topics.* Newbury Park, CA: Sage.

Alderson, P. (1995) *Listening to Children.* London: Barnardo's.

Alexander, G. (1995) Children's rights in their early years: from plaiting fog to knitting treacle, in B. Franklin (ed.) *The Handbook of Children's Rights: Comparative Policy and Practice.* London: Routledge.

Alexander, R. (1996) *Other Primary Schools and Ours: Hazards of International Comparison.* Centre for Research in Elementary and Primary Education Occasional Paper. Coventry: University of Warwick.

American Psychological Association (APA) (1992) Ethical principles of psychologists and code of conduct, *American Psychologist*, 47: 1597–1611.

Anderson, G. L., Herr, K. and Nihlen, A. S. (1994) *Studying your Own School: An Educator's Guide to Qualitative Practitioner Research.* London: Sage.

Audit Commission (1992) *Getting In on the Act. Provision for Pupils with Special Educational Needs: The National Picture.* London: HMSO.

Ayella, M. (1993) 'They must be crazy': some of the difficulties in researching 'cults', in C. M. Renzetti and R. M. Lee (eds) *Researching Sensitive Topics.* London: Sage.

Bailey, E. (1998) *Implicit Religion: An Introduction.* London: Middlesex University Press.

Bainham, A. (1998) *Children: The Modern Law.* Bristol: Family Law.

Ball, S. (1991) Power, conflict, micropolitics and all that!, in G. Walford (ed.) *Doing Educational Research.* London: Routledge.

Ball, S. (1993) Self doubt and soft data: social and technical trajectories in ethnographic fieldwork, in M. Hammersley (ed.) *Educational Research: Current Issues*. London: Paul Chapman in association with The Open University.

Ball, S. J., Bowe, R. and Gerwitz S. (1994) Market forces and parental choice, in S. Tomlinson (ed.) *Educational Reform and its Consequences*. London: Institute for Public Policy Research and Rivers Oram Press.

Barker, E. (1983) Supping with the devil: how long a spoon does the sociologist need? *Sociological Analysis*, 41: 128–36.

Barratt, M. and Price, J. (1996) *Meeting Christians Book 1: Teacher's Resource Book*. Oxford: Heinemann.

Barton, L. and Meighan, R. (eds) (1979) *Schools, Pupils and Deviance*. Driffield: Nafferton.

Beckford, J. A. (1985) *Cult Controversies*. New York: Tavistock.

Begley, A. and Lewis, A. (1998) Methodological issues in the assessment of the self-concept of children with Down Syndrome, *Child Psychology and Psychiatry Review*, 3: 33–40.

Bell, D. (1998) Accessing science: challenges faced by teachers of children with learning difficulties in primary schools, *Support for Learning*, 13(1): 26–31.

Bendelow, G., France, A. and Williams, S. (1998) *Beliefs of Young People in Relation to Health, Risk and Lifestyles*. Final Report to the NHS Executive. Coventry: University of Warwick.

Bennett, J. (1996) Supporting family responsibility for the rights of the child: an educational viewpoint, *International Journal of Children's Rights*, 4: 45–56.

Billig, M. (1987) *Arguing and Thinking: A Rhetorical Approach to Psychology*. Cambridge: Cambridge University Press.

Blaxter, L., Hughes, C. and Tight, M. (1996) *How to Research*. Buckingham: Open University Press.

Breakwell, G. M. (1990) *Interviewing*. London: British Psychological Society with Routledge.

British Educational Research Association (BERA) (1992) *Ethical Guidelines for Educational Research*. Edinburgh: BERA and Scottish Council for Research in Education.

British Psychological Society (BPS) (1996) *Code of Conduct, Ethical Principles and Guidelines*. Leicester: BPS.

British Sociological Association (BSA) (1993) *Statement of Ethical Practice*. London: BSA.

Bronfenbrenner, U. (1979) *The Ecology of Human Development*. Cambridge, MA: Harvard University Press.

Brown, G. and Yule, G. (1983) *Discourse Analysis*. Cambridge: Cambridge University Press.

Brown, R. (1973) *A First Language: the Early Stages*. London: Allen & Unwin.

Bryant, P. (1974) *Perception and Understanding in Young Children*. London: Methuen.

Bryant, P. E. (1984) Piaget, teachers and psychologists, *Oxford Educational Review*, 10(3): 215–59.

Bryman, A. and Burgess, R. (ed.) (1994) *Analysing Qualitative Data*. London: Routledge.

Bull, R. (1995) Interviewing children in legal contexts, in R. Bull and D. Carson (eds) *Handbook of Psychology in Legal Contexts*. Chichester: Wiley.

Bulmer, M. (1979) Concepts in the analysis of qualitative data, *Sociological Review*, 27: 651–77.

Burgess, R. (ed.) (1982) *Field Research: A Sourcebook and Field Manual*. London: Allen & Unwin.

Burgess, R. G. (1995) Gaining access to pupil perspectives, in M. Lloyd-Smith and J. D. Davies (eds) *On the Margins: The Educational Experience of 'Problem' Pupils*. Stoke-on-Trent: Trentham.

Burns, R. B. (1982) *The Self-Concept: In Theory, Measurement, Development and Behaviour*. London: Longman.

Bushnell, H. (1967) *Christian Nurture*. New Haven, CT: Yale University Press (first published 1847).

Butler, I. and Williamson, H. (1994) *Children Speak: Children, Trauma and Social Work*. London: Longman.

Canadian Psychological Association (CPA) (1992) *Companion Manual to the Canadian Code of Ethics for Psychologists, 1991*. Quebec: CPA.

Carrington, B. and Short, G. (1992) Researching 'race' in the 'all-white' primary school: the ethics of curriculum development, in M. Leicester and M. Taylor (eds) *Ethics, Ethnicity and Education*. London: Kogan Page.

Caul, L. (ed.) (1990) *Schools under Scrutiny: The Case of Northern Ireland*. London: Macmillan.

Ceci, S. (1991) The suggestibility of child witnesses. Paper to the British Psychological Society. Annual conference, Bournemouth, March.

Ceci, S. J. and Bronfenbrenner, U. (1985) 'Don't forget to take the cupcakes out of the oven': prospective memory, strategic time monitoring and context, *Child Development*, 56, 152–64.

Chaudhary, V. (1998) School leagues blamed for boom in exclusions, *The Guardian*, 23 March.

Children's Rights Office (CRO) (1995) *Making the Convention Work for Children*. London: CRO.

Childright (1996) At what age can I . . . ? *Childright* 128.

Clark, D. (1995) Whose case Is It anyway? MPhil thesis, University of Sussex.

Cleaver, H. and Freeman, P. (1995) *Parental Perspectives in Cases of Suspected Child Abuse*. London: HMSO.

Cochran-Smith, M. and Lytle, S. L. (1993) *Inside Outside: Teacher Research and Knowledge*. New York: Teachers College Press.

Coffey, A. and Atkinson, P. (1996) *Making Sense of Qualitative Data*. London: Sage.

Cohen, L. and Manion, L. (1994) *Research Methods in Education*, 4th edn. London: Routledge.

Connolly, P. (1998) *Racism, Gender Identities and Young Children: Social Relations in a Multi-ethnic, Inner City Primary School*. London: Routledge.

Cooper, P., Smith, C. and Upton, G. (1994) *Emotional and Behavioural Difficulties: Theory to Practice*. London: Routledge.

Council of Europe (1985) *Teaching and Learning about Human Rights in Schools*. Appendix to Recommendations of the Committee of Ministers to Member States, Strasbourg: Council of Europe.

Coupe, J., Barton, L., Barber, M. *et al.* (1985) *Affective Communication Assessment (Leading to Intervention, for Use with Developmentally Young Pupils).* Manchester: Hester Adrian Research Centre.

Crafts, L. W., Schneila, T. C., Robinson, E. E. and Gilbert, R. W. (1938) *Recent Experiments in Psychology.* New York: McGraw-Hill.

Crompton, M. (1996) *Children, Spirituality and Religion: A Training Pack.* London: Central Council for Training and Education in Social Work.

Crozier, J. and Anstiss, J. (1995) Out of the spotlight: girls' experience of disruption, in M. Lloyd-Smith and J. Davies (eds) *On the Margins: The Educational Experience of Problem Pupils.* Stoke-on-Trent: Trentham.

Cuskelly, M. and de Jong, I. (1996) Self-concept in children with Down Syndrome, *Down Syndrome: Research and Practice,* 4: 59–64.

Dalrymple, J. and Burke, B. (1996) *Anti-Oppressive Practice: Social Care and Law.* Buckingham: Open University Press.

Davie, R. and Galloway, D. (eds) (1996) *Listening to Children in Education.* London: David Fulton.

Davies, B. (1982) *Life in the Classroom and Playground.* London: Routledge & Kegan Paul.

Davies, B. (1989) *Frogs and Snails and Feminist Tails: Pre-School Children and Gender.* Sydney: Allen & Unwin.

Davies, L. (1978) The view from the girls, *Educational Review,* 30(2): 103–9.

Dawtry, L., Holland, J., Hammer, M. and Sheldon, S. (eds) (1995) *Equality and Inequality in Education Policy.* Clevedon: Multilingual Matters.

Denny, T. (1978) In defence of story telling as a first step in educational research. Paper presented at the International Reading Association Conference, Houston.

Denscombe, M. and Aubrook, L. (1992) 'It's just another piece of school work': the ethics of questionnaire research on pupils in schools, *British Educational Research Journal,* 18(2): 113–31.

Department for Education (DfE) (1994a) *Code of Practice for the Identification and Assessment of Children with Special Educational Needs.* London: HMSO.

Department for Education (DfE) (1994b) Statistics of schools in England: January 1993. *Statistical Bulletin,* 8/94. London: DfE.

Department for Education and Employment (DfEE) (1997a) *Excellence for All Children: Meeting Special Educational Needs.* London: DfEE.

Department for Education and Employment (DfEE) (1997b) *Statistics on Women and Men in Education, Training and Employment.* London: HMSO.

Department for Education and Employment (DfEE) (1998) *Teaching: High Status, High Standards: Requirements for Courses of Initial Teacher Training,* Circular 4/98. London: DfEE.

Department of Education and Science (DES) (1978) *Special Educational Needs: Report of the Committee of Enquiry into the Education of Handicapped Children and Young People.* London: HMSO.

Department of Education and Science (DES) (1989) *Discipline in Schools (The Elton Committee Report).* London: HMSO.

Department of Health (DoH) (1991) *Working Together under the Children Act 1989.* London: HMSO.

Department of Health (DoH) (1994) Child Protection: Medical Responsibilities – an Addendum to Working Together under the Children Act 1989. London: HMSO.

Department of Health (DoH) (1995) *Not Alone: A Children's Guide to Care Proceedings*. London: HMSO.

Department of Health and Social Security (DHSS) (1974) *Report of the Committee of Inquiry into the Care and Supervision Provided in Relation to Maria Colwell*. London: HMSO.

Detheridge, T. (1996) The role of information technology in bridging the communication competence/production gap in pupils with profound and multiple learning difficulties. Unpublished MPhil thesis, University of Warwick.

Detheridge, T. and Detheridge, M. (1997) *Literacy through Symbols*. London: David Fulton.

Deutscher, I. (1973) *What We Say, What We Do: Sentiments and Acts*. Glenview, IL: Scott, Foresman.

Diener, E. and Crandall, R. (1978) *Ethics in Social and Behavioural Research*. Chicago: University of Chicago Press.

Dockrell, J. and Joffe, H. (1992) Methodological issues involved in the study of young people and HIV/AIDS: a social psychological view, *Health Education Research: Theory and Practice*, 7(4): 509–16.

Dockrell, J. and McShane, J. (1993) *Children's Learning Difficulties: A Cognitive Approach*. Oxford: Blackwell.

Doherty, P. (1997) Engaging students on the margins in educational research, *Emotional and Behavioural Difficulties*, 2(3): 29–37.

Donaldson, M. (1978) *Children's Minds*. London: Fontana.

Dunn, J. (1988) *The Beginnings of Social Understanding*. Oxford: Blackwell.

Edwards, A. (1988) A child of four could tell you: a study of identity in the nursery school using situations grids, in F. Fransella and L. Thomas (eds) *Experimenting with Personal Construct Psychology*. London: Routledge & Kegan Paul.

Edwards, A. D. and Westgate, D. P. G. (1994) *Investigating Classroom Talk*, 2nd edn. Lewes: Falmer Press.

Elliot, J. (1990) Validating Case Studies, *Westminster Studies in Education*, 13: 47–60.

Elliot, J. (1991) *Action Research for Educational Change*. Buckingham: Open University Press.

EPOCH Worldwide (1996) *Hitting People is Wrong – and Children are People Too*. London: Approach.

Ericsson, K. A. and Simon, H. A. (1990) Verbal reports as data, *Psychological Review*, 87: 215–51.

European Federation of Professional Psychologists Associations (EFPPA) (1995) *Meta-code of Ethics*. Leicester: British Psychological Society for EFPPA.

Everington, J. (1996a) A question of authenticity: the relationship between educators and practitioners in the representation of religious traditions, *British Journal of Religious Education*, 18(2): 69–78.

Everington, J. (1996b) *Meeting Christians: Book 2: Teacher's Resource Book*. Oxford: Heinemann.

Farberow, N. L. (1963) Introduction, in N. L. Farberow (ed.) *Taboo Topics*. New York: Atherton.

Finch, J. (1987) The vignette technique in survey research, *Sociology*, 21(1): 25–34.

Fine, G. and Sandstrom, K. (1988) *Knowing Children: Participant Observation with Minors*. Newbury Park, CA: Sage.

Forster, E. M. (1953) *The Hill of Devi*. London: Arnold.

Foucault, M. (1977) *Discipline and Punish: The Birth of the Prison*. Harmondsworth: Penguin.

Foucault, M. (1980) Two lectures, in C. Gordon (ed.) *Power/Knowledge: Selected Interviews and Other Writings 1972–77: Michel Foucault*. London: Harvester Wheatsheaf.

Fox Harding, L. (1991) *Perspectives in Child Care Policy*. London: Longman.

France, A. (1996) Youth and citizenship in the 1990s, *Youth and Policy*, 53: 28–43.

Franklin, B. (ed.) (1995) *The Handbook of Children's Rights: Comparative Policy and Practice*. London: Routledge.

Freire, P. (1993) *Pedagogy of the Oppressed*. Harmondsworth: Penguin.

Galloway, D., Rogers, C., Armstrong, D. and Leo, E. (1998) *Motivating the Difficult to Teach*. London: Longman.

Gardner, F. (1994) The quality of joint activity between mothers and their children with behaviour problems, *Journal of Child Psychology and Psychiatry*, 45, 935–48.

Garner, P. (1995) Schools by scoundrels: the views of 'disruptive' pupils in mainstream schools in England and the United States, in M. Lloyd-Smith and J. Davies (eds) *On the Margins: The Educational Experience of Problem Pupils*. Stoke-on-Trent: Trentham Books.

Gathercole, S. E. and Baddeley, A. D. (1992) *Working Memory and Language*. Hove: Erlbaum.

Geaves, R. (1998) The borders between religions: a challenge to the world religions approach to religious education, *British Journal of Religious Education*, 21, 1, 20–31.

Geertz, C. (1973) *The Interpretation of Cultures*. New York: Basic Books.

Geertz, C. (1983) *Local Knowledge*. New York: Basic Books.

Gerwitz, S., Ball, S. J. and Bowe, R. (1995) *Markets, Choice and Equity in Education*. Buckingham: Open University Press.

Glaser, B. and Strauss, A. (1967) *The Discovery of Grounded Theory*. New York: Aldine de Gruyter.

Glenn, S. and O'Brien, Y. (1990) Encouraging contingent responding in children with severe and profound learning difficulties, in W. I. Fraser (ed.) *Key Issues in Mental Retardation Research*. London: Routledge.

Glenn, S. and O'Brien, Y. (1994) Microcomputers: do they have a part to play in the education of children with PMLDs?, in J. Ware (ed.) *Educating Children with Profound and Multiple Learning Difficulties*. London: David Fulton.

Glinert, L. (1993) Language as quasilect: Hebrew in contemporary Anglo-Jewry, in L. Glinert (ed.) *Hebrew in Ashkenaz: A Language in Exile*. Oxford: Oxford University Press.

Golby, M. (1994) *Case Study as Educational Research*. Exeter: University of Exeter.

Goodson, I. and Walker, R. (1995) Telling tales, in H. McEwan and K. Egan (eds) *Narrative in Teaching, Learning, and Research*. New York: Teachers College Press.

Griffiths, M. (1985) Doubts, dilemmas and diary keeping: some reflections on teacher-based research, in R. G. Burgess (ed.) *Issues in Educational Research: Qualitative Methods*. Lewes: Falmer Press.

Griffiths, T. (1997) Obituary to Albert Kushlick. Care for all the children, *The Guardian*, 2 September.

Gross, M. (1993) *Exceptionally Gifted Children*. London: Routledge.

Grove, N., Porter, J., Bunning, K. and Olsson, C. (in press) Interpreting the meaning of communication by people with severe and profound intellectual disabilities, *Journal of Applied Research in Intellectual Disabilities*.

Gurney, P. (1990) The enhancement of self-esteem in junior classrooms, in J. Docking (ed.) *Education and Alienation in the Junior School*. London: Falmer Press.

Hall, C. S. (1952) Crooks, codes and cant, *American Psychologist*, 7, 430–1.

Hamilton, C. and Hopegood, L. (1997) Offering children confidentiality: law and guidance, *Childright*, 140: 1–8.

Hamilton, D. (1995) *Peddling Feel-Good Fictions (Reflections on Key Characteristics of Effective Schools)*. Liverpool: Department of Education, University of Liverpool.

Hamilton, D. (1997) Peddling feel-good fictions, in M. Barber and J. White (eds) *Perspectives on School Effectiveness and School Improvement*. London: Institute of Education, University of London.

Hammersley, M. (1992) *What's Wrong with Ethnography?* London: Routledge.

Hammersley, M. (1997) Partnership and credibility: the case of anti-racist educational research, in P. Connolly and B. Troyna (eds) *Researching Racism in Education: Politics, Theory and Practice*. Buckingham: Open University Press.

Hammersley, M. and Atkinson, P. (1984) *Ethnography: Principles in Practice*. London: Routledge.

Handy, C. (1990) *The Age of Unreason*. London: Arrow.

Harper, D. (1992) Small N's and community case studies, in C. Ragin and H. Becker (eds) *What is a Case?* Cambridge: Cambridge University Press.

Harris, J. (1994) Language, communication and personal power: a developmental perspective, in J. Coupe-O'Kane and B. Smith (eds) *Taking Control*. London: David Fulton.

Harris, J. R. (1995) Where is the child's environment? A group socialisation theory of development, *Psychological Review*, 102: 458–89.

Harter, S. (1990) Developmental differences in the nature of self-representations: implications for the understanding, assessment and treatment of maladaptive behaviour, *Cognitive Therapy and Research*, 14: 113–42.

Harter, S. and Pike, R. (1981) *The Pictorial Scale of Perceived Competence and Acceptance for Young Children*. Plates – first and second grades. University of Denver.

Harter, S. and Pike, R. (1984) The pictorial scale of perceived competence and social acceptance for young children, *Child Development*, 55: 1969–82.

Hazel, N. (1996) *Elicitation Techniques with Young People*. Social Research Update. Guildford: University of Surrey.

Henry, L. and Gudjohnson, G. (1998) Eye witness memory and suggestibility in children with learning disabilities. Paper presented to the London Conference of the British Psychological Society, London, December.

Her Majesty's Inspectorate (HMI) (1991) *National Curriculum and Special Needs: Preparation to Implement the National Curriculum for Pupils with Statements in Special and Ordinary Schools, 1989–90*. London: HMSO.

Hillage, J., Pearson, R., Anderson, A. and Tamkin, P. (1998) *Excellence in Research on Schools*. London: DfEE.

Homan, R. (1991) *The Ethics of Social Research*. London: Longman.

Hornby, G. (1995) *Working with Parents of Children with Special Educational Needs*. London: Cassell.

Howarth, C., Kenway, P., Palmer, G. and Street, C. (1998) *Key Indicators of Poverty and Social Exclusion*. London: New Policy Institute.

Huberman, M. (1995) Working with life-history narratives, in H. McEwan and K. Egan (eds) *Narrative in Teaching, Learning, and Research*. New York: Teachers College Press.

Hudson, C. (1996) Unethical research with children? Paper presented to Ethnography in Education Conference, Oxford, March.

Hudson, C. (1998) Time: a neglected dimension in fieldwork? Explorations of the concept of time in qualitative research. Paper presented to Case Study Research in Education Conference, University of Warwick, March.

Hughes, C. (1994) From field notes to dissertation: analysing the stepfamily, in A. Bryman and R. Burgess (eds) *Analysing Qualitative Data*. London: Routledge.

Hughes, M. and Grieve, R. (1980) On asking children bizarre questions, *First Language*, 1: 149–60.

Hull, J. (1984) *Studies in Religion and Education*. Lewes: Falmer Press.

Hull, J. (1991) *God-Talk with Young Children*. Birmingham Papers in Religious Education 2, University of Birmingham and the Christian Education Movement/Philadelphia, PA: Trinity Place International.

Hunt, J. and Macleod, A. (1997) *The Last Resort: Child Protection, The Courts and the 1989 Children Act*. Bristol: Centre for Socio-Legal Studies, University of Bristol.

Hyde, K. (1990) *Religion in Childhood and Adolescence: A Comprehensive Review of the Research*. Birmingham, AL: Religious Education Press.

Jackson, R. (1997) *Religious Education: An Interpretive Approach*. London: Hodder.

Jackson, R., Barratt, M. and Everington, J. (1994) *Bridges to Religions Teacher's Resource Book*. Oxford: Heinemann.

Jackson, R. and Nesbitt, E. (1993) *Hindu Children in Britain*. Stoke-on-Trent: Trentham.

James, A. and Prout, A. (eds) (1990) *Constructing and Reconstructing Childhood*, 1st edn. London: Falmer Press.

James, A. and Prout, A. (1996) Strategies and structures: towards a new perspective on children's experiences of family life, in J. Brannen and M. O'Brien (1996) *Children in Families: Research and Policy*. London: Falmer Press.

James, A. and Prout, A. (eds) (1997) *Constructing and Reconstructing Childhood*, 2nd edn. London: Falmer Press.

Jenkins, P. (1993) *Children's Rights: A Participative Exercise for Learning about Children's Rights in England and Wales*. London: Longman.

Jenks, C. (ed.) (1982) *The Sociology of Childhood: Essential Readings*. London: Batsford.

Jenks, C. (1995) The centrality of the eye in western culture: an introduction, in C. Jenks (ed.) *Visual Culture*. London: Routledge.

John, P. (1996) Damaged goods? An interpretation of excluded pupils' perceptions of schooling, in E. Blyth and J. Milner (eds) *Exclusion from School: Inter-Professional Issues for Policy and Practice*. London: Routledge.

Jones, M. (1996) No angel, *Sunday Times*, 27 October.

Karmiloff-Smith, A. (1992) *Beyond Modularity: A Developmental Perspective on Cognitive Science*. London: MIT Press.

Kelly, G. A. (1955) *The Psychology of Personal Constructs*. New York: Wiley.

Kennedy, I. (1988) *Treat Me Right*. Oxford: Clarendon Press.

Keys, W. and Fernandes, C. (1993) *What Do Students Think about School?* Slough: National Foundation for Educational Research (NFER).

King, R. (1987) No best method – qualitative and quantitative research, in G. Walford (ed.) *Doing Sociology of Education*. London: Falmer Press.

Klee, T., Carson, D., Gavin, W., Hall, L., Kent, A. and Reece, S. (1998) Concurrent and predictive validity of an early language screening program, *Journal of Speech, Language and Hearing Research*, 41: 627–41.

Knight, A. (1998) *Valued or Forgotten Independent Visitors and Disabled Young Children*. London: National Children's Bureau.

Knott, K. (1992) *The Changing Character of the Religions of the Ethnic Minorities of Asian Origin in Britain: Final Report of a Leverhulme Project*. Community Religions Project Research Papers (new series). Leeds: Department of Theology and Religious Studies, University of Leeds.

Kraat, A. W. (1985) *Communication Interaction between Aided and Natural Speakers: An IPCAS Study Report*. Toronto: Canadian Rehabilitation Council for the Disabled.

Kurtz, P., Gaudin, J., Wodarski, J. and Howing, P. (1993) Maltreatment and the school aged child: school performance consequences, *Child Abuse and Neglect*, 17(5): 581–9.

Lahey, M. (1988) *Language Disorders and Language Development*. New York: Macmillan.

Lansdown, G. and Newell, P. (1994) *UK Agenda for Children*. London: Children's Rights Development Unit.

Landis, C. (1924) Studies of emotional reactions: general behaviour and facial expressions, *Journal of Comparative Psychology*, 4: 447–50.

Lansdown, G., Waterston, T. and Baum, D. (1996) Implementing the UN Convention on the Rights of the Child, *British Medical Journal*, 313: 21–8.

Leaman, O. (1996) cited in G. Haigh, Death in the classroom, *Times Educational Supplement*, 22 November.

Lee, L. (1965) *Cider with Rosie*. London: Hogarth.

Lee, R. (1993) *Doing Research on Sensitive Topics*. London: Sage.

Lee, S. (1986) *Laws and Morals: Warwick, Gillick and Beyond*. Oxford: Oxford University Press.

Lewis, A. (1992) Group child interviews as a research tool, *British Educational Research Journal*, 18(4): 413–21.

Lewis, A. (1995) *Children's Understanding of Disability*. London: Routledge.

Light, J., McNaughton, D. and Parnes, P. (1986) *A Protocol for the Assessment of the Communicative Interaction Skills of Non-speaking Severely Handicapped Adults and their Facilitators*. Toronto: Hugh Macmillan Medical Centre.

Lindley, B. (1994) *On The Receiving End*. London: Family Rights Group.

Lindsay, G. (1992) Educational psychologists and Europe, in S. Wolfendale, T. Bryans, M. Fox, A. Labram and A. Sigston (eds) *The Profession and Practice of Educational Psychology*. London: Cassell.

Lindsay, G. (1995) Values, ethics and psychology, *The Psychologist: Bulletin of the British Psychological Society*, 8: 448–51.

Lindsay, G. (1998) Baseline assessment: a positive or malign influence? in B. Norwich and G. Lindsay (eds) *Baseline Assessment*. Tamworth: National Association for Special Educational Needs (NASEN).

Lindsay, G. and Clarkson, P. (1999) Ethical dilemmas of psychotherapists, *The Psychologist: Bulletin of the British Psychological Society*, 12: 182–5.

Lindsay, G. and Colley, A. (1995) Ethical dilemmas of members of the Society, *The Psychologist: Bulletin of the British Psychological Society*, 8: 214–17.

Lindsay, G. and Desforges, M. (1998) *Baseline Assessment: Practice, Problems and Possibilities*. London: David Fulton.

Lindsay, G. and Dockrell, J. E. (in preparation) The behaviour and self esteem of children with specific speech and language difficulties.

Lipman, M. (1980) *Philosophy in the Classroom*. Philadelphia, PA: Temple University Press.

Llewellyn, M. (1980) Studying girls at school: the implication of confusion, in R. Deem (ed.) *Schooling for Women's Work*. London: Routledge & Kegan Paul.

Lloyd Bennett, P. (1993) Stockpiling the unsaleable goods, *Education*, 13 September: 126–7.

Lloyd-Smith, M. and Davies, J. (eds) (1995) *On the Margins: The Educational Experience of Problem Pupils*. Stoke-on-Trent: Trentham.

McDougall, W. (1921) *An Introduction to Social Psychology*, 16th edn. London: Methuen.

McTear, M. (1985) *Children's Conversation*. Oxford: Blackwell.

Martinsen, H. and von Tetzchner, S. (1996) Situating augmentative and alternative communication intervention, in S. von Tetzchner and M. Hygum Jensen (eds) *Augmentative and Alternative Communication: European Perspectives*. London: Whurr.

Mason, J. (1996) *Qualitative Researching*. London: Sage.

May, T. (1993) *Social Research: Issues, Methods and Processes*. Buckingham: Open University Press.

Mayall, B. (1996) *Children, Health and the Social Order*. Buckingham: Open University Press.

Measor, L. and Woods, P. (1984) *Changing Schools: Pupil Perspectives on Transfer to a Comprehensive*. Milton Keynes: Open University Press.

Melton, G. B., Koocher, G. P. and Saks, M. J. (1983) *Children's Competence to Consent*. New York: Plenum.

Merson, M. (1995) Political explanations for economic decline in Britain and their relationship to policies for education and training, *Journal of Education Policy*, 10(3): 303–15.

Mertens, D. and McLaughlin, J. (1995) *Research Methods in Special Education*. London: Sage.

Miles, M. B. and Huberman, A. M. (1994) *Qualitative Data Analysis*, 2nd edn. London: Sage.

Milgram, S. (1963) Behavioural study of obedience, *Journal of Abnormal and Social Psychology*, 67: 391–8.

Mill, J. S. (1964) *Utilitarianism, On Liberty and Considerations on Representative Government*. London: Dent.

Mills, R. and Mills, J. (1993) *Bilingualism in the Primary School*. London: Routledge.

Moore, M., Beazley, S. and Hargie, O. (1998) *Researching Disability Issues*. Buckingham: Open University Press.

Moore, S. (1993) Children of our times, *Observer*, 25 November.

Mortimore, P., Sammons, P., Stoll, L., Lewis, D. and Ecob, R. (1988) *School Matters: The Junior Years*. Wells: Open Books.

Murch, M. and Hooper, D. (1992) *The Family Justice System*. Bristol: Family Law.

Musslewhite, C. and St Louis, K. (1982) *Communication Programming for the Severely Handicapped: Vocal and Non-Vocal Strategies*. San Diego, CA: College Hill Press.

Neilson, I. and Dockrell, J. E. (1981) Cognitive tasks as interactional settings, in G. Butterworth and P. Light (eds) *Social Cognition*. Brighton: Harvester.

Nesbitt, E. (1993a) Children and the world to come: the views of children aged eight to fourteen years on life after death, *Religion Today*, 8(3): 10–13.

Nesbitt, E. (1993b) Photographing worship: ethnographic study of children's participation in acts of worship, *Visual Anthropology*, 5: 285–306.

Nesbitt, E. (1995) Many happy returns: some British South Asian children's birthday parties, *Multicultural Teaching*, 14(1): 34–5, 40.

Nesbitt, E. (1998) Bridging the gap between young people's experience of religious tradition at home and school: the contribution of ethnographic research, *British Journal of Religious Education*, 20(2): 98–110.

Nesbitt, E. (1999a) 'The impact of Morari Bapu's *kathas* on Britain's young Hindus', unpublished paper.

Nesbitt, E. (1999b) Being religious shows in your food: young British Hindus and vegetarianism, in T. S. Rukmani (ed.) *Hindu Diaspora: Global Perspectives*. Montreal: Concardia University.

Nesbitt, E. (1999c) The contribution of nurture in a *sampradaya* to young British Hindus' understanding of their tradition, in J. Hinnells and W. Menski (eds) *From Generation to Generation: Religious Reconstruction in the South Asian Diaspora*. London: Macmillan.

Nesbitt, E. and Jackson, R. (1994) Aspects of cultural transmission in a diaspora Sikh community, *Journal of Sikh Studies*, 18(1): 49–67.

Nesbitt, E. and Jackson, R. (1995) Sikh children's use of 'God': ethnographic fieldwork and religious education, *British Journal of Religious Education*, 17(2): 108–20.

Neumark, V. (1997) Father and son reunion, *Times Educational Supplement 2*, (13 June): 6.

Newell, P. (1991) *The UN Convention and Children's Rights in the UK*. London: National Children's Bureau.

Newsom, J. and Newsom E. (1990) *The Extent of Parental Physical Punishment in the UK*. London: Approach.

Nisbett, R. E. and Wilson, T. D. (1977) Telling more than we can know: verbal reports on mental processes, *Psychological Review*, 84: 231–59.

Oakley, A., Bendelow, G., Barnes, J., Buchanan, M. and Nasseem Husain, O. A. (1995) Health and cancer prevention: knowledge and beliefs of children and young people, *British Medical Journal*, 310: 1029–33.

Oakley, M. W. (1997) Representing children. The law, the UN Convention on the Rights of the Child, children's rights and research, in the Foundation Section of the *Turning Points* Pack. London: NSPCC.

Oakley, M. W. (1998) Approaching the millenium: representing young people, in A. Poyser (ed.) *Approaching the Millenium: Children and the Guardian Service within the Family Justice System*. Panel Managers' Annual Workshop. London: SSI Social Care Group, DoH.

O'Brien, M., Alldred, P. and Jones, D. (1996) Children's constructions of family and kinship, in J. Brannen and M. O'Brien (1996) *Children in Families: Research and Policy*. London: Falmer Press.

OFSTED (1996) *Effective Teaching Observed in Special Schools*. London: DfEE.

O'Neill, J. (1995) On the liberal culture of child risk, in A. James, C. Jenks and A. Prout (eds) *Theorizing Childhood*. Cambridge: Polity.

Organization for Economic Cooperation and Development (OECD) (1997) *Education and Equity in OECD Countries*. Paris: OECD.

Palmer, J. (1997) A charter of rights for citizens of EU. *The Guardian*, 18 June.

Parsons, C. (1996) The cost of primary school exclusions, in E. Blyth and J. Milner (eds) *Exclusion from School: Inter-Professional Issues for Policy and Practice*. London: Routledge.

Piaget, J. (1929) *The Child's Conception of the World*. New York: Harcourt Brace.

Pollard, A. (1987) Studying children's perspectives: a collaborative approach, in G. Walford (ed.) *Doing Sociology of Education*. Lewes: Falmer Press.

Pollard, A. and Tann, S. (1993) *Reflective Teaching in the Primary School*, 2nd edn. London: Cassell.

Pope, K. S. and Vetter, V. A. (1992) Ethical dilemmas encountered by members of the American Psychological Association, *American Psychologist*, 47: 397–411.

Powney, J. and Watts, M. (1987) *Interviewing in Educational Research*. London: Routledge & Kegan Paul.

Pridmore, P. and Bendelow, G. (1995) Images of health: exploring beliefs of children using 'draw and write' techniques, *Health Education Journal*, 54: 473–88.

Priel, B. and Leshem, T. (1990) Self-perceptions of first- and second-grade children with learning disabilities, *Journal of Learning Disabilities*, 23: 637–42.

Punch, M. (1986) *The Politics and Ethics of Fieldwork*. London: Sage.

Qualifications and Curriculum Authority (QCA) (1998) *Education for Citizenship and the Teaching of Democracy in Schools: Final Report of the Advisory Group on Citizenship*. London: QCA.

Qvortrup, J. (1997) A voice for children in statistical and social accounting: a plea for children's rights to be heard, in A. James and A. Prout (eds) *Constructing and Reconstructing Childhood*. London: Falmer Press.

Reder, P., Duncan, S. and Gray, M. (1993) *Beyond Blame: Child Abuse Tragedies Revisited*. London: Routledge.

Renzetti, C. M. and Lee, R. M. (eds) (1993) *Researching Sensitive Topics*. London: Sage.

Robson, C. (1993) *Real World Research*. Oxford: Blackwell.

Romaine, S. (1989) *Bilingualism*. Oxford: Blackwell.

Rosaldo, R. (1993) *Culture and Truth: The Remaking of Social Analysis*. London: Routledge.

Rose, S. A. and Blank, M. (1974) The potency of context in children's cognition: an illustration through conservation, *Child Development*, 45: 499–502.

Roseneil, S. (1993) Greenham revisited: researching myself and my sisters, in D. Hobbs and T. May (eds) *Interpreting the Field*. Oxford: Clarendon.

Rowan, J. (1998) Qualitative vs quantitative (letter), *The Psychologist: Bulletin of the British Psychological Society*, 11: 578.

Rubin, H. J. and Rubin, I. S. (1995) *Qualitative Interviewing: The Art of Hearing Data*. London: Sage.

Ruddock, J., Chaplain, R. and Wallace, G. (1996) *School Improvement: What Can Pupils Tell Us?* London: David Fulton.

Rutter, M., Maughn, B., Mortimer, P. and Ouston, J. (1979) *Fifteen Thousand Hours*. London: Open Books.

Save the Children (1996) *Towards a Children's Agenda: New Challenges for Social Development*. London: Save the Children UK.

Sawyer, C. (1995) *The Rise and Fall of the Third Party*. Oxford: Centre for Socio-Legal Studies, University of Oxford.

Scott, D. (1995) Methods and data in educational research, in D. Scott and R. Usher (eds) *Understanding Educational Research*. London: Routledge.

Shaw, C. (1998) *Remember My Messages*. London: Who Cares? Trust.

Shaw, I. (1996) Unbroken voices: children, young people and qualitative methods, in I. Butler and I. Shaw (eds) *A Case of Neglect*. London: Avebury.

Sheldon, F. (1994) Children and bereavement: what are the issues? *European Journal of Palliative Care*, 1(1): 42.

Sheurich, J. J. (1997) *Research Method in the Postmodern*. London: Falmer Press.

Shotter, J. (1973) Acquired powers: the transformation of natural into personal powers, *Journal for the Theory of Social Behaviour*, 3(2), 141–56.

Shotton, J. (1993) *No Master High or Low*. Bristol: Libertarian Education.

Simons, H. (1995) The politics and ethics of educational research in England: contemporary issues, *British Educational Research Journal*, 21: 435–91.

Sinclair Taylor, A. (1995a) A 'dunce's place': pupils' perceptions of the role of a special unit, in M. Lloyd-Smith and J. D. Davies (eds) *On the Margins: The Educational Experience of 'Problem' Pupils*. Stoke-on-Trent: Trentham Books.

Sinclair Taylor, A. (1995b) 'Less better than the rest': perceptions of integration in a multi-ethnic special needs unit, *Educational Review*, 47(3): 263–74.

Sinclair Taylor, A. and Costley, D. (1995) Effective schooling for all: the special needs dimension, in J. Siraj-Blatchford and I. Siraj-Blatchford (eds) *Educating the Whole Child: Cross Curricular Skills, Themes and Dimensions*. Buckingham: Open University Press.

Smart, N. (1968) *Secular Education and the Logic of Religion*. London: Faber and Faber.

Smart, N. (1971) *The Religious Experience of Mankind*. London: Fontana.

Smith, M. (1996) The medium or the message: a study of speaking children using communication boards, in S. von Tetzchner and M. Hygum Jensen (eds) *Augmentative and Alternative Communication: European Perspectives*. London: Whurr.

Solicitors' Family Law Association (SFLA) (1995) *Guide to Good Practice for Solicitors Acting for Children*, 2nd edn. Orpington, Kent: SFLA.

Solicitors' Family Law Association (SFLA) (1997) *Guide to Good Practice for Solicitors Acting for Children*, 4th edn. Orpington, Kent: SFLA.

South Glamorgan Advocacy Scheme for Children and Young People Who Are Looked After (1994) *First Year Report August 1993 to September 1994*. Cardiff: Children's Society.

Spann, M. L. (1988) Code-switching among bilingual Punjabi-English nursery school children: co-operation and conflict in relation to familiarity. Unpublished PhD thesis, University of York.

Spencer, J. and Flin, R. (1993) *The Evidence of Children*. London: Blackstone.

Spradley, J. (1980) *Participant Observation*. New York: Holt, Rinehart and Winston.

Stalker, K. (1998) Some ethical and methodological issues in research with people with learning difficulties, *Disability and Society*, 13(1): 5–19.

Stalker, K. and Harris, P. (1998) The exercise of choice by adults with intellectual disabilities: a literature review, *Journal of Applied Research in Intellectual Disabilities*, 11(1): 60–76.

Stanley, B., Sieber, J. E. and Melton, G. B. (1995) Empirical studies of ethical issues in research: a research agenda, in D. N. Bersoff (ed.) *Ethical Conflicts in Psychology*. Washington, DC: American Psychological Association.

Starkey, H. H. (ed.) (1991) *The Challenge of Human Rights Education*. London: Cassell.

Stevenson, O. and Parsloe, P. (1993) *Community Care and Empowerment*. London: Joseph Rowntree Foundation.

Stratford, B. and Gunn, P. (1996) *New Approaches to Down Syndrome*. London: Cassell.

Swain, J., Heyman, B. and Gillman, M. (1998) Public research, private concerns: ethical issues in the use of open-ended interviews with people who have learning difficulties, *Disability and Society*, 13: 21–36.

Tannock, J. (1997) Bereavement and the young child. Unpublished MA thesis, University of Warwick.

Thane, P. (1981) Childhood in history, in M. King (ed.) *Childhood, Welfare and Justice*. London: Batsferd.

Thomas, G. and Jolley, R. (1998) Drawing conclusions: a re-examination of empirical and conceptual bases for psychological evaluation of children from their drawings, *British Journal of Clinical Psychology*, 37: 127–39.

Thomas, G. and Silk, A. (1990) *An Introduction to the Psychology of Children's Drawings*. London: Harvester Wheatsheaf.

Thompson, N. (1993) *Anti-Discriminatory Practice*. London: Macmillan.

Thorne, B. (1993) *Gender Play: Girls and Boys in School*. New Brunswick, NJ: Rutgers University Press.

Times Educational Supplement (TES) (1993) What about the boys? *Times Educational Supplement*, 8 October.

Tisdall, G. and Dawson, R. (1994) Listening to the children: interviews with children attending a mainstream support facility, *Support for Learning*, 9(4): 179–83.

Tite, R. (1993) How teachers define and respond to abuse: the distinction between theoretical and reportable cases, *Child Abuse and Neglect*, 17: 591–603.

Tizard, B. and Hughes, M. (1984) *Young Children Learning*. London: Fontana.

Tomlinson, S. (1982) *A Sociology Of Special Education*. London: Routledge & Kegan Paul.

Tooley, J. and Darby, D. (1998) *Educational Research: A Critique*. London: OFSTED.

Townsend, P. (1996) Too many rights don't make a wrong, in M. John (ed.) *Children in Charge*. London: Jessica Kingsley.

Troyna, B. and Hatcher, R. (1992) *Racism in Children's Lives*. London: Routledge.

US Department of Health and Human Services (1995) Policy for protection of human research subjects, in D. N. Bersoff (ed.) *Ethical Conflicts in Psychology*. Washington, DC: American Psychological Association.

Utting, Sir W. (1997) *People Like Us: The Report of the Review of the Safeguards for Children Living Away from Home*. London: DoH.

van Balkom, H. and Welle Donker-Gimbrere, M. (1996) A psycholinguistic approach to graphic language use, in S. von Tetzchner and M. Hygum Jensen (eds) *Augmentative and Alternative Communication: European Perspectives*. London: Whurr.

von Tetzchner, S., Grove, N., Lonke, F., Barnett, S., Woll, B. and Clibbens, J. (1997) Preliminaries to a comprehensive model of augmentative and alternative communication, in S. von Tetzchner and M. Hygum Jensen (eds) *Augmentative and Alternative Communication: European Perspectives*. London: Whurr.

Vulliamy, G. and Webb, R. (1991) *Teacher Research and Special Educational Needs*. London: David Fulton.

Wade, B. and Moore, M. (1993) *Experiencing Special Education*. Buckingham: Open University Press.

Wagner, P. (1993) *Children and Bereavement, Death and Loss: What Can the School Do?* Coventry: National Association for Pastoral Case in Education.

Walford, G. (1991) Researching the City Technology College, Kingshurst, in G. Walford (ed.) *Doing Educational Research*. London: Routledge.

Walker, R. (1989) The conduct of educational studies: ethics, theory and procedures, in M. Hammersley (ed.) *Controversies in Classroom Research*. Milton Keynes: Open University Press.

Ward, L. (1997) *Seen and Heard*. York: York Publishing Services.

Warner Report (1992) *Choosing with Care: The Report of the Committee of Enquiry into the Selection, Development and Management of Staff in Children's Homes*. London: HMSO.

Warren, S. (1997) 'Who do these boys think they are?' An investigation into the construction of masculinities in a primary classroom, *International Journal of Inclusive Education*, 1(2): 207–22.

Watts, J. (1997) A future in the balance, *The Guardian*, 25 June.

Watts, M. and Ebbutt, D. (1987) More than the sum of the parts: research methods in group interviewing, *British Educational Research Journal*, 13(1): 25–34.

Wayne, E. and Everington, J. with Kadodwale, D. and Nesbitt, E. (1996) *Hindus*, Interpreting Religions Series, Oxford: Heinemann.

Webb, R. (1990) The processes and purposes of practitioner research, in R. Webb (ed.) *Practitioner Research in the Primary School*. Basingstoke: Falmer Press.

Webster, A., Wood, D. J. and Griffiths, A. J. (1981) Reading retardation or linguistic deficit? 1: Interpreting reading test performances of hearing-impaired adolescents, *Journal of Research in Reading*, 4: 136–47.

Whyte, W. F. (1943) *Street Corner Society: The Social Organisation of a Chicago Slum*. Chicago: University of Chicago Press.

Williams, D. T., Wetton, N. and Moon, A. (1989) *A way in: five key areas of Health Education*. London: Health Education Authority.

Williamson, H. (1996) So much for 'participation': youth work and young people, in I. Butler and I. Shaw (eds) *A Case of Neglect*. London: Avebury.

Willis, P., Jones, S., Canaan, J. and Hurd, G. (1990) *Common Culture: Symbolic Work at Play in the Everyday Cultures of the Young*. Buckingham: Open University Press.

Willow. C. (1997) *Hear! Hear! Promoting Children and Young People's Democratic Participation in Local Government*. London: Local Government Information Unit.

Woods, P. and Hammersley, M. (eds) (1993) *Gender and Ethnicity in Schools: Ethnographic Accounts*. London: Routledge.

Wylie, R. C. (1974) *The Self-Concept, vol. 1*. Lincoln, NB: University of Nebraska Press.

Wynnejones, P. (1985) *Children, Death and Bereavement*. Milton Keynes: Scripture Union.

Yin, R. K. (1994) *Case Study Research: Design and Methods*, 2nd edn. London: Sage.

 Index

CRITICAL ISSUES IN SOCIAL RESEARCH
POWER AND PREJUDICE

Suzanne Hood, Berry Mayall and Sandy Oliver

Social science research is a political activity. It stands at the intersection of three interest group: the researchers; the funders and policymakers; and the people whose lives and views are being explored, including frail elderly people, children, ethnic minorities, gays, people with disabilities and other disempowered groups. This book addresses the questions:

- Whose interests are served by research?
- For whom is it undertaken?
- What research methods are appropriate?
- How can those researched find a voice in the research process?

The authors consider inter-relations between theory and method and the processes of doing empirical research with disadvantaged people, from design through to dissemination. All the authors are experienced empirical researchers and draw on their own as well as other people's research.

The book will be of central interest to researchers in both policy-oriented and academic institutions; to their teachers; and to service-providers who need to think about the relevance of research to their work with minorities.

Contents
Introduction – Children and childhood – Children in the majority world: is Outer Mongolia really so far away? – Learning disabilities: the researcher's voyage to planet Earth – Disturbed young people: research for what, research for whom? – 'Unhistoric acts': women's private past – Black people's health: ethnic status and research issues – Frail elderly people: difficult questions and awkward answers – Gay men: drowning (and swimming) by numbers – The 'targets' of health promotion – Users of health services: following their agenda – People's ways of knowing: gender and methodology – Index.

192pp   0 335 20140 7   (Paperback)   0 335 20141 5 (Hardback)